The Roots of Our Children's War

Identity and the War on Terrorism

By R. Brad Deardorff

AGILE PRESS

An imprint of Agile Research and Technology, Inc.

THE ROOTS OF OUR CHILDREN'S WAR

Published in the United States by Agile Press,
an imprint of Agile Research and Technology, Inc.
Williams, CA

Printed in the United States of America
First printing, March 2013

ISBN 978-0-9830745-0-2

Cover design by Matthew Prichard

info@agilepress.com
www.agile-rt.com

THE ROOTS OF OUR CHILDREN'S WAR

CONTENTS

THE ROOTS OF OUR CHILDREN'S WAR

Acknowledgements

I would first like to express my appreciation to Drs. Anders Strindberg and David Brannan, whose field-tested pursuit of knowledge has proven both inspiring and challenging. By bringing together academic study and practical experience, they continue to challenge both "thinkers" and "doers" to find effective solutions to some of the most formidable security-related issues of our generation and the generation to follow.

This book also would not have been possible without the assistance and mentoring of Paul Jonathan Smith, who encouraged and supported my effort to pursue a greater understanding of how counterterrorism organizations and processes work, and how they might work better. I appreciate his willingness to share his experiences and expertise, and am proud to call him a friend.

My friend and colleague Mohamed Elibiary, whose personal experience spans the spectrum of the homeland security enterprise, was an invaluable resource. He is regularly attacked by those on both sides of the West vs. Islam narrative, which means he must be doing something right. I am also particularly grateful for his assistance as a bridge-builder between the American government and the Muslim community.

Drs. Christopher Bellavita and William Pelfrey of the Center for Homeland Defense and Security: The opportunity to study under the tutelage of experts and within a diverse group of proven practitioners was an unparalleled experience in my professional life. These men are doing some very great things at the Naval Postgraduate School, and they have my gratitude for welcoming me into such an environment.

For Kerrick and Gareth

If we could all see the world through your eyes, this book wouldn't be necessary.

I am thankful for your laughs, smiles and patience.

I look forward to our next adventures, both large and small.

Elizabeth

It is impossible to express how much

I appreciate your encouragement and unwavering support of this project,

even when it made a complicated and hectic life together even more so.

You are amazing, and I am very lucky.

THE ROOTS OF OUR CHILDREN'S WAR

THE CHANGING FACE OF TERRORISM

On May 1, 2011, the President of the United States announced that al Qaeda's leader, Osama bin Laden, had been killed in Pakistan by a team of Navy SEALs. That night, the New York Times reported on the event:

> "For over two decades, Bin Laden has been Al Qaeda's leader and symbol," the president said in a statement broadcast around the world. "The death of Bin Laden marks the most significant achievement to date in our nation's effort to defeat Al Qaeda. But his death does not mark the end of our effort. There's no doubt that Al Qaeda will continue to pursue attacks against us. We must and we will remain vigilant at home and abroad."[1]

Minutes after bin Laden's death, fingerprints, photographs and DNA samples were taken at the scene, as scientific confirmation of his demise was essential. Forty minutes allowed for a hasty search of the compound. Computers, cell phones and documents were recovered. A specially designed and equipped Blackhawk helicopter landed in the compound as another lay burning nearby. The SEAL team was extracted along with the corpse of a murderer—a man that some consider a martyr. Subsequently, the President of the United States announced bin Laden's body had been buried at sea, in accordance with Islamic rites.

How much will bin Laden's elimination really affect our national security, or the security of any Western country? The treasure trove of information taken from bin Laden's compound will most likely assist counterterrorism efforts against remaining al Qaeda leadership. Had the events described above occurred in 2002 rather than 2011, al Qaeda's "global Islamist jihad" might have fizzled out long ago. More than a decade since al Qaeda's most dramatic attack on the United States, however, al Qaeda has changed. Al Qaeda is not just an organization: it is a violent political *ideological movement*,[2] justified by an ultraconservative and anachronistic interpretation of Islam. And, despite the fact that al Qaeda, as an organization, is "greatly diminished,"[3] the appeal

---

1   Peter Baker, Helen Cooper, and Mark Mazzetti. "Bin Laden is Dead, Obama Says" New York Times

2   Jonathan Paris. "Discussion Paper on Approaches to Anti-Radicalization and Community Policing in the Transatlantic Space." Washington, DC, June 27-28, 2007.

3   Mike Leiter (2010). "The Aspen Institute: The Terror Threat Picture and Counterterrorism Strategy." Aspen, Colorado, Federal News Service, 2010.

of its narrative has increased dramatically during the past half-decade. As pointed out in stark terms by Seth G. Jones, a counterterrorism expert with first-hand knowledge of both the threat and the strategies employed to combat al Qaeda overseas,

> ...several indicators suggest that al Qaeda is growing stronger. First, the size of al Qaeda's global network has dramatically expanded since the 9/11 attacks. Al Qaeda in Iraq, al Qaeda in the Arabian Peninsula, al Qaeda in the Islamic Maghreb, and Somalia's al-Shabab have formally joined al Qaeda, and their leaders have all sworn bayat -- an oath of loyalty—to bin Laden's successor, Ayman al-Zawahiri.[4]

Now more than ever, it is critical to our national security to consider not just the whereabouts of the remaining cadre of al Qaeda leadership, but also the factors that result in the creation of new terrorists as a pervasive threat. As noted in the National Strategy for Counterterrorism, "As the threat continues to evolve, our efforts to protect against those threats must evolve as well."[5]

For more than a decade, the United States' national security apparatus, along with its state and local partners, has successfully prevented domestic terrorist attacks *after* the plans for these attacks had been developed and initiated. Though it has been somewhat effective, this approach is analogous to the "Whac-A-Mole" arcade game, in which a player uses a mallet to repeatedly bat down moles as they pop up from holes in the game's cabinet. Though it should have happened sooner, bin Laden's demise offers our nation an opportunity to truly prevent terrorism for the next generation. It is time to unplug the machine—to transition from a preemptive to a preventative strategy.

Bin Laden is gone. Now what?

First, we must recognize the threat for what it is. Salafi-jihadi ideology[6] and its associated goals are existential threats; they do not endanger the physical or material United States—its buildings, critical infrastructure, and the lives of its citizens—but our ideals, our culture, our way of life. The threat of terrorism (and our understanding of it) has changed over the past decade.

---

4   Seth G. Jones (2012). Think Again: al Qaeda: A year after Osama bin Laden's death, the obituaries for his terrorist group are still way too premature., Foreign Policy..

5   National Strategy for Counterterrorism (2011). in whitehouse.gov [database online]

6   For the purpose of this book, the term "Salafi-jihadist" refers to an adherent to an ultraconservative form of Islam who subscribes to the notion that Islam and democracy are incompatible and that the violent defeat of non-believers is necessary to restore the Muslim world to its rightful place of social dominance.

Recent trends indicate that terrorist activity in the United States is increasing, even though al Qaeda doesn't seem to have entrenched operational networks in the United States. Instead, the terrorist threat seems to be less organized, and to be inspired by Salafi-jihadist political goals and grievances, rather than by core al Qaeda leadership –not from Islam itself.

The concept of a continuously evolving threat frames the fundamental challenge of developing a national counterterrorism doctrine. When the threat is dynamic, ideological, and impacts a diverse population, lines of delineation between "us" and "them," free speech and violent rhetoric, and positive messaging and propaganda can become substantially blurred. These terms are understood differently depending on an individual's personal experience and the cultural context in which one lives. The terms are all subjective.

A few things though, are certain: according to Seth Jones, "military force is too blunt an instrument to defeat most terrorist groups,"[7] and how the nation implements a counter-radicalization strategy to prevent terrorism will inevitably alter the context surrounding those vulnerable to radicalization.

The focus of this study is Salafi-jihadist terrorism, but the lessons noted herein are derived from the experiences of those fighting various strains of terrorism. As such, the lessons learned may serve more broadly to inform strategies for combating other forms unconventional threats; for instance, right or left wing terrorists, ethno-nationalist groups, separatists and single-issue terrorists. In order to make substantial progress against these threats at the strategic, regional and local levels, the counterterrorism effort ought to be a national affair. This means that counterterrorism ought not be solely a federal responsibility, the job of law enforcement, or an action left to be decided by local jurisdictions and the traditional roles assigned to individuals within these constructs. In order to realize a national effort, paradigms must shift.

While reading this book, some practitioners will find academic validation for the approach they have been taking for years. Others might find that engagement with those hostile to current government policies is distasteful, politically risky or otherwise uncomfortable. Some in the general public and

---

7   Seth Jones. How Terrorist Groups End, 107. Santa Monica, California: Rand Corporation, 2008.

the American Muslim community may question how they might contribute to the fight against terrorism, or even why they should. If you fall into the latter categories, please read on–this book is also written for you.

Much of the literature on terrorism—especially much of the popular kind published after 2001—amounts to political posturing, or represents the far right or far left of the political spectrum. Too often, this kind of literature is based on undifferentiated analysis. The theme of a "clash of cultures" appeals to the marketplace because we are naturally wired and conditioned to compete with and be suspicious of the "other." These one-dimensional works tend to be heavy on anecdotal evidence and political vitriol rather than a serious consideration of the causes of terrorism, its potential solutions and the necessary steps to enhance the American public's resilience to violent Islamist ideologies. My attempt here is to provide a pragmatic approach to understanding the evolving threat and a measured argument for a change in the way the nation addresses terrorism. My sincerest hope is that this work will provide a realistic framework for discussion and debate as the nation continues its efforts to "prevent" terrorism.

Most important, I hope the points made herein will contribute to the creation of a greater, more nuanced counterterrorism community: one that incorporates government, the American Muslim community, industry and the general public. After all, we are in this together, as are our children.

Many academics, like real-world practitioners, have aggressively pursued the nation's top national security concern. The psychosocial study of terrorists and terrorist groups provides insight regarding the radicalization process, how seemingly "normal" people progress to violent extremism and how they might just as easily (and perhaps more frequently) reject violence. And, of course, there has been significant research on why terrorist ideologies appeal to segments of the populations and lose their appeal to others–essentially, how terrorist groups end and why they survive.

Court filings, government studies and Congressional testimony further supplement the material provided by recognized subject-matter experts to inform this study. Some of the nation's greatest minds have contributed to the study of terrorism by applying what the academic community knows about individual and group motivation and behavior to the known backgrounds of confirmed terrorists–those already dead or convicted. Many of their insights are explored here to help define the challenge of preventing violent extremism, and provide potential strategies to do so.

Before the United States can successfully address the challenges of terrorism, we must first try to understand why terrorist ideology appeals to even a miniscule fraction of the American population; the impact of external factors that influence the threat; and how the government, the American Muslim community, non-government organizations and private industry might work together to mitigate homegrown terrorism.

CHAPTER 1

CREATING TERRORISTS

A FRAMEWORK FOR VIOLENCE

"No problem can be solved from the same level of consciousness that created it."

–Albert Einstein

What motivates the Salafi-jihadi terrorist to commit violence? Counterterrorists, whether they are government agents, religious leaders, community activists or individual citizens, require an understanding of how and why terrorist groups form. The answers they find inform practical efforts to prevent terrorist group formation and growth. Unfortunately, in seeking an answer to this question, many turn to sources that seem to explain the current war on terrorism in terms of a conflict between the West and the Muslim world. Most media coverage relates to terrorist events, not terrorist motivations, and most advice to the public pertains to defensive measures and perhaps warnings of what might indicate the existence of a physical threat. Actions resulting from these types of information can, and has, helped foil attacks; nevertheless, a more thorough and practical understanding of terrorist group formation and how individuals become terrorists is necessary to truly stave off terrorism.

Since most of the world sees no justification for the taking of "innocent" life, it is easy to assume that terrorists are simply crazy and/or filled with hate; after all, their actions seem evidence of this theory. But how have we come to our understanding of the current conflict, and on what basis have we developed our counterterrorism strategies?

The research of Robert Benford, of the University of Nebraska, seeks to explain how group grievances are converted to group action in terms of "collection action frames." He defines "collective action frames" as "action-oriented sets of beliefs that inspire meaning and legitimate social movements and campaigns."[1] Citing his own previous research, Benford further asserts that collective action frames are used to "underscore and embellish the seriousness and injustice of a particular social condition or redefine as unjust

---

1   Robert Benford, "An Insider's Critique of Social Movement Framing Perspective," *Sociological Inquiry* 67, no. 4 (1997), 416.

and immoral what was previously seen as unfortunate but perhaps tolerable."[2] Well prior to 9/11, influential ideologues in both the Muslim and Western worlds employed religious "framing" as a basis to understand and explain conditions that seemed to justify the use of force to settle long-standing geopolitical conflicts. By reviewing the most prevalent of these frames, it is possible to better understand the descent from mere competition to violent asymmetrical conflict.

That said, an in-depth exploration of the religious underpinnings of violent conflict between Muslims and Christians or Catholics and Protestants is beyond the scope of this work,[3] and is perhaps better left to students of religion. Herein, we will instead review "counterterrorism" efforts by national governments and the results of their different approaches. But since those on both sides of the threat often use religious framing to define the nature of terrorism, some exploration is necessary. For instance, the United States' top intelligence official, Director of National Intelligence James R. Clapper, used explicitly religious terms that may be unfamiliar to many when he testified before Congress on January 12, 2012. Clapper said that, despite important losses to core al Qaeda and an increasingly decentralized Salafi-jihadi threat,

> [the] global jihadist movement …will continue to be a dangerous transnational force, regardless of the status of core al-Qa'ida, its affiliates, and its allies. Terrorist groups and individuals sympathetic to the jihadist movement will have access to the recruits, financing, arms and explosives, and safe havens needed to execute operations.[4]

It is therefore worth considering how such terrorist groups use religion, ethnicity and culture to further their political agendas. In doing so, one should keep in mind what Clapper identified as a "key challenge for the West"—conducting "aggressive [counterterrorism] operations," without "exacerbating anti-Western global agendas and galvanizing new fronts in the movement."[5]

---

2   Ibid.

3   For those interested in a more complete exploration of the roots of Islamist conflict and political activism against Western influences from an "identity" perspective, consider referring to Islamism (2011) by Anders Strindberg and Mats Warn. This work includes a great deal of first-hand sources, interviews with Muslim religious, activist, and political leaders as well as a thorough review of Islamist thought. The first-hand sources—some of them considered terrorists—provide unique insight to the Islamist narrative and its variations.

4   James R. Clapper, "Unclassified Statement for the Record on the Worldwide Threat Assessment of the US Intelligence Community for the Senate Select Committee on Intelligence" Office of the Director of National Intelligence.

5   Ibid, 2.

The challenge Clapper described recognizes that deeply-held identities like religion, ethnicity, culture and nationalism can be used to inspire individuals to action in order to protect the group to which they most closely associate themselves and share a sense of perceived interdependence –their perceived "ingroups." Those falling outside this mental construct constitute an "outgroup." Individuals motivated by ingroup/outgroup competition might also seek to reclaim the group's "rightful" place and dignity when offense is perceived or its status threatened.

Clapper's challenge should be considered in the domestic environment, as well as abroad. If domestic counterterrorists continue (or are perceived to continue) to employ only coercive tactics, there is a risk that punishing actions might be counterproductive to the counterterrorism effort. This concept, whether Clapper realized it or not, lays the groundwork for a discussion of Social Identity Theory (SIT), a matter that will be examined in closer detail subsequently in this chapter.

As we consider the impact of domestic security strategies in the United States, it is necessary to develop an understanding of the dynamics of the American Muslim experience both nationally and locally. Specifically, we should identify what is "normal" behavior and behaviors that deviate from "normal." Understanding such baselines of behavior for groups from which Salafi-jihadists recruit might assist counterterrorists in assessing and ultimately predicting what the impact or influence of a particular action is likely to have in a given locality.

Prior to 9/11, the United States rarely experienced terrorist attacks that were linked to Islamist groups, those who described themselves as "Muslims," or even the broader description of "Arabs." The baseline of violent activity conducted by American Muslims in the United States was relatively low. In fact, a review of data from 1970-2000, collected by the National Consortium for the Study of Terrorism and Responses to Terrorism (START), found that only 20 of 1,961 terrorist attacks in the United States were linked to Muslim or Arab terrorist groups.[6] During this 30-year period, Muslim and Arab terrorist

---

6   Global Terrorism Database, National Consortium for the Study of Terrorism and Responses to Terrorism (START). Data provided by the START Global Terrorism Database (GTDB) met the following criteria: I: The act must be aimed at attaining a political, economic, religious, or social goal; II: There must be evidence of an intention to coerce, intimidate, or convey some other message to a larger audience (or audiences) than the immediate victims; III: The action must be outside the context of legitimate warfare activities, i.e. the act must be outside the parameters permitted by international humanitarian law (particularly the admonition against deliberately targeting civilians or non-combatants).

groups were responsible for the deaths of six and the wounding of 11 within the United States; in contrast, other groups that claimed religious motivation were far more active during the same period. The Jewish Defense League (JDL) conducted 32 attacks, killing two and wounding 43, while the Army of God, a group operating under a Christian ideology, carried out 21 attacks, killing three and wounding 121. Clearly, even in the United States, perverse interpretations of what it means to be a "true" adherent to a particular religious identity can serve as a powerful motivator for violent actions.

For many groups (including Salafi-jihadists, Irish Republicans, and Dutch Malaccans), political grievances can be, and have been, wrapped in the cloak of religious and ethnic identity in order to appeal to other individuals sharing those common backgrounds. As demonstrated above, perverted religious ideologies can be potent motivating factors when ingroup members sense an external threat. In some cases, predatory recruiters are able to convince a recruit that violence is religiously justified in order to achieve the group's political goals.

The way many American Muslim and non-Muslim populations in the United States viewed and dealt with one another changed drastically after 9/11. This shift led some, or perhaps many, Muslims living in the United States to feel as though they were simultaneously rejected by fellow Americans and their foreign co-religionists with whom they might otherwise closely identify. When second- and third-generation American Muslims now ask themselves, "Who am I?," what might their answer be? In too many instances, Salafi-jihadi ideology and the Salafi-jihadi culture has strong appeal, precisely because this ideology rejects both western and mainstream Muslim culture. It is critical that counterterrorists confront this dangerous ideology now, before it becomes a core component of the identity of a rising generation and its children.[7]

When conflicts become entrenched in a population's collective identity and the struggle becomes multi-generational, it will likely take a long time to return to a non-violent, "normal" state (in this case, a pre-9/11 security posture). There are plenty of historic examples of this social phenomenon. For instance: Hindu Tamils invaded Sri Lankan Buddhist communities in the early second century B.C.E., and the polytheist Roman Empire repressed

---

7   This concern is supported by data that indicates the possibility of a long-term threat as addressed in detail in Chapter 5.

Jewish communities in the first century C.E. [8] In these instances the religious framing of the conflict employed by the protagonists became ingrained in society: the conflict in India continues today, and the Roman actions resulted in the formations of the Sicarii —perhaps the world's first terrorists. These examples demonstrate that terrorist groups that present their narrative in the form of an existential threat to religious identity can be effective and long-lasting causes for concern. And, as we'll see in Chapter 2, modern conflicts demonstrate similar results

Many on either side of the Global War on Terrorism view the world in terms of irreconcilable conflict, ideas developed and promoted by the arguments of Samuel P. Huntington in the West and Sayyid Qutb in the Muslim world, among many others. Those who subscribe to Huntington-Qutbian perspective perceive an existential threat from either the Arab/ Muslim or Western (Judeo-Christian/secular) societies, respectively. As such, conflicting parties are able to employ a clearly defined "us-versus-them" psychosocial framework that may be passed from one generation to the next.

For the critical thinker, the Huntington-Qutbian construct might seem disappointingly reductionist and counterproductive—an artificial and incomplete explanation of conflict born of undifferentiated analysis —analysis that dangerously oversimplifies the relationship between Arab/Muslim and Western (Judeo-Christian/secular) cultures. Though it's gained traction in the policymaking world, the Huntington-Qutbian construct is, in effect, a call to action, not a sound basis for effective counterterrorism strategy.

In contrast to the Huntington-Qutbian construct, Daniel Bar-Tal provides a more thoughtful explanation of the "Clash of Civilizations" as the confluence of "real issues such as territories, natural resources, self-determination, statehood, religious dogmas, and/or basic values…that have to be addressed in conflict resolution."[9]

Bar-Tel argues that when government and non-government entities use a reductive model as a foundation for long-term policies, the sociopsychological infrastructure that evolves "includes collective memory, ethos of conflict, and collective emotional orientations," [10] making the already difficult job of countering terrorism even more so: trust is undermined, communication

---

8   David C. Rapoport , Fear and Trembling: Terrorism in Three Religious Traditions. The American Political Science Review, Vol. 78, No. 3 (Sep., 1984), 668-672

9   Daniel Bar-Tal, "Sociopsychological Foundations of Intractable Conflicts," *The American Behavioral Scientist* 50, no. 11 (2007), 1430-1436, 1438-1453.

10   Ibid,1431.

becomes and remains hostile, and government and communities become isolated from one another, increasing the likelihood of conflict. More than a decade after 9/11, the nation is increasingly at risk of entering what Bartel described as an "intractable conflict" as a result of such thinking.

Writing from Tel-Aviv University, Bar-Tal described "intractable conflict" in terms of its psychosocial foundation. In order to meet his definition of an intractable conflict, a relationship between societies, states or groups must meet the following seven criteria[11]:

1. **Protracted:** lasting at least one generation, thus resulting in at least one generation whose life experience includes only that conflict.

2. **Violent:** often resulting in what each side perceives as intentional and malicious death that is inflicted by the other side without justification.

3. **Perceived as irresolvable.**

4. **Demands extensive investment:** parties involved make huge material and emotional investment in protecting their ingroup.

5. **Total:** neither side is willing nor capable of compromising its fundamental goals, and focuses exclusively on its own needs.

6. **Perceived as zero-sum in nature:** any loss suffered by the other side is its own gain; conversely, any gains of the other side are their own losses.

7. **Central:** engagement in the conflict is a core component in the party's social identity and salient under most or all circumstances.

By its nature, once such deep-seated identity issues are activated, they can be a long-lasting behavioral driver for those who maintain religion (or ethnicity, culture, nationalism, etc.) as a core part of their social identities. The call to protect core components of one's social identity is strong, as evidenced in the number of American Muslims who leave the United States to engage in combat against fellow Americans abroad and the disturbing increase in domestic plots since 2009[12].

How did the environment in the United States change in a way that began producing new, homegrown Salafi-jihadi terrorists at an increasing rate? In today's globalized environment where information can be transmitted instantaneously and migration from one side of the world to another can occur within hours, it is critical to consider the "us-versus-them" narrative that has developed and grown in the Muslim world since the Industrial

---

11   Ibid.

12   Bergen, Peter, Andrew Lebovich, Matthew Reed, Laura Hohnsbeen, Nicole Salter, Sophie Schmidt, William Banks, et al. Post-9/11 Jihadist Terrorism Cases Involving U.S. Citizens and Residents: An Overview. Washington, DC: New America Foundation and Syracuse University's Maxwell School of Public Policy., 2011.

Revolution, and particularly since the end of World War I. Are the anti-Western sentiments in the Muslim world tied more closely to religious dogma or common political grievances found in Muslim-majority nations during this period?

For more than a century and a half, the Muslim world and the Western world have become increasingly divided. Though polarization initially developed slowly, it quickened and became more violent in the wake of World War I and World War II. Differences in culture became more obvious in the United States following 9/11, as both Western and Muslim nations questioned which groups were 'with' or 'against' them. In a manner remarkably similar in both the Muslim and Western worlds, native majority populations came to view Western and Muslim minorities, respectively, as a danger to the indigenous demography and cultural landscape.[13] These existential threats were addressed through violence and repression (both real and perceived, as well as intentionally and unknowingly) by both sides of the conflict. How did we come to this state of affairs?

From an Islamist perspective, the past 150 years saw the majority of the world's Muslims as colonial subjects of non-Islamic Western powers. For the faithful of Islam, "the notion of Islam's divinely appointed universal superiority had become little more than a joke."[14] Repressed by kings and other political despots, much of the Muslim world lived (and continues to live) in environments with little opportunity for social progression. The fact that many in the general populations in these countries resented their governments, viewing their leaders as puppets of colonial Western powers, is not surprising. In the view of many Muslim intellectuals,

> [C]olonial powers were steadily Westernizing their subservient local clients—royal families and local business elites molded entirely in the image of their Western masters—which in turn impacted the social norms and cues of society at large. ...As a reaction to this situation, Islam was gradually forged into Islamism; Islam as a modern, action-oriented political language, in addition to its traditional theological, ethical, and philosophical content.[15]

---

13 Asef Bayat, "When Muslims and Modernity Meet." *Contemporary Sociology*, 36 (6), 507-511.

14 Anders Strindberg and Mats Warn. 2011. *Islamism*. United Kingdom: John Wiley and Sons Ltd, 68.

15 Ibid, 68-69.

Despite the obvious benefits of modernity, technological development and material advantages of Western society enjoyed by Westerners, many Muslims resisted the embrace of Western culture at the perceived cost of their religious identity. In a sense, "Islamism" developed as "the language of self-assertion to mobilize those (largely middle-class high achievers) who felt marginalized by the dominant economic, political or cultural processes in their societies...those for whom the language of morality (religion) [became] a substitute for politics."[16] Accordingly, Islamic intellectuals sought "to plan ways of action to stop and then reverse the decline of the Islamic communities; and to imagine the contours of a future world where Islam would reach equality with, if not supremacy over, the West."[17]

This Islamist thought, in turn, spawned a response in direct opposition to Western societal norms—a "back to basics" approach to Islam, deeply intertwining religion and governance. To "Salafis," those who follow this "pure" Islamic way, the practice of Islam is based on strictly interpreted Islamic law as understood by the prophet Mohammed's contemporaries, commonly referred to as "*salafiyya*." In the modern world,

> contemporary Salafis articulate a very demanding interpretation of monotheism, which has the consequence of making unbelief more likely. They also advocate an expansive definition of innovation, which narrows the scope of acceptable Islamic practice, and they remain wary of extrascriptural influences and sources of knowledge in religious matters.[18]

While there are a multitude of contributors to contemporary Islamist and Salafist thought, a particular current that can be directly traced to the radical thought that underpins the Salafi-jihadi threat to the Western world is especially pertinent to understanding and confronting this particular terrorist ideology.

Perhaps the most effectual political discourse on Salafi-jihadi ideology was initiated by Jamal al-Din Afghani (1838-1897) and his protégé Muhammad Abdu (1849-1905). These Salafist thinkers framed "Muslimness" with "sharp ingroup/outgroup boundaries and a matrix for thought and action, thus forging a new and enlarged ingroup out of previously fragmented

---

16   Bayat (2007), "When Muslims and Modernity Meet." 509-510.

17   Hakan Yilmaz. (2007). Islam, Sovereignty, and Democracy: A Turkish View. *The Middle East Journal*, 61(3), 477-493.

18   Henri Lauzière. "The Construction of Salafiyya: Reconsidering Salafism from the Perspective of Conceptual History." *International Journal of Middle East Studies* 42, no. 3 (2010): 369-389.

communities."[19] Afghani and Abdu feared the influence of Western culture would gradually pollute Muslim society until it ceased to exist. They saw Muslims as a threatened class, drawing on religion, commonly one of the most salient features of an individual's identity, as a mechanism of differentiation. The contributions of Afghani and Abdu are relevant because of their influence on those who most visibly led the progression of Salafi-jihadi thought to violent action: Hasan al-Banna (1906-1949) and Sayyid Qutb (1906-1966).

Hassan al-Banna founded the Muslim Brotherhood (MB) in Egypt in 1928 with the intent to "operationalize the ideas of al-Afghani and Abdu."[20] Immersed in the context of colonialism and the fear of religious and cultural subservience, the MB launched a campaign of violence in Egypt, targeting rulers whom it perceived to be puppets of secular western powers, businesses with western clientele and British soldiers. Like al-Banna, Sayyid Qutb "believed that the establishment of an Islamic state was the solution to all problems and expected that violence would be necessary to remove obstacles in the way of [his] vision."[21] This conviction became clear in Qutb's writing as his thoughts progressively came to justify violence.

In Qutb's early adult life, he was a poet, philosopher and teacher. His literary efforts initially focused on personal and public morality. Sponsored by the Egyptian government, Qutb studied and lived in the United States from 1948-1950. When he returned to Egypt, Qutb's experience in the United States seemed to have expanded his concerns from a predominately individualist moral perspective to a broader concern, at the cultural level. Qutb promoted the concept of "Islamic nationalism," a perspective that welcomed all ethnicities and people from all nations who embraced "true Islam" and rejected all of its other forms. [22] After his sojourn in the United States, Qutb condemned not just British imperialism, but Western society as a whole, viewing Western culture as an existential threat to the Islamic way of life, as he saw it:

> Already concerned with the corrosive influence of British colonialism, and deeply anti-colonial in his thinking, Qutb's time in the United States prompted him to re-diagnose his country's

19   Strindberg and Warn. 2011. Islamism. United Kingdom: John Wiley and Sons Ltd, 77.

20   Ibid.

21   Ana Belén Soage. 2009. Hasan al-Banna and Sayyid Qutb: Continuity or Rupture? The Muslim World 99 (2) (Apr 2009): 294-311

22   Sayed Khatab, 2004. "Arabism and Islamism in Sayyid Qutb's Thought on Nationalism." The Muslim World 94 (2): 217, 217-244.

ailment. He came to understand the challenge as both more generic and more intrusive, viewing British colonialism as merely an aspect of a secularist, materialist, individualist and capitalist West.[23]

Upon his return to Egypt, Qutb promoted the concept of a religious obligation for all Muslims to aggressively expand, not just defend, Islam until it attained world dominance. In pursuit of this goal, Qutb joined the Muslim Brotherhood in 1952 and was chosen to lead its Section for Propagation of the Call and Publishing, the MB's propaganda department.[24] In this capacity, he engaged in political activism against the Egyptian state and was arrested in a broad government crackdown on the Muslim Brotherhood in 1954, following an attempt by the group to assassinate the Egyptian ruler.[25] This crackdown crippled the MB movement in Egypt, but it did not silence Qutb, and may have served to strengthen his convictions.

Many fellow MB members were sentenced to death, but Qutb himself was sentenced to 15 years of hard labor. The years in prison turned out to be the most productive literary years of Qutb's life. His writings became increasingly radical while he wrote from his jail cell, as his belief that violence was necessary to attain the Brotherhood's Islamist goals became more pronounced. Qutb first wrote an extensive commentary on the Quran, *In the Shade of the Quran*, which he used to develop his personal understanding of the holy text. Selections from this work, which appeared in installments throughout his imprisonment (with the consent of the Egyptian government), were printed separately in the volume called *Signposts Along the Road*, also published under the title *Milestones*.

Milestones included an idealized history of "true" Islam characterized by religious tolerance and brotherhood and called for "true" Muslims to confront "*jahili* society," [26] which he described as:

> ...any society other than the Muslim society...any society...that does not dedicate itself to submission to God alone, in its beliefs and ideas in its observances of worship and its legal regulations.[27]

---

23   Strindberg and Warn. *Islamism*, 80.

24   Ibid.

25   William E. Shepard. (2003). "Sayyid Qutb's Doctrine of Jahiliyya." *International Journal of Middle East Studies*, 35:4, 521-545.

26   James Aho. "The Terrorist Identity: Explaining the Terrorist Threat." Contemporary Sociology 36, no. 4 (2007): 372-373.

27   Sayyid Qutb, *Milestones*, Chapter 5: La Ilaha Illa Allah – The way of life (Mississauga, Canada: Young Muslims, 2008): 52.

Qutb further suggested that God's will was for humankind to live according to Islamic law, implying that Muslim society should dominate the global political and social spheres. According to Seth Jones, Qutb's "philosophy allowed for no gray areas. The difference between true Muslims was the same as between good and evil and just vs. unjust,"[28] conclusions that are reminiscent of the works of al-Afghani and Abdu. *Signposts Along the Road* was published and reprinted five times; despite having provided approval for the work to be published, Egyptian authorities used its contents to sentence Qutb to death. He was hanged in 1966. *Milestones* , however, lived on to became one of the most influential texts of modern Salafi-jihadist thought.

Qutb made a religious argument for the violent overthrow of the existing world order, but Qutb's ideology was well outside most Muslim conventions. For instance, Qutb's accusations that all contemporaneous Muslim governments were heretical represent a position well outside the Muslim mainstream.[29] In contrast, the Salafi mainstream might interpret religious texts in this way:

> A leader only becomes an apostate if he willingly implements non-Islamic law, understands that it does not represent Islam, and announces that it is superior to Islam. Otherwise, the leader could be ignorant, coerced, or driven by self-interest, failings that signify sinfulness, not apostasy.[30]

Qutb's interpretation of Islamic texts was inherently tainted by his personal experiences of repression and the geopolitical circumstances in which he lived. Qutb, along with and the Salafi anti-colonialist predecessors who helped shape his thought, offered a new understanding of Islamic texts that challenged dominant interpretations and marked a radical deviation from the mainstream. Qutb used his developing religious beliefs to justify his political goals, appealing to those in the Muslim community who felt similarly alienated, exploited and humiliated by Western colonization and other related projects. Little new thought has since emerged in the Salafi-jihadi paradigm; instead, the present generation of Salafi-jihadi terrorists "for the most part,

---

28   Seth G. Jones. *In the Graveyard of Empires: America's War in Afghanistan.* New York: W.W. Norton & Company, 2009, 101.

29   Quintan Wiktorowicz. 2005. A genealogy of radical Islam. Studies in Conflict and Terrorism 28, (2): 75-97, 77.

30   Ibid, 77

merely adapted [al-Banna's and Qutb's] understandings to new issues, often stretching them to their logical conclusion in a way that increased the scope of permissible violence."[31]

It is therefore important to note that Qutb and his ideological predecessors framed the world's population in an "us vs. them" paradigm: "Islam knows only two kinds of societies, the Islamic and the *jahili*."[32] Unfortunately, the prominence of Qutb's manifesto has also shaped the way many on both sides of the conflict view each other, despite attempts by other senior leaders of the Muslim Brotherhood to refute and distance themselves from Qutb's call for violence.[33]

In the West, the idea of "a central focus of conflict for the immediate future... between the West and several Islamic-Confucian states,"[34] and "the perhaps irrational but surely historic reaction of ancient rival [Islam] against our Judeo-Christian heritage, our secular present, and the worldwide expansion of both,"[35] has informed the opinion of many influential policy advisors and historians. This evaluation of the geopolitical landscape helped shape the foreign policy of the United States for a quarter of a century. Authors like Bernard Lewis and Samuel P. Huntington recognized and encouraged an increased understanding of the Muslim world in order to inform policy and avoid "inter-civilization" conflict, but they also considered violent turmoil inescapable. According to Huntington:

> The great divisions among humankind and the dominating source of conflict will be cultural. Nation states will remain the most powerful actors in world affairs, but the principal conflicts of global politics will occur between nations and groups of different civilizations. The clash of civilizations will dominate global politics.[36]

These authors point to the cultural differences between Islamic society and the West as the causal factors behind what they viewed as inevitable conflict. This position seems logical because, as noted by Oliver Roy, it draws "a straight

---

31   Ibid, 77.

32   Sayyid Qutb, *Milestones*, Chapter 5: La Ilaha Illa Allah – The way of life (Mississauga, Canada: Young Muslims, 2008): 64.

33   See *Preachers Not Judges*, by the second MB chairman counselor, Hassan al-Hudhaibi, as well as Ana Belén Soage's exploration of these writings in "Hasan Al-Banna and Sayyid Qutb: Continuity Or Rupture?" *The Muslim World* 99: 2 (2009): 294-311, 294.

34   Samuel P. Huntington. "The Clash of Civilizations?" Foreign Affairs 72, no. 3 (1993): 48.

35   Bernard Lewis, "The Roots of Muslim Rage." *Atlantic Monthly* 266:3 (1990): 60.

36   Huntington. "The Clash of Civilizations?" 48.

line from Islamic fundamentalism to terrorist operations. ...[A] 'global war on terrorism' makes sense because [Huntington and Lewis conclude] similar trends and ideas are at work among most of the Muslims involved in local as well as global conflicts."[37]

However, Huntington's macro-level analysis provided little useful insight to prevent violence or stop terrorist groups from developing over the next 30 years. The prescient observations of Western policy advisors did not translate into long-range policies designed to mitigate the observable and documented rise of militant political Islam. And, while Western states did experience violent clashes with Salafi-jihadists, conflict with Muslims was not universal. For instance, Indonesia, the country with the world's largest Muslim population, has proven a powerful ally in the Global War On Terror (GWOT). Similarly, Turkey, Saudi Arabia, Pakistan and Egypt (each to varying degrees) entered into conflict with various "Muslim" terrorist organizations. In the past decade, each of these nations has been targeted and has suffered more terrorist attacks than the United States. In fact, al Qaeda and its affiliates have conducted more terrorist attacks in Muslim-majority nations and killed more Muslims in those attacks than any Westerners, Christian or otherwise. [38] These facts support the conclusion that the broad-based assertion of a "Clash of Civilizations" is unfounded. The Salafi-jihadists appear to be at war with most of the world's population, including fellow Muslims who do not accept the Salafi-jihadi interpretation of Islam. Is it possible that the war on terror is about something more than a religious struggle?

This is a vital question, as the United States has faced domestic attacks by international terrorists in the past. For instance, in the 1970s, terrorists opposed to Puerto Rican annexation responded violently to what they considered colonization: the Fuerzas Armadas de Liberación Nacional (FALN) conducted 86 domestic attacks between 1974 and 1979, the Armed Revolutionary Independence Movement conducted 22 domestic attacks between 1970 and 1973, and the Independent Armed Revolutionary Commandos (CRIA) conducted 16 attacks in 1973 and 1974.

There were, of course, international groups composed of adherents to their version of Islam forming in the Muslim world during in this period; however, non-Muslim international terrorists also were emerging, and with

---

37   Oliver Roy, *Al Qaeda in the West as a Youth Movement: The Power of a Narrative.* Brighton: MICROCON, (2008).

38   National Consortium for the Study of Terrorism and Responses to Terrorism (START). (2011).

similar ideologies. These terrorist groups were simply striking out against what they regarded as the "imperialism" of the Western world, and were specifically targeting Americans. Some of the most prominent of these groups include; the Revolutionary People's Struggle (ELA), Revolutionary Organization 17 November, and the Japanese Red Army (also known as the Anti-Imperialist Brigade), among others.[39]

Those promoting the Clash of Civilizations might ask, "If this is not a conflict based on religion, why is the United States not in conflict with Buddhists or Hindus, for example?" And while this question recognizes a correlation between religion and the current conflict, we might be wiser in asking, "What is the commonality between groups with which we are in conflict?" According to one authority with unique insight to al Qaeda,[40] bin Laden's "reasons [for launching a global Salafi-jihadi insurgency] have nothing to do with our freedom, liberty, and democracy, but have everything to do with U.S. policies and actions in the Muslim world."[41]

In fact, the Clash of Civilizations frame might tell us more about Qutb, Huntington, Lewis, and those they most influenced, than about how to counter terrorism itself. These thinkers saw the West and Islam in starkly polar terms, arguing that the competition between these two very different cultures would (or should) result in violence. Their prediction came to pass during the last two decades, as the ingroup/outgroup framing of their pre-9/11 works had a substantial influence on both Western policies and Islamist ideologies.

If counterterrorists cannot move beyond this problematic political model, the zero-sum game of violent, cyclical confrontation between the Western and Muslim worlds will continue. However, macro-level observations of social evolution and predation are insufficient to explain why and how terrorist groups form, merely noting conflicting interests and identities that exist.

---

39   Department of State. "Patterns of Global Terrorism 1996." Department of State.

40   Anonymous has been revealed as Michael Sheuer, a senior U.S. intelligence official with nearly two decades of experience in national security issues related to Afghanistan and South Asia. He was identified as "anonymous" as the condition for securing his employer's permission to publish *Imperial Hubris* and *Through Our Enemies' Eyes*.

41   Micheal Scheuer, *Imperial Hubris: Why the West is Losing the War on Terror.* 1st ed. Washington, D.C.: Brassey's, 2004.

Irreconcilable religious difference, the common theme of both the "Clash of Civilizations" and "Muslim-*jahili*" frameworks, provides the basis for only a superficial understanding of the root causes of the conflict at hand. While there is a correlation between religion and the current struggle, the relationship is too often incorrectly described as a causal one. Such conflict theories, presuppose

> …certain categories and category relations as the basis of human action are quite literally useless to those who have an interest in understanding or producing change… By contrast, they are all too helpful to those who wish to keep the social world as it is." [42]

In the interest of efficiency and effectiveness, it is necessary for the savvy counterterrorist to look far deeper into circumstances surrounding terrorism than those superficially (and much more readily) available through extant explanations. A more refined assessment is called for in order to overcome what may be considered this "fundamental attribution error."[43]

To truly understand and combat the threat of Salafi-jihadi terrorism, it is necessary to first understand its roots in local contexts. Rather than dismiss terrorist motivations as "irrational," it is necessary to understand that, from a terrorist's perspective, his or her actions may be quite logical. In this context, terrorists and their supporters may act as, not violent maniacs, but "uncompromising moralists who see the world in starkly polar terms."[44] From their vantage point, some terrorists view their actions as altruism, intending to support their co-religionists, ethnic group or family.

It is undeniable that geopolitical circumstances, foreign policies and interpretations of religious ideology provide material to be exploited by Islamic extremists. But, it takes something more to move an individual to violence, and something more again to result in the formation of a terrorist group. Any successful counterterrorism strategy must address the underlying needs of the mass population in order to be effective in the long run. Careful

---

42   Stephen Reicher. "The Context of Social Identity: Domination, Resistance, and Change," *International Society of Political Psychology* 25, no. 6 (2004): 941-942.

43   Lee Ross, "The Intuitive Psychologist and His Shortcomings: Distortions in the Attribution Process," *Advances in Experimental Social Psychology*, edited by L. Berkowitz. Vol. 10, 174-214. New York: Academic Press, 1977.

44   Jeff Victoroff, "The Mind of the Terrorist: A Review and Critique of Psychological Approaches." *The Journal of Conflict Resolution* 49, no. 1 (Feb., 2005): 3-42, 25.

analysis of these motivating factors is critical because a poorly fielded counterterrorism strategy might induce some of the phenomena it intends to eliminate.[45]

The West vs. Islam explanation for our current conflict is fundamentally flawed, as neither the "West" nor "Islam" is a monolithic entity. The majority of the Muslim world rejects violence as a legitimate tool to defend Islam, and American Muslims—regardless of whether or not they disagree with U.S. policies, values or even the Western principle of separation between church and state—reject violence against civilian targets to defend Islam from its enemies.[46] Cultural differences exist but are themselves insufficient to explain why terrorist groups form, and far less capable of explaining why American Muslims (and especially Americans who convert to Islam) engage in terrorism against their fellow citizens. In the words of one analytical team,

> Blaming Islam is a simple answer, easier and less controversial than re-examining the core political issues and grievances that resonate in much of the Muslim world.[47]

The Huntington-Qutbian models rely on the assumption of a fundamental competition between democratic Western civilization and the Muslim world. But what does that mean for the domestic United States, where the Muslim community represents less than one percent of the general population?[48] The ingroup/outgroup framing might be expected to justify policies of either "authoritarian integration" where majorities rule with little regard for minorities or multiculturalism,[49] in which cultures exist separate from one another within the same nation. These kinds of policies run contrary to civil liberties, civil rights and the notion of an integrated and egalitarian society. How we choose to characterize the root causes of terrorism and thereby the foundation of counterterrorism strategies is critical. With the Muslim population in the United States expanding rapidly,[50] policies that encourage feelings of alienation or isolation might tend to promote increasing instances

---

45   Oliver Roy, "Al Qaeda as a Youth Movement', 1.

46   The Pew Forum on Religion and Public Life. *Little Support for Terrorism among Muslim Americans.* Washington, DC: Pew Research Center, 2009.

47   John L. Esposito and Dalia Mogahed, *Who Speaks for Islam?: What a Billion Muslims Really Think.* New York, NY: Gallup Press, 2007.

48   *The Future of the Global Muslim Population: Projections for 2010-2030.* Washington, DC: Pew Research Center's Forum on Religion and Public Life, 2011.

49   Oliver Roy, *Al Qaeda in the West as a Youth Movement: The Power of a Narrative*, 2.

50   The Pew Research Center estimates that the Muslim population in the United States is approximately 2,595,000, or 0.8 percent of the United States population. The number of Muslims in the United States is expected to double by 2030.

of civil unrest or acts of violence. As evidenced by social activism and domestic terrorist organizations of the 1960s and 1970s, social polarization is a real threat. The potential threat is magnified not by massive numbers of aggrieved American citizens, but because in today's technologically advanced and interconnected world, grievances (real or fabricated) can be shared instantaneously, and even small numbers of violent actors have the potential to do great damage. In worst-case scenarios of social polarization a cycle of violence and retribution might be triggered.

The United States government recognizes that the counterterrorism effort must include

> ...capabilities related to border protection and security; aviation security and screening; aerospace control; maritime/port security; cargo security; cyber security; nuclear, radiological, biological, and chemical materials and the ability to detect their illicit use; biometrics; critical infrastructure protection; force protection; all hazards preparedness; community engagement; and information sharing among law enforcement organizations at all levels.[51]

The challenge for government, however, is developing doctrine: "how" we execute this kind of strategy in a way that ensures an integrated national security effort is implemented in a way that avoids alienating our own citizens.

Globalization, electronic media and ease of trade and travel expose various cultures to one another more rapidly, more frequently and in greater depth today than at any other time in history. The United States may indeed, as Bernard Lewis suggested, be "facing a mood [of disillusionment and hostility from much of the Muslim world] and a movement far transcending the levels and policies and the governments that pursue them."[52] But it is a mistake to attribute the resulting political violence to an entire culture without considering the political, social and historical contexts that might influence an individual's decision to engage in political activism on the one hand, or terrorist acts on the other.

The principal flaw of Huntington's "Clash of Civilizations" theory then is that millions of Muslims, even radical *salafists*, do not become terrorists. Thus, for the practitioner, it is counterproductive to develop policy based on reductive and, frankly, inaccurate analytical framework. The conclusions it

---

51   United States, "National Strategy for Counterterrorism (2011)," 11.

52   Lewis, "The Roots of Muslim Rage," 60.

generates are too vague to yield concrete, practical value in preventing either
terrorist attacks or the development of new terrorists.[53] So, we will turn to
other possible explanations.

PSYCHOLOGICAL DISORDERS AS AN EXPLANATION FOR TERRORISM

At the other end of the explanatory spectrum is the individual approach,
an alternative that posits that terrorists represent the "irrational other" and
social misfits—that the intentional murder of innocent civilians connotes
a character devoid of a moral compass. To better assess the plausibility
of this explanation, it is worth visiting an authoritative reference. The
Diagnostic and Statistical Manual of Mental Disorders (DSM) is the mental
health professional's "Bible" for diagnosis in the United States and in many
nations abroad.   It defines psychological disorders, their symptoms and
potential guides for treatment. Western psychologists, use a "multiaxial or
multidimensional approach to diagnosing because rarely do other factors in
a person's life not impact their mental health." [54] The five axes described by
the DSM IV are provided below:[55]

- **Axis I: Clinical Syndromes -** This is what we typically think of as the
  diagnosis (e.g., depression, schizophrenia, social phobia).

- **Axis II: Developmental Disorders and Personality Disorders -**
  Developmental disorders include autism and other disorders which are
  typically first evident in childhood.

- **Axis III: Physical Conditions which play a role in the development,
  continuance, or exacerbation of Axis I and II Disorders -** This includes
  physical conditions such as brain injury or HIV/AIDS that can result in
  symptoms of mental illness.

- **Axis IV: Severity of Psychosocial Stressors -** Events in a person's life, such
  as the death of a loved one, starting a new job, college, unemployment, and
  even marriage can impact the disorders listed in Axis I and II.

- **Axis V: Highest Level of Functioning -** On the final axis, the clinician rates
  the person's level of functioning both at the present time and the highest level
  within the previous year.

---

53   Strindberg and Warn. *Islamism*, 14-34.

54   *Diagnostic and Statistical Manual of Mental Disorders,* Fourth Edition. IV ed. American
     Psychiatric Association, Washington, DC: 1994.

55   Ibid.

Conditions along these five axes may drive individuals to act in ways that are abnormal or dysfunctional to self or others, and in some cases can result in violence. Those who demonstrate behavior that is inconsistent with group norms are unable to contribute productively toward group goals. For the counterterrorist, it is important to note that it is unlikely that individuals suffering severe mental disorders are capable of maintaining the interpersonal relationships and the confidence of fellow members of a covert organization to be core components of a terrorist organization. Thus, the mentally or emotionally challenged might serve terrorist organizations as expendable "tools" (suicide bombers, for instance), but, generally speaking, the mentally unstable are incapable of leading or participating in a sustained terrorist threat to society.

There is, however, anecdotal evidence that a small number of terrorists may suffer psychological disorders, one prominent example of which might be Abu Musab al-Zarqawi, the former leader of al Qaeda in Iraq. His lifetime of truancy and criminal activity meets several of the indicated behaviors that are attributable to Antisocial Personality Disorder (APD). [56] [57] His behavior also exemplifies the risks incurred by a terrorist organization when a psychopath[58] is included in a covert organization. Based on his willingness to conduct acts of extreme violence without sympathy or moral qualm, it might seem that a person like al-Zarqawi would be an ideal candidate for recruitment to a terrorist group. But other characteristics that are typical of the psychopath, including impulsive actions, irresponsible behavior and lack of concern for social norms, argue against the antisocial candidate's induction into a covert organization that is engaged in high-risk activity. Simply put, the psychopath cannot be trusted to act in accordance with the covert organization's goals, and if an individual's irresponsible actions compromise the terrorist group' ability to act covertly, the terrorist group is likely to fail to accomplish its goals.

---

56   Ellen Knickmeyer and Jonathan Finer,"Insurgent Leader Al-Zarqawi Killed in Iraq," *Washington Post*, June 8, 2006.

57   *Diagnostic and Statistical Manual of Mental Disorders Third Edition, Revised (1989)*, Third Edition (Revised) ed. Washington, DC: American Psychiatric Association, 1989.

58   This term is used by the to illustrate the risk of including a person suffering from mental illness in a covert organization. The term "psychopath" is often associated with the more exact diagnosis of Anti-Social Personality disorder. The author lacks specialized clinical training that provides both a body of knowledge and clinical skills to properly diagnose Zarqawi's mental condition. A clinical diagnosis, however, is unnecessary to illustrate this risk.

Consistent with the clinical description of APD, al-Zarqawi was unwilling to conform to guidance from al Qaeda's senior leadership. This resulted in turmoil within the al Qaeda organization when al-Zarqawi expanded his targets from American forces to Shia Muslims and indiscriminant attacks on women and children. Al Qaeda's senior leaders felt these actions in Iraq undermined the appeal of al Qaeda to its target audience, as evidenced by a letter of rebuke from al Qaeda's second-in-command, Ayman al-Zawahiri.[59]

It is likely that al-Zarqawi was accepted by senior al Qaeda leaders only because "core" al Qaeda, the close network of individuals who ran the organization at the strategic level, had little presence in or capability to organize in Iraq, and were therefore compelled to bring al-Zarqawi in to their fold to avoid being overshadowed on the world stage.[60] Al-Zarqawi's propensity for extreme violence –particularly against fellow Muslims –and egomaniacal need for publicity undermined the leadership of core al Qaeda leaders and worked against al Qaeda's strategic goals.

Ultimately, the negative attention al-Zarqawi drew to his local organization demonstrated al Qaeda's inability to fully control subordinate affiliates, diminished the status of al Qaeda amongst the Muslims al Qaeda sought to attract, fractured the al Qaeda in Iraq organization and may have diminished to the organization's ability to recruit. Al Zarqawi's relationship with al Qaeda's senior leaders remained tumultuous and divisive until he was killed by the U.S. military in June 2006.

While there is more relative "probability of some degree of psychopathology for those moved to act alone"[61] than for other mechanisms of radicalization, psychopaths do not represent an existential threat to national security. Their actions are inherently self-limiting. Psychopaths are usually unable to develop or maintain the mutual commitment necessary to act in groups that could present a threat to the social fabric and the way citizens go about daily life. Studies of terrorist organizations almost uniformly conclude that while groups that resort to terrorism act outside the norms of society at large, individual group members do not commonly suffer from psychological dysfunction. Many Islamist terrorists are from middle and upper class

---

59   Jim Garamone, "Al Qaeda Leader's Letter Questions Zarqawi Tactics," *American Forces Press Service,* October 17, 2005.

60   It is another matter altogether to determine if al-Zarqawi's organization was principally a "terrorist group" or a counterinsurgency, or criminal band that employed terrorist tactics for separate motives.

61   Clark McCauley and Sophia Moskalenko, *Friction: How Radicalization Happens to Them and Us,* New York: Oxford University Press, 2011, 25.

backgrounds and grew up in traditional families where they maintained apparently loving relationships with parents and siblings. In fact, a study of more than 500 al Qaeda-affiliated terrorists by Marc Sageman (a forensic psychiatrist and former CIA officer) discounted economic deprivation, brainwashing, religious knowledge, poor education and sexual frustration as common motivators for terrorist activity.[62] Many of the "known terrorists" Sageman studied lived in the West and amongst westerners for years, [63] many had positively contributed to their local communities, and most were considered completely normal by friends and associates.[64] Such individuals might demonstrate no dysfunctional behavior along Axes I, II, and III.

The stressors identified in the DSM's Axis IV, however, are of more interest to the student of the radicalization process. These stressors may trigger "cognitive openings" that figure prominently in radicalization models where life changing events cause abnormal stress to the subject and can increase the subject's vulnerability to recruitment to a group or cause.[65] All humans are vulnerable to external influences like moving away from home, the death of a loved one, divorce, loss of employment, and other events that can result in personal paradigm shifts and new searches for identity (or searches for new identity). During the period surrounding these events, the searcher may experience cognitive dissonance, a feeling of discomfort caused by holding conflicting beliefs simultaneously. At the same time, the searcher may reassess his or her fundamental beliefs about his or her place in the world, which in turn may lead the newly recruited terrorist to the conclusion that self-determination is inseparable from the impulse for destruction.[66]

---

62 Marc Sageman, *Leaderless Jihad: Terror Networks in the Twenty-First Century*. Philadelphia: University of Pennsylvania Press, 2008. In this book and in *Understanding Terror Networks*, Sageman details studies of "known" and convicted terrorists. These books provide great insight in to the biographical history of the subjects and useful detail regarding terrorist backgrounds.

63 "Known terrorists" refers to those convicted of crimes of terrorism, killed as a result of their own terrorist acts and those publically identified by the United States as belonging to terrorist groups.

64 Sageman, *Leaderless Jihad*.

65 Fathali M. Moghaddam, *From the Terrorists' Point of View: What they Experience and Why they Come to Destroy*, Westport, Conn.: Praeger Security International, 2006, 33-113, and Mitchell D. Silber and Arvin Bhatt, *Radicalization in the West: The Homegrown Threat*. New York: New York (City) Police Department, 2007.

66 Victoroff, *The Mind of the Terrorist*, 23. Victoroff references Freud's conclusion self-determination is inseparable from the impulse for destruction.

The influence of Axis IV stressors implies support for an approach that takes contextual circumstances into account in order to explain the appeal of terrorism. Understanding the psychological progression of an individual is critical to accurately assessing the threat he or she may pose, and what influences might mitigate or exacerbate that threat. Likewise, individuals' interactions within certain social contexts can lead to the formation of similarly motivated groups or movements that might not have happened in another social context.

PSYCHO-SOCIAL THEORIES

Psychosocial theories suggest that self-identity is developed only in the context of interpersonal and group processes: "the self is meaningful only in the context of one's relationship to others and one's position in social groups."[67] Identity and group dynamics theories argue that individual contexts and interactions between those belonging to the West and those in the Muslim world can have direct impact on security in a number of ways.

For instance, both the Bush and the Obama Administrations have suggested that al Qaeda exploits local grievances to recruit new members or co-opt existing groups to support or engage in in terrorism.[68] [69] This implies that where local grievances exist, regardless of their nature (for example, feelings of political disenfranchisement, repressive policies, failing economies, corrupt government, economic exploitation by international companies, etc.), Salafi-jihadi ideology might appeal to the aggrieved population by offering an alternative to the status quo and a chance to enhance the status of the ingroup (and, thus, how group members view themselves).

Targeting the West, al Qaeda can apply anti-colonial arguments to justify political violence and lead the aggrieved to blame the United States or other "heretical" governments benefitting from U.S. support for any or all of its problems. In this scenario, the aggrieved population might identify with the anti-colonial perspective of Salafi-jihadists and recognize the potential benefit of aligning with a sophisticated and well-financed terrorist organization, without necessarily agreeing with all of al Qaeda's tenets or

---

67   Marilynn B. Brewer and Miles Hewstone, eds. *Self and Social Identity*, 2nd ed. Malden, MA: Blackwell Publishing, 2005, 3.

68   *National Strategy for Combating Terrorism (Updated 2006)*. Retrieved from on 09/05/2011. Washington, DC: United States Government, 2006.

69   Obama Administration, "National Strategy for Counterterrorism (2011)," whitehouse. gov.

accepting direction from core al Qaeda leaders. By aligning with al Qaeda's Salafi-jihadi cause, members of the aggrieved population might win needed resources and training, but just as importantly, they may develop an activist identity that compares favorably to their previous identity as helpless victims.

As McCauley notes, "the foundation of large-scale intergroup conflict is the human capacity for group identification."[70] To the faithful of this approach, religion plays little role in radicalization; instead, the driving force is the Islamist narrative: the West's war against Islam and oppression of Muslims.[71] From a psychosocial perspective, "the success of Osama Bin Laden is not to have established a modern and efficient Islamist political organisation, but to have invented a narrative that could allow rebels without a cause to connect with a cause."[72]

At both the individual and group levels, terrorist motivations may include (but are not limited to): the redress of individual and group grievances, altruism and narcissism, paranoia, absolutist moral beliefs and apocalyptic faiths, and revenge for individual or group humiliation.[73] [74] Each of these potential motivations suggests, "[T]he most effective way to root out terrorism is to change the contexts that give rise to a morality supporting terrorism."[75] This is why the *National Strategy for Counterterrorism*, published in 2011, advocates "supporting community leaders and influential local stakeholders as they develop solutions tailored to their own particular circumstances," as an integral part to combating violent extremism.[76]

The motivating factors that lead an individual to political violence may be real or perceived notions of injustice. The "reality" of the offense can only be construed through the eyes of the potential recruit to terrorism, as "their involvement in political violence is a result of a series of understandable factors which combined result in a process of deepening involvement in

---

70 McCauley and Moskalenko. *Friction*, 28.

71 Roy, "Al Qaeda as a Youth Movement," 2.

72 Roy, "Al Qaeda as a Youth Movement," 1

73 McCauley and Moskalenko. *Friction*. McCauley and Moskalenko provide a clear and concise examination of how normal people can be moved toward criminal and violent behavior by normal psychological influences.

74 Victoroff, *The Mind of the Terrorist*. Victoroff addresses specific psycho-social theories related to these themes.

75 Fathali Moghaddam, *From the Terrorist Point of View*, 11. Moghaddam provides a provocative radicalization model of value to those interested in counter-radicalization in this work, as well as "The Staircase to Terrorism: a psychological exploration."

76 National Strategy for Counterterrorism (2011), 11.

violent extremism."[77] It is therefore necessary to examine a range of factors that may contribute to the formation of movements whose membership might resort to violence in order to attain politico-religious goals, "if we want to develop mechanisms for combating such malevolent transformations, then it seems essential to learn to appreciate the extent that ordinary people can be seduced or initiated into the performance of evil deeds."[78]

If counterterrorists are to understand the root causes of terrorism, we need a model that accounts for the interaction of multiple factors that shape behavior in both individuals and groups. "[B]oth the origins and effects of terrorist acts are anchored in group dynamics,"[79] writes Clark McCauley. The ability to prevent terrorism is necessarily about building a capacity to change the *context* of the potential terrorist in a way that is beneficial to national security.

SOCIAL IDENTITY THEORY

First described in detail by Henri Tajfel and John Turner in 1979, these three theoretical principles that serve as Social Identity Theory's (SIT) foundation:

1.   Individuals strive to achieve or maintain positive social identity.

2.   Positive social identity is based on favorable comparisons between ingroups and relevant outgroups: the ingroup must be perceived as positively differentiated or distinct from relevant outgroups.

3.   When these comparisons yield unsatisfactory results, individuals will strive to leave their existing group and join some more positively distinct group and/ or make their existing group more positively distinct. [80]

Over the past three decades, the theory has been supported and refined, both in the laboratory and in practical experience. If an SIT approach to counterterrorism is to be taken by policymakers and practitioners as they

---

77   Silke, Andrew. "Becoming a Terrorist." *Terrorists, Victims and Society: Psychological Perspectives on Terrorism and its Consequences*, edited by Andrew Silke. West Sussex, England: Wiley & Sons, 2003, 30.

78   Philip Zimbardo, "A Situationist Perspective on the Psychology of Evil: Understanding how Good People are Transformed into Perpetrators," *The Social Psychology of Good and Evil*, edited by Arthur G. Miller, (New York: Guilford Press, 2004), 26.

79   Clark McCauley, "Psychological Issues in Understanding Terrorism and the Response to Terrorism," *The Psychology of Terrorism*, Volume III, edited by Chris E. Stout (Westport, Connecticut: Praeger, 2002), 24-25.

80   H. Tajfel, and J. Turner. "An Integrative Theory of Intergroup Conflict." *The Social Psychology of Intergroup Relations*, edited by W. G. Austin and S. Worchel (Monterey, CA: Brooks-Cole, 1979), 94-109.

develop strategies, it is necessary that they weigh heavily "the significance of the subject's social situation, the group member's internally constructed social identity, and the context in which a cohesive group consciousness is installed in the minds and hearts of the members."[81]

According to SIT, individuals define themselves based on the groups to which they belong. When groups and communities isolate themselves or perceive themselves to be rejected by the general population, the likelihood of successful coexistence is inherently limited. Naturally, and especially when searching to define one's place in the world, individuals "segment, classify and order the social environment in order to form a basis of self-orientation."[82] Tajfel and Turner predicted, "when a group's action for positive distinctiveness is frustrated, impeded, or in any way actively prevented by an outgroup, this will promote overt conflict and hostility between groups."[83] For the terrorist groups considered by this book, the outgroup is represented by Western governments and groups that are seen as extensions of this larger group (i.e. its military, affiliated private sector companies and in some instances, even its citizens).

An SIT approach to counterterrorism demands purposeful contact between ingroups and outgroups, as well as an effort to develop new interactions that might attract members of the terrorist recruiting pool to membership into expanded, more inclusive groups. It is true that this will require agents of the government to work outside traditional roles as enforcers and bureaucrats. It will also require non-government entities to acknowledge that pockets of radicalization prone to violent action exist and to actively work to create alternative groups that might have positive appeal to the terrorist recruiting pool. These efforts by government and non-government counterterrorists should not be aimed at eliminating the salience of ascribed identities, but rather at understanding how local policies and actions can be used to for positive influence. At a minimum, policymakers need to reduce the impact of policies that might negatively influence members of the terrorists' potential recruiting pool. Unlike the sociohistorical perspective of the War on Terrorism and some elements of the psycho-social paradigm,[84] an SIT approach has the potential to attract those undergoing the radicalization process away from terrorism.

---

81 Brannan, Esler, and Strindberg, "Talking to 'Terrorists,'" 17.

82 Tajfel and Turner. "An Integrative Theory of Intergroup Conflict," 40.

83 Ibid, 41.

84 Especially those based on a genetic disposition.

Positive influence is possible because group cohesion and intergroup conflict are based on individuals' perceptions and social surroundings:

> Both individual differences and societal norms shape intergroup contact effects. The deeply prejudiced both avoid intergroup contact and resist positive effects from it. Societies suffering intergroup conflict both restrict and undercut intergroup contact.[85]

This is to say that each individual views the world differently and defines him or herself in terms of associations that are shaped by cultural history, group and individual experience. Additionally, each individual also has his or her own biases regarding those individuals and groups with which we are not affiliated. The complexity inherent in the development of a group member's social identity consists of multiple layers, and the most salient identity may shift based on the circumstances surrounding a potential terrorist. In some cases, these influences may be related to Axis IV stressors. One's sense of self-worth might be positively or negatively affected by changes in familial relationships, employment status, or change of status within a group or between subsets of one's ingroup. Counterterrorists aware of such dynamics can take advantage of these circumstances to positively change the contexts that surround an individual or group.

If one considers "the idea that intergroup prejudice and discrimination can be reduced by interpersonal contact between members of the respective social groups under conditions of equal-status, cooperative, and personal interaction,"[86] as articulated in Pettigrew's Contact Hypothesis, the necessity for counterterrorists to develop positive engagement strategies becomes apparent. Another conclusion is also made quite clear: to be most effective, leaders of those bent on countering terrorism must directly engage with those having similar influence from the outgroup they wish to influence.

If individuals seek to define themselves positively, they might fabricate rationales to justify positive self-evaluation, change their environment by leaving groups with negative value, or take action to increase the status of their own group. It is at this point that competing counter-narratives and counter-ideologies should be available and be applied. It is at this critical juncture that attraction instead of coercion promises the opportunity to disintegrate al Qaeda as an ideological movement. Though some critics might

---

85   Thomas Pettigrew, "Intergroup Contact Theory." *Annual Review of Psychology* 49, no. 00664308 (1998): 65-65-85, 80.

86   Marilynn B Brewer, "Reducing Prejudice through Cross-Categorization: Effects of Multiple Social Identities," *Reducing Prejudice and Discrimination*, edited by Stuart Oskamp,(Mahwah, NJ: Erlbaum, 2000), 165-183.

argue that disintegrating a terrorist organization is not as simple as providing positive alternatives to its members, for potential or actual terrorists without attractive alternatives to violent extremism, the outcome is all but certain. A one-sided counterterrorism strategy based on coercion alone is likely to produce more terrorists over the long run. With that said, it is understood that an SIT approach will not prevent terrorism by itself. What is needed is an appreciation for how counterterrorist actions impact the terrorists' recruiting pool, and, consequently, a balanced strategy of Hard- and Soft-Power (coercion and attraction, respectively).

How can government officials reduce violent conflict by influencing the social context of potential terrorist recruits? The only viable answer is through the community. Members of the perceived ingroup (American Muslims, in this case) likely have more influence than those from outgroups (like government agents). As a result, the effort to counter violent extremism is inherently reliant on partnerships between government and figures outside government who belong to non-violent groups that may nevertheless express opposition to government policies and practices.

Countering violent extremism might therefore be viewed by government and community members not just as a component of counterterrorism strategy, but as a superordinate goal—one that acts as a basis for intergroup relationships and the formation of a new superordinate group identity shared by those working together to this common end. This is true because interrupting the flow of new terrorists is often "compelling and highly appealing to members of two or more groups in conflict but which cannot be attained by the resources and energies of the groups separately."[87]

Collaboration between government, non-government and community members (even those opposed to government policies, so long as they adhere to constitutional values) is the prescribed path to diminish the appeal of terrorist ideologies. The effort requires a willingness from all parties to take political risks, especially when collaborating groups might be perceived to be in competition with one another, as in concerns of civil liberties and national security.

The reward for taking such risks has a direct and positive impact on the social context of groups whose members participate in activities designed to counter violent extremism (CVE). When government, non-government

---

87   Muzafer Sherif, "Superordinate Goals in the Reduction of Intergroup Conflict," *Intergroup Relations:Essential Readings*, edited by Michael A. Hogg and Dominic Abrams (Ann Arbor, Michigan: Edwards Brothers, 2001), 64.

and community groups work, and are perceived to work, together, this circumstance directly undermines the credibility of the dangerous "us versus them" narrative. Widespread and coordinated efforts at collaboration should be encouraged, because

> [g]oals and goal relations undoubtedly play a critical role in intergroup behavior, and are an important component of social-psychological explanations of intergroup relations. There is little doubt that groups that can only see themselves as competing over a zero-sum resource are likely to have conflictual intergroup relations, and that this relationship could be improved if those groups could only view themselves as having superordinate goals or non-zero-sum goal relations.[88]

SIT suggests that altering the social context surrounding a potential recruit, particularly an individual who encounters an Axis IV stressor, can determine the path chosen to address real and perceived grievances. In fact, according to SIT, one's categorization of those viewed as "ingroup and outgroup, whom we see as ally or enemy, and the bases upon which we treat those so categorized, are all in constant motion."[89] Thus, for the counterterrorist, an SIT perspective opens a wide field of opportunity and provides a theoretical basis and motivation for building cooperative relationships, increasing information-sharing, and the ability to more accurately assess and prevent conflict—especially in a domestic setting where an ingroup—in this case, an American ingroup—already exists.

An SIT approach compels counterterrorists to facilitate intergroup contact and to develop relationships with the "other." Intergroup relationships can serve as the mechanism for "four interrelated processes [that]...mediate attitude change: learning about the outgroup, changing behavior, generating affective ties, and ingroup reappraisal."[90] For counterterrorist strategists, this means creating platforms for and participating in frank dialogue with the Muslim community at both group and individual levels.

Dialogue is, simply in itself, inadequate. An SIT approach means incorporating these concepts in to a counterterrorism doctrine aimed squarely at terrorist ideology. This doctrine should be explicitly geared to make government agents better informed about local communities. It should

---

88   Michael A. Hogg and Dominic Abrams, eds. *Intergroup Relations: Essential Readings*, (Philadelphia: Psychology Press, 2001), 4.

89   Reicher, "The Context of Social Identity: Domination, Resistance, and Change," *International Society of Political Psychology* 25, no. 6 (2004): 941-942, 924.

90   Thomas Pettigrew, *Intergroup Contact Theory*, 85.

be expected that increased understanding might change the nature of actions taken to disrupt terrorist activities, that new approaches might contribute to increased cooperation, and ultimately, to improved trust between the government and the American Muslim community.

Positive engagement might, for instance, result in a series of meetings between government officials and community leaders. Since "groups provide people [with] social identity and people have as many social identities as the number of groups to which they feel they belong,"[91] the mere act of consistent engagement can help shape the identity of those participating. If these individuals are influential within their social networks and purposeful in their efforts, the experience can be expected to have a much wider positive influence. In this way, relatively small behavioral inputs result in attitudinal changes that increase trust and information-sharing on a larger scale. When groups see those they look to as leaders act outside of ingroup norms (like meeting with the FBI only in the presence of an attorney), the norms change. Thus, the social stigma assigned to interaction with the "other," by both those in American Muslim and government ingroups that are uncomfortable with engagement, can be altered.

The study of intergroup processes provides solid basis for understanding why and how intergroup conflict can be diminished. As a result, guiding actions for counterterrorists can be discerned. SIT offers the opportunity to address the threat of violent extremism through the psycho-social processes of recategorization, decategorization and crosscategorization.

Recategorization, a contact situation between groups that is structured "so as to focus attention on superordinate category identification that encompasses both the ingroup and outgroup in a single social group representation,"[92] might be facilitated between government, the American Muslim population or a non-government agency. For example, for American Muslims who are interested in partnering with the U.S. government in order to confront Salafi-jihadi ideology, recategorization first requires willingness to frankly engage with government officials. Those who share in and contribute to the superordinate goal of diminishing violent extremism (from any engaged party) would likely come to feel part of a group created for this purpose. Ultimately, any gains made by the new, superordinate group would

91   Michael A. Hogg and Dominic Abrams, eds. *Intergroup Relations: Essential Readings.* Philadelphia: Psychology Press, 2001), 4.

92   Marilynn B. Brewer, "When Contact is Not Enough: Social Identity and Intergroup Cooperation," *International Journal of Intercultural Relations* 20, no. 3/4 (1996): 294.

provide its members with positive social status in many social networks, as well as tangible benefit for their community or salient ingroup. The development of superordinate groups should therefore be a primary goal of counterterrorism efforts. If it is possible to develop or attract a cadre of influential leaders who agree on and are committed to common goals, this new, collaborative ingroup would be well postured to influence those who also identify with it.

This is exactly the desired effect of strategic engagement between leaders from different ingroups (government, NGOs, and members of diverse groups in the American Muslim community) for whom "preventing" terrorism is salient. Recategorization might be considered the first step in a linear process to interrupt the development of new terrorists because

> [r]ecategorization is thought to result in a reduction of the saliency of intergroup boundaries. Prejudice between groups can then be reduced to the extent that the group members see themselves as members of a single superordinate group. So, for example, one reason that contact with mutual goals may be effective in reducing bias is because it functions to reduce the saliency of group boundaries.[93]

Members of "dissimilar other" groups (i.e. government officials and representatives of American Muslim communities) would necessarily be included in this new group of counterterrorists and help define the new superordinate group's identity.

To follow this scenario in its natural progression, if the described meetings are purposeful and consistent, those who attend might identify superordinate goals and work to achieve them. For instance, if Muslim Americans in the community felt local police forces neglected Muslim neighborhoods, the police department might respond by altering patrol patterns or by increasing the amount of time police officers spent outside their patrol cars and interacting with Muslim shop owners. If the Muslim community perceived the FBI to only approach the Muslim community when there is a terrorist threat, the community might invite the FBI to provide education regarding internet fraud or child predators to Muslim audiences in order to increase positive contact between the agency and the community.

---

93   Catherine Seta, John Seta, and Jenifer Culver. "Recategorization as a Method for Promoting Intergroup Cooperation: Group Status Matters." *Social Cognition* 18, no. 4 (2000), 355.

But there are readily apparent challenges to recategorization, and recategorization may backfire in some cases.[94] What if the intergroup contact results in a negative or hostile interaction? Negative experiences might exacerbate intergroup conflicts. If there is a history of bad experiences or mistrust between groups, how can the recategorization process even begin? These concerns emphasize the point that partners must be chosen carefully by all potential subordinate group members in order to maximize the likelihood of successful partnerships. It also means individuals leading the effort must be willing to take some degree of educated risk.

Those beginning such a process must be prepared to confront opposing views with intent to first understand the other's perspective, and then act in a way that is inconsistent with negative stereotypes. By regularly demonstrating behavior that is consistent with the superordinate goal (countering violent extremism) and empathetic toward the other, mutual trust can be garnered (though depending on the context of a given situation, progress may be slow, and it may be useful to consider alternative processes).

Another mechanism to diminish intergroup conflict is decategorization. Decategorization also draws heavily on the concept that increased engagement between outgroup members can change attitudes. Decategorization, however does not focus on building a new superordinate group; instead, decategorization refers to a process where individual attitudes and biases are changed based on personal experiences with members of the outgroup who behave in ways that contradict stereotypes.[95]

In order for interpersonal relationships to form, members of outgroups must necessarily share information related to each other's personal and (ingroup) interests, affording all parties a better understanding of the "other." In order to optimize the potential for personalized relationships, outgroup members should hold similar status within their own groups, be intent on cooperative interaction and willing to discuss personal concerns. Over time, "repeated personalized contact with a variety of outgroup members should…undermine the value and meaningfulness of the social category stereotype as a source of information about the group." [96] Thus, not only does interaction between centers of influence and government leadership

---

94   Hogg and Abrams, eds. *Intergroup Relations: Essential Readings*, 354.

95   Marynn B Brewer and Samuel L. Gaertner, "Toward Reduction of Prejudice: Intergroup Contact and Social Caterorization," *Self and Social Identity*, 2nd ed., edited by Marilynn B. Brewer and Miles Hewstone (Malden, MA: Blackwell Publishing, 2005), 304-305.

96   Ibid.

present a straightforward and transparent way of learning about the intents, concerns and needs of others, it also creates the opportunity to reduce bias and improve the way the government executes its mission both within and beyond security work. In this way, engagement directly influences the government's ability to understand more precisely the context of a potential threat and the community's ability to articulate its needs and grievances.

Recategorization and decategorization represent conflict resolution models based on assimilation in to a new, superordinate group. These methods may delineate the initiation of a CVE effort, but it is unlikely that they are fully scalable to a society-level population because they do not fully account for an individual or group's need for differentiation.

Cross-categorization, or mutual differentiation "recommends maintaining social category distinctions in the context of mutual interdependence —a model which comes closer to pluralistic philosophies of intergroup relations." [97] Crossed categorization is a more complex identity mechanism that comes into play when an individual identifies with more than one social group. For instance, an individual may belong to the following groups: American, Muslim, female, doctor and parent.

It is important for counterterrorists to recognize the opportunities presented by cross cutting identities. Depending on the situational context, any one of the described identities may become most salient for the individual at a given time. The immediate salience of a certain identity provides an opportunity to contact and positively engage with individuals whose social identities overlap with outgroup members.

SIT indicates that these types of actions are important in cases where the meaning or value associated with an ascribed identity (Muslim or Arab, in this case) is diminished, [98] the self-esteem associated with that group becomes more negative. [99] This appears to be the situation for many second- and

---

97   Marilynn B. Brewer, "Reducing Prejudice Through Cross-Categorization: Effects of Multiple Social Identities," 166.

98   *"Ascribed"* characteristics—like ethnicity, religion, culture and nationality—are neither earned nor chosen by the individual. Rather, in many cases, ascribed characteristics are assigned naturally at birth or through early childhood and can be very difficult for the individual as well as others to alter. For this reason, there may be a fundamental need for individuals and groups to pursue a positive valuation of these characteristics. When individuals are unable to positively alter the valuation of an ascribed characteristic and the salience of this characteristic is high, then conflict between the individual and outgroup is likely.

99   Hogg and Abrams, eds. *Intergroup Relations: Essential Readings*, 256.

third-generation American and European Muslims who have grown up in the context of the Global War on Terrorism, especially when the conflict is framed as a "Clash of Cultures."

Benefits to the government in the described scenario might not be readily apparent to the casual reader. But for those who collect raw intelligence and those who execute law enforcement actions, these interactions represent opportunities to better understand the local environment. With a better understanding of the community, it is easier to build trust and develop information that might assist in determining who and what constitute an actual threat, and who and what are not threats at all.

The capacity and mechanisms for government and American Muslims to share information about grievances and potential threats is crucial. Frank communication might provide local and higher-level government, as well as the Muslim community, with opportunities to develop strategies and policies to mitigate the radicalization process. Likewise, the government and the community would benefit from early warning of potential threats and gain insight to behaviors indicating that perceived threats have dissipated. Such outcomes are in the interest of government, community and even the supposed terrorism subject. When non-traditional partners collaborate—as described later using the British and Netherlands models—leaders within these groups have proven successful in preventing terrorist attacks.

At an individual level, SIT-informed counterterrorists might be alerted to the context surrounding individuals in their group, or a group considered at risk of recruitment to terrorism. When community or government members become aware that an individual is vulnerable to recruitment to Salafi-jihadi ideology *and* is subject to Axis IV stressors (like the loss of a job, loss of a spouse and cultural conflicts that pose a threat to identity or challenge the meaning or value of an individual's identity), appropriate courses of action might be taken by both the government and the Muslim community simultaneously.

Of course, if overt steps toward terrorist actions are taken, the responsibility of the government is to intervene. But at the same time, when sufficient information is not developed to apply judicial process, the Muslim community might itself intervene to counter terrorist messages, providing positive avenues in which to channel frustration and a theological argument to counter the Salafi-jihadi ideology. The SIT lens compels practitioners to delineate roles and responsibilities between government and community partners. And, at a local level, SIT affords practitioners the psychosocial framework to develop precise strategies to fit the immediate environment.

What does an SIT lens tell us about the unique context of the "American Muslim experience" and local environmental factors that may influence an individual or group's worldview? Applied in terms of Salafi-jihadi terrorism, and especially homegrown terrorists in the United States, it is necessary to ascertain how unique contexts affect radicalization –and it is important to remember that cultural context will vary from location to location and individual to individual. According to some terrorism experts, SIT

> ...accounts for the dynamics of group identity and belonging within a framework of profound cultural difference... the way human identity develops in groups that takes seriously the critical issues of culture and social environment... social identity theory offers a means of integrating insights from a variety of analytical models within an intercultural framework.[100]

Thus, for counterterrorists within and outside government, an SIT framework opens a wide field of opportunity and provides a theoretical basis for building cooperative relationships, increasing information-sharing, and the ability to more accurately assess and *prevent* conflict.

In order to move the Homeland Security community toward prevention of Salafi-jihadi terrorism, it is useful to adopt a unifying theory of how intergroup conflict, like terrorism, develops. Ideally, the analytical model should be grounded on principles that are broadly applicable across different types of terrorist groups, not only Salafi-jihadi terrorism (which appears to consist of a hybrid of ethno-nationalist and religious motivations). Such a model would allow governments at the federal, state and local levels to create scalable structures and strategies designed to counter both local and national threats in ways that make sense in local contexts. It might also increase the salience of the national security mission in areas where the threat of international terrorism is perceived to be low.

Ultimately, a unifying theory (and an associated strategy with dedicated resources) might lead to an intelligence-minded counterterrorism culture that employs common language, training, and alertness that increases our ability to quickly adjust rapidly evolving threats. These capabilities are crucial in today's security environment because "terrorism is a single species, but with local variation. While ideologies uniquely shape some aspects of clandestine

---

100 Brannan, Esler and Strindberg, "Talking to Terrorists,'" 1.

violence, the deeper wellsprings of transnational terrorism can be found in the basic contexts of social life."[101] Social Identity Theory offers a holistic approach to achieve these desirable outcomes.

Concerned with the interactions of both individuals and groups, SIT requires investigators to look beyond superficial behaviors. The theory is certainly broadly applicable, because SIT "is based on an insistence that human action needs to be understood in its social context,"[102] a condition which allows counterterrorists to tailor counterterrorism strategies to the local circumstances.

One caveat, though: applying an SIT-based counterterrorism strategy would necessarily require a more refined understanding of the terrorist and the local context in which he lives than other theories that are currently employed for risk-based counterterrorism planning.[103] Analysis, operations and strategic plans based on SIT provide a "big picture" approach, not an effort to stop imminent threats—the function of tactical planning. Rather, SIT should define the "how, why and when" of operations, messaging and outreach.

AMERICAN MUSLIMS PERSPECTIVES

There is little peer-reviewed research regarding the attitudes of Muslim-Americans and their willingness or ability to accept an identity that has more affinity to "American-ness" than ethnic and religious roots. Sparse research is documented regarding likely sources of support and influence in countering Islamic radicalization, although the academic community is now beginning to turn with interests to foreign efforts at de-radicalization, in places like Saudi Arabia, Singapore and some European countries. Academia seems to accept that Muslim-Americans enjoy better relationships with government and the general public than in other Muslim-minority countries, and the Muslims I personally have met and interacted with over a decade and a half of counterterrorism work almost universally support this assumption.

---

101   Kristopher K. Robison, Edward M. Crenshaw, and J. Craig Jenkins, "Ideologies of Violence: The Social Origins of Islamist and Leftist Transnational Terrorism." *Social Forces* 84, no. 4 (2006): 2009-2026, 2023.

102   Reicher, "The Context of Social Identity: Domination, Resistance, and Change," *International Society of Political Psychology* 25, no. 6 (2004): 941-942, 921.

103   David W. Brannan, Philip F. Esler, and N. T. Anders Strindberg, "'Talking to Terrorists'": Towards an Independent Analytical Framework for the Study of Violent Substate Activism," *Studies in Conflict and Terrorism* 24, no. 1 (2010): 3-24.

Both professional and academic fieldwork (interviews, conversations and a limited survey of self-identified "conservative, devout, faithful, and practicing" Muslims) inform this work. The interviews contained herein were performed in a liaison capacity, with both long-standing and newly-established contacts. Access to some of these individuals was facilitated through these first-level interpersonal contacts. Each interview subject was identified based on their public status as a Muslim leader, the author's professional assessment of their influence or at the referral of non-government organizations.[104] The material provided by these individuals served as a basis on which to gauge the effectiveness of current outreach efforts by federal, state and local government organizations; to identify needs and grievances of the local Muslim population; to better understand what local factors contribute to positive and negative assessments of "the other"; and to generate discussion about how the government and community, at multiple levels, might increase trust between one another.

In addition to regular and ongoing dialogue with members of the Muslim community, on four occasions (including the survey), conversations were held in group settings. In these conversations, the author was aware of the identities of only some of the participants (those who arranged the group meetings) prior to the meeting itself. In one instance, discussions were held in a public forum wherein the author received ad hoc questions from an audience of approximately 150 self-identified Salafi students. It is likely that the anonymity of these settings encouraged participation and increased the participants' willingness to speak frankly, despite the author's official position. It is also likely that some participants refrained from overtly hostile comments due to the nature of the setting and the fact that the interviewer was invited as a guest to these venues. Continuing contact with some of these individuals and an increasing willingness from the local Muslim community to engage in dialogue indicate that they perceived some value in the three-to-four hour meetings.

Some American Muslims were overtly interested in conversations about radicalization. Other interviews were more difficult to arrange. Some meetings were arranged only after personal recommendations were given by high-status figures in the local community, or at the urging of the leadership of local religious and ethnic organizations. The information gleaned from

---

104 The NGOs which facilitated these interviews and the survey have acted as intermediaries between the Muslim community, the federal government and the families of known extremists with a recognized Salafi-jihadi influence (including convicted terrorists).

this research may identify group or individual characteristics that indicate a willingness to assist the homeland security community in countering "Islam versus the United States" rhetoric. In order to preserve the sanctity of these relationships, and at their request the individuals interviewed, cooperating NGOs and survey participants are not identified herein.

The fieldwork described above indicates my effort to understand the perspective of the portion of the local community that is perhaps most vulnerable to recruitment or radicalization by terrorists. I felt an understanding of local Muslim perspectives was important, because the essence of counterterrorism is similar to insurgent warfare. The terrorist, like an insurgent, must have at least the passive support of the population in order to succeed against the existing government. As Irish Republican Army Chief of Staff Cathal Goulding admitted in 1962, "Without the support of the majority of the people, we just couldn't succeed."[105] Similarly, global jihadists must have the support of a segment of the population, [106] albeit much less support is needed for these terrorists to accomplish their goals in the United States than for an insurgency that intends to overthrow and replace a standing government. The importance of public support has resonated through insurgent and terrorist organizations during the last half-century and has been employed for over a decade and a half by al Qaeda and similarly inclined Islamist militants in the United States. As Steven Metz notes of insurgency, it:

> …combines continuity and change, an enduring essence and a shifting nature. Its essence is protracted, asymmetric violence; political, legal, and ethical ambiguity; and the use of complex terrain, psychological warfare, and political mobilization. It arises when a group decides that the gap between their political expectations and the opportunities afforded them is unacceptable and can only be remedied by force.[107]

Therefore, it is incumbent on the counterterrorist, like the counterinsurgent, to understand the grievances and concerns of the adversary and the population in which the terrorist hides himself: these are the elements of most concern

---

105 Tony Geraghty. *The Irish War: The Hidden Conflict between the IRA and British Intelligence.* Johns Hopkins ed. Baltimore: Johns Hopkins University Press, 2000; 1998, 351.

106 While it is recognized that the term "jihadist" may have both positive and negative connotations based on its context, for the purpose of this thesis, the term is used to describe Islamists who support, promote, participate in, or otherwise subscribe to the use of violence to further Islamist ideology.

107 Steven Metz, *Rethinking Insurgency.* Carlisle, PA: Strategic Studies Institute, U.S. Army War College, 2007, 1.

in an ideology-driven conflict. Furthermore, in order to develop an accurate understanding of local dynamics, it is necessary for the counterterrorist to collect information that informs his view from a variety of sources.

It is also critical that the counterterrorist avoid mistaking the intent of the majority of that population, which maintains grievances (real or perceived), but nevertheless rejects violence. As demonstrated in the analysis that will follow, a poor understanding of local dynamics—the result of poor intelligence and limited engagement—can result in inappropriate government and public responses that, in turn, exacerbate the conditions that enable terrorism.

For the purpose of this book, the information regarding these matters "that has been analyzed and refined so that it is useful to policymakers in making decisions—specifically, decisions about potential threats to our national security" is referred to as "intelligence." [108] There are five main intelligence disciplines in the United States Intelligence Community (USIC): Imagery Intelligence (IMINT), generally speaking, the use of satellite imagery to understand physical attributes surrounding a threat or vulnerability; Measurement and Signatures Intelligence (MASINT), which concerns weapons capabilities and industrial activities; Open-Source Intelligence (OSINT), a broad array of information and sources that are generally available, including information obtained from the media (newspapers, radio, television, etc.), professional and academic records (papers, conferences, professional associations, etc.), and public data; Signals Intelligence (SIGINT), which in the domestic environment refers primarily to information collected through authorized wiretaps and other electronic intercepts of information that are subject to judicial oversight; and Human Intelligence (HUMINT), the collection of information from human sources.[109]

When "intelligence" is referred to in the pages that follow, it is important to remember that the term is commonly used to describe only intrusive and clandestine activities that are intended to solve crimes and prevent attacks. In fact, the true purpose of "intelligence" is to inform policymakers so they can make sound decisions. The best intelligence will include analysis from a variety of intelligence disciplines and multiple sources within each discipline that provide context to individual pieces of information. When only a few

---

108 Intelligence Defined," Federal Bureau of Investigation, accessed May 15, 2012.

109 "Intelligence Collection Disciplines (INTs)," Federal Bureau of Investigation, accessed May 7, 2012.

sources of information or only those that conform to the policymakers' personal agendas are considered, the result is undifferentiated analysis, and the chances of a poor decision are substantial.

WINNING ASYMMETRICAL CONFLICTS

Due to the prominence of asymmetrical warfare in modern history and its impact on foreign policy, the literature available on this topic is dense and rich in military tactics. Multiple studies of successful counterinsurgency (COIN) operations are available in academic work and peer-reviewed journals. The experiences of the United Kingdom in Malaysia and Ireland, the Peruvian struggle versus the Shining Path, and the United States' experience in El Salvador all lend broad principles for the development of a domestic counterterrorist strategy, but the body of work is less informative when applied to the domestic sociological and political tactics. The literature is sufficient only to scope key points of COIN strategies, points also readily available in Western counterterrorism practices.

While core al Qaeda does not appear to seek replacement of the governmental system in the United States, it does seek to alternately coerce the American public to alter its government's foreign policy and to promote a "United States versus Islam" narrative in the segment of the population from which it seeks funding, material, and recruits. Some of the characteristics of insurgent warfare, as described above by Goulding and Metz, have parallels in the homeland security community's counterterrorism efforts.

Like the creation of the DHS and the restructuring of the FBI after the attacks of September 11, recent struggles with insurgents abroad necessitated a complete overhaul of United States military strategy for counterinsurgency operations in Iraq and Afghanistan.[110] The Department of Defense altered its structure and its tactics to focus on the "mass base"– followers of the insurgent ideology; it may likewise be necessary for the domestic security community to assess the value of "Soft Power" in order to frustrate and disrupt the appeal of violent Islamist ideologies in the homeland.[111]

---

110 United States Army.,FM 3-24.2: *Tactics in Counterinsurgency*. Washington, DC: Department of the Army, 2009.

111 Nye, Joseph S., Jr. "The Velvet Hegemon: how Soft Power can Help Defeat Terrorism." *Foreign Policy* (2003).

The concept of Soft Power was introduced in 1990 by Joseph S. Nye, a Distinguished Service Professor at Harvard and former dean of the Kennedy School of Government.[112] According to Nye, "'Power' is the ability to produce the outcomes you want,"[113] and there are three basic ways to achieve power: 1) coercion 2) payments –both these "sticks and carrots" are considered "Hard Power,"—and 3) attraction –"Soft Power."[114] Nye described Hard and Soft Power in relation to foreign policy; naturally, his descriptors are concerned with national level interests. But despite the fact that the conflict at hand is based on ideologies that transcend geographical boundaries, it is nonetheless helpful and logical to consider Nye's concept in terms of domestic security.

Hard Power employs "carrots" and "sticks" to achieve its goals. Overseas, the United States might employ Hard Power in the form of direct military action, sanctions (or the threat of either), foreign aid or trade agreements, or other explicit incentives or disincentives.

A nation's Soft Power generates from three basic sources: "its culture (in places where it is attractive to others), its political values (when it lives up to them at home and abroad), and its foreign policies (when they are seen as legitimate and having moral authority)."[115] Nye argues:

> "[t]he current war on terrorism is not a clash of civilizations but a struggle whose outcome is closely tied to a civil war between moderates and extremists within Islamic civilization. The United States will win only if moderate Muslims win, and the United States' ability to attract moderates is critical to victory.[116]

Do these concepts apply in the domestic environment? If the homegrown Salafi-jihadi threat is to be viewed as an international, sub-state movement, domestic applications of Hard- and Soft Power have direct bearing on the war for hearts and minds. In domestic terms, Hard Power might connote arrest, deportation, seizure of funds, the issuance of visas, reduced sentences for convicts, etc. Soft Power, however, does not translate so clearly.

One might assume that it is not necessary for a nation to attract its own citizens. Though this may seem an appealing assumption, when the government and general population are perceived to reject a minority

---

112 Ibid.

113 Ibid.

114 Joseph S. Nye Jr., "Think Again: Soft Power. *Foreign Policy,* February 23, 2006, 1.

115 Joseph S. Nye Jr. "The Velvet Hegemon." *Foreign Policy* no. 136 (May/Jun 2003, 2003): 74-75.

116 Ibid.

population this assumption proves false, as will be demonstrated by the experiences recounted in this book of the British, Dutch and post-9/11 United States. Efforts to attract segments of the indigenous population are important, and can be vital, because to a minority population feeling rejected by the mainstream, the culture in power is not attractive, political values are not shared, and policies (particularly those relating to security) can be viewed as illegitimate and lacking moral authority. In order to attract potential recruits to terrorism away from terrorist groups, a nation must garner "credibility and legitimacy" as assessed by the disaffected minority group [117]; this is the primary measure of Soft Power's effectiveness. How can this be accomplished?

A good starting point would be an overarching national strategy. This is a common theme across the spectrum of asymmetrical conflict, from COIN to foreign counterterrorism. Nations that successfully confront asymmetrical enemies have almost uniformly developed doctrine that is administered by a centralized authority and serves as a base of context for independent actions by subordinate components. Successful strategies for low-intensity conflict are flexible and decentralized in their execution, with great emphasis on diminishing or preventing the spread of the opposition's influence on the local population. The United States should develop a grand strategy, a formal doctrine that is informed by the results of preceding ideological struggles.

Several Western countries have successfully coordinated governmental responses to the threat of terrorism. Their approaches and success vary, as does the applicability of these strategies in the United States. But it is a valuable practice (one exercised by all European Union countries and many progressive states in Asia) to consider the counterterrorism strategies, structures, tools and implementation of multiple nations in the construction and refinement of our own.

For instance, the United Kingdom and the Netherlands have developed specific "radicalization models" that identify key points where intervention might stop or reverse the radicalization process. The U.K. proposed community-based interaction with an aim "to reduce the risk [to the state] ... and its interests overseas from international terrorism, so that people can go about their lives freely and with confidence."[118] Similarly, the

---

117 Ibid.

118 United Kingdom. *Prevent Review: Summary of Responses to the Consultation.* London: National Archives, 2011, 5.

Netherlands executes "a broad-based policy aimed at increasing resistance to radicalization, "a society that is resilient enough to resist the growth of violent radicalization."[119]

These nations fundamentally changed their way of operating in order to more effectively counter the new threat of militant Islamist ideologies. The U.K. and the Netherlands created joint service centers to coordinate the counterterrorism analysis and reports across multiple government agencies. The Netherlands went a step further, endowing its coordination component with responsibility for operations, as well. Counterterrorism specialists permeate the national security effort from the national level to local police forces. These steps assure that local strategies to counter radicalization adhere to the national security mission, and that national-level policies can be informed by those who understand local threats in local contexts.

In the U.K. and the Netherlands, local and municipal decision makers coordinate social strategies to prevent polarization in individual communities based on national-level analysis. The common philosophy behind these strategies is that government at all levels must understand and act on "new terrorism" as an ideological battle. Militant, dictatorial ideologies—not race, or ethnic derivation, or cultural identity— are perceived as existential threats and are explicitly targeted for disruption.

Conversely, in the United States, "integrating and harmonizing the efforts of federal, state, local and tribal entities remains a challenge."[120] Counterterrorism efforts are predominantly reactive and tend to function in ways that address identified plots rather than radicalization. As such, the homeland security community faces the dynamic nature and complexity of terrorism threats with no "end game" goal, multiple definitions of the domestic security mission,[121] and overlapping jurisdictions that can cause internecine rivalries.

As the United States struggles to "get our arms around the problem" of domestic radicalization,[122] we might do well to consider how these Western nations address the "war of ideas." The U.K. and the Netherlands provide

---

119 J.P.H. Donner. and J. W. Remkes. *Counterterrorism: Letter from the Minister of Internal Affairs and Kingdom Relations and the minister of Justice* (Letter No 30. The Hague: NCTb, 2004, 2.

120 "National Strategy for Counterterrorism (2011)." whitehouse.gov. 11.

121 Christopher Bellavita, "Changing Homeland Security: What is Homeland Security" *Homeland Security Affairs Journal* IV, No.2, June 2008, 1.

122 Andrea Elliot. "Why Yasir Qadhi Wants to Talk about Jihad." *New York Times,* March 17, 2011.

models set in liberal Western democracies. They have enjoyed varying degrees of success fighting domestic terrorist groups across an extended period of time, and have recently adjusted their tactics in order to better counter what they perceive to be an existential threat. These nations have succeeded in diminishing homegrown terrorist threats; they have also made notable and acknowledged mistakes. The United States should consider the strengths and weaknesses of British and Dutch approaches as we struggle to shape our own. Neither the British nor the Dutch model is likely to translate directly to the United States, but aspects of either—or both—might assist policy makers at federal, state and local levels who aim to diminish the threat of homegrown terrorism. This book examines British and Dutch counterterrorism efforts and their impact on domestic terrorism based on their actions across four parameters:

1. Strategy
2. Structure
3. Tools for Fighting a War of Ideas
4. Impact of the doctrine

Regardless of the geographical setting, homegrown terrorism bears some commonality to a fight for "hearts and minds" in an insurgency, although there are significant differences as well. The current threat in the United States is not set in the context of violent civil unrest, therefore domestic counterterrorism efforts should logically be much less aggressive and severe than in a COIN scenario where military forces are involved. Moreover, it should be carefully considered that even in military contexts like the COIN efforts in Iraq and Afghanistan, the United States has experienced the most success in weakening al Qaeda and minimizing radicalization with "a light footprint approach" that works with and through local communities.[123]

Only a very small portion of the indigenous population of the United States supports Islamic extremist ideology; thus, propaganda and "messaging" efforts should be commensurately constrained. That said, it must be noted that al Qaeda has declared a "war of ideas" against the United States.[124] The domestic intelligence community and counterterrorists in other communities must engage on the same "battlefield" in order to be successful.

---

123 Seth G. Jones, *Hunting in the Shadows: The Pursuit of Al Qa'Ida since 9/11*. New York: W.W. Norton & Company, 2012, 27.

124 Bin Laden Lieutenant Admits to September 11 and Explains Al-Qa'ida's Combat Doctrine. Washington, DC: The Middle East Media Research Institute, 2002.

To craft an effective strategy that can truly prevent terrorism, the homeland security community must come to understand local American Muslims within the context of local environments, and the inherent distrust of many in immigrant communities in domestic law enforcement and intelligence services should be considered perhaps in light of both cultural echoes from their nations of origin, and the impact of missteps taken by the government and the public in the wake of September 11. These issues need to be addressed from an ideological perspective: as will be demonstrated in the chapters that follow, the unwillingness or inability to engage in the war of ideas is akin to surrendering this central element of the struggle.

In the pages that follow, I have used an SIT lens to review strategic approaches and practical mechanisms that other nations have employed and are employing to diminish the threat of terrorism to their domestic security. This is a pragmatic approach, as it is understood that the implications of our nation's foreign policy and foreign actions will continue to contribute to increased or diminished threat of attacks against the United States. My focus will be on those elements of the counterterrorism environment of which a nation has most control, those matters that can be improved within its national and state boundaries, as well as within local communities. As such, the SIT lens may provide a different level of consciousness that can assist counterterrorists in their work at both the tactical and strategic level.

CHAPTER 2

HARD-WON LESSONS

"OLD" COUNTERTERRORISM IN THE UNITED KINGDOM AND THE NETHERLANDS

"Experience: that most brutal of teachers. But you learn, my God do you learn."

–C. S. Lewis

A Social Identity perspective affords counterterrorists a perspective into both the physical environment and the mental context that produces terrorists because it takes into account "who" the terrorists are and "why" terrorist groups form and disintegrate. SIT also acknowledges that identities can shift with circumstances, which in turn allows informed counterterrorists the ability to apply different models when analyzing terrorist activity. Simply put, SIT

> …posits [the terrorists point of view] itself as the critical starting point for the investigative project. Rather than forcing the subject into externally constructed and ill-fitting frameworks, Social Identity Theory offers a means of integrating insights from a variety of analytical models within an intercultural framework.[1]

Some might ask, "Why would the counterterrorist care what the terrorist thinks?" First, let's consider the question at the most basic level: a thorough understanding of the subject's social identity and the context that produced it affords the counterterrorist the ability to influence the subject. This holds true whether a government agent seeks to elicit information, or a favorite uncle or religious leader seeks to de-radicalize a potential terrorist recruit.

An individual's social identity is made up of multiple layers—identities that for most wax and wane in their salience. As discussed in Chapter 1, these multiple layers can result in internal conflicts and opportunities to overcome stereotypes and build trust, particularly in the context of Axis IV stressors.

For the counterterrorist (and the terrorist) competing identities and processes represent the key to recruitment and resilience, as well as cooperation and resistance. This is why, SIT principles can be effectively employed in interviews and interrogations, even in the case of "true believers," and even

---

1   Brannan, Esler, & Strindberg, "Talking to 'Terrorists,'" 5.

if the application is merely intuitive. For practitioners like Ali Soufan,[2] the internal mechanisms of an individual terrorist subject played a critical role in interrogations. Each interrogation required a different approach, and was based on the subject's most salient identities at the time of an interview.

> With Ali al-Bahlul…we played on his commitment to al Qaeda and religious knowledge, with L'Houssaine Kherchtou the important point was al Qaeda's refusal to pay for a Cesarean section for his wife, and with (1 word deleted), it was his childhood feelings toward his brother that flipped him.[3]

The interview strategies described by Soufan connote an SIT approach that required the interrogator know as much about the subject as possible, and use that information to gain the subject's cooperation—not through physical abuse and intimidation, but by creating a context in which the subject was compelled to assess his social identity under new conditions.

In the examples above, the subjects were faced with cognitive dissonance. Al-Bahlul was forced to confront religious arguments that undermined his confidence in al Qaeda's religious authority. Kherchtou's assessment of al Qaeda leadership and justification for his loyalty to the group were diminished because he felt they did not hold up their moral responsibilities and didn't value the health of his family. Finally, with the unnamed subject, the interrogators capitalized on the subject's familial relationship, an ascribed identity that was more salient than the suspect's Salafi-jihadi conviction.

Through their cooperation with Soufan, the subjects may have perceived an enhanced condition in life: Al-Bahlul was able to cooperate because he assessed the al Qaeda's ideology and religious knowledge was inferior to the perspective of his interrogator. Kerchtou, who felt betrayed by al Qaeda, was able to strike back against the injustice and disrespect it inflicted. The unnamed subject simply sought to redeem himself in his brother's eyes.

When the interrogator or the counselor is able to understand the factors that underlie multiple layers of identity, he is able to attract the subject to a new way of thinking and assessing his place in the world. But, is an SIT strategy scalable? Can it assist in dealing with terrorist groups? If the answers to these questions are positive, then SIT can be used to shape strategies and tactics of the counterterrorist.

---

2   Soufan has been recognized as one of the FBI's most effective al Qaeda interrogators and was extensively used in interrogations of high-value al Qaeda terrorists.

3   Ali H. Soufan. The Black Banners: The Inside Story of 9/11 and the War Against Al Qaeda. New York: W.W. Norton & Company, 2012, 449

One requisite for an SIT-based strategy is the application of "Balanced Power." While Hard Power tactics (arrest, detention, seizure of property, coercive source recruitment and deportation, for instance) are necessary and justifiable in order to preempt terrorist attacks, the tactical application of Hard Power should be precise. As evidenced in Ireland and the Netherlands, the precise and measured application of Hard Power is most effective if such tactics negatively impact the mass base as little as possible. For law enforcement and the domestic intelligence community, this means it is necessary to consider how coercive actions might be perceived in the community from which terrorists recruit as soon as it becomes apparent that Hard Power tactics will be necessary. Decision-makers should, therefore, ask themselves how they might develop the capacity to communicate credibly to, and through, that community.

It is not enough to uncover plots and preempt attacks. We must realize that the actions of counterterrorists (how and when they govern, represent and police) can impact the community's response - based upon whether their actions are perceived to conform with the terrorists' narrative. If the way counterterrorists behave toward the American-Muslim population conforms to the West-versus-Islam narrative of Salafi-jihadists, terrorist recruitment is likely to increase. Conversely, when actions to thwart terrorist activity are precise and the community's rejection of terrorism is acknowledged, only the terrorist's very close associates might be burdened with the stigma of association, and fewer in the community have reason to view the government as a threat. Thus, the community enjoys a more positive social identity and is more likely to consider the counterterrorists' actions to be valid. Decision-makers should know their local communities well enough to be capable of understanding what factors in their area might initiate political violence. They ought to be able to adjust policies, communication strategies and behaviors in a way that diminishes (or at least avoids exacerbating) adverse reactions from the mass base.

Just as the approach to every interview is necessarily different and based on individual experiences for Soufan, so must be the local government's approach to countering violent extremism. There is no magic bullet or common recipe for success. An SIT approach will, however, require governments and organizations within each locality to respond to threats and grievances in a coordinated way. The SIT framework allows for multiple identities to drive behavior depending on local contexts: the same group may behave as rational actors, for what they perceive as altruistic goals, or be driven by religion, nationalism or ethnicity (amongst other motivations), depending on the immediate circumstances.

As we will now explore, British and Dutch governments developed frameworks to support localized approaches as part of much more formalized and expansive national strategies. The results of these changes have been significant.

CONFLICTS AND CONTEXT

In order to better appreciate the counterterrorism efforts in Ireland and the Netherlands, some readers may find it useful to explore the historical contexts of the terrorist groups discussed. The following section is devoted to the underlying social grievances of the PIRA and Dutch Moluccans, and the sociopolitical environments from which these terrorists groups emerged.[4]

While the history of the Irish-British conflict dates back at least to the Norman Conquest of 1066 C.E., the scope of this analysis will limit itself to the conflict between the British and the Provisional Irish Republican Army (PIRA). This conflict, commonly referred to as the "Troubles," began in 1969. Today's PIRA is an outgrowth of, but separate from, the Irish Republican Army (IRA). Too often these similarly named groups are conflated because some of their interests overlap. The IRA fought what was essentially an asymmetrical military conflict that began with the Easter Rebellion of 1916–1921, and challenged the British claim to rule in Ireland. Reacting to IRA violence in an attempt to maintain control of the Irish populous, British forces employed tactics including martial law, cordon and search operations, the use of IRA prisoners as hostages on high-risk patrols, rigid media control and even firing squads.[5]

These tactics initially succeeded in quelling immediate threats of IRA violence, but caused resentment from the Catholic population in Ireland that identified religiously with the IRA and opposed British (Protestant) rule. The U.K.'s heavy-handed tactics diminished its popular support and credibility with an Irish Catholic population that, from its perspective, had

---

4   If the reader is unfamiliar with Irish or Dutch-Moluccan history, please read on. For those familiar with the historical grievances of these groups, it may be more efficient to proceed to the section titled "Common themes of British and Dutch Strategy Adjustments" near the end of this chapter, where government approaches and their impact are explored in terms of SIT.

5   Geraghtly, 340.

been repressed by the Crown for hundreds of years. In this way, the U.K.'s "retaliation policy" ultimately undermined its ability to provide security for the population in Ireland until the British were compelled to make significant political concessions to the separatists. The British ultimately acquiesced to a treaty partitioning the island into the Republic of Ireland in the South, where a predominately Catholic population achieved self-rule, and a British province in the North, where the majority population was Protestant.[6] As a result of this geographical division, the six northernmost counties became what is now known as the Province of Northern Ireland.[7]

This "Irish victory" resonated in Irish Catholics' social identity, serving as a siren song for a hard-core element within the IRA's "Republican" movement. Republicans opposed the partition altogether and instead sought to establish Catholic rule throughout the country, ignoring the sentiment of the Protestant majority (Loyalists) in Northern Ireland who preferred to remain a part of the U.K. Republicans instead sought unification of all of Ireland's 32 counties into a single independent state. The Republicans' preferred strategy to accomplish unification was to oust the local Protestant government in Ulster and the British Army through the use of terrorism.

Conflict in Northern Ireland would not be driven solely by a small group of individuals seeking control of the whole of Ireland, however; there were other underlying factors resulting from the partition that also contributed to social unrest. Despite concessions made by the U.K. and achieving some degree of political independence, many viewed the British as an occupying security force in the North. Catholics in Ulster were subject to discrimination and maltreatment by the Loyalist Protestant population. Individual grievances derived from personal injustices merged with the Catholic community's political grievances to create a stable and enduring platform for intergroup conflict.[8] These circumstances lay mostly below the surface, dormant, until after World War II and the rise of civil protest that permeated Western society in the 1960s.

Legitimate social grievances and the Protestant government's inability or unwillingness to constructively address them created a situation in which frustrated Catholics increasingly came to the conclusion that organized

6   Geraghty, *The Irish War: The Hidden Conflict between the IRA and British Intelligence*, 330–342.

7   Kathryn Gregory, *Provisional Irish Republican Army (IRA) (Aka, PIRA, "the Provos," Óglaigh Na hÉireann) (UK Separatists)*. Washington, D.C.: Council on Foreign Relations, 2010

8   McCauley and Moskalenko describe this phenomenon as the "Synergism of personal and group grievance."

protest might be the only option or redress. Local communities divided themselves along religious lines and became isolated from one another. Societal polarization had already occurred, and it persisted, leaving both sides of the conflict unable to accurately assess the intentions of the other.

In 1968, Catholic frustration and widespread perceptions of discrimination resulted in a campaign of mass civil rights protests that attracted international attention to the cause of the Irish Catholics. The Royal Ulster Constabulary (RUC), Northern Ireland's police service, misread the motivation of civil rights protesters. While in fact, the demonstrators sought to emulate contemporaneous protests by African Americans in the United States, the RUC assessed the civil disobedience as veiled separatism led by Republicans. The Ulster government responded impotently. It conceded to some grievances of the "Catholic community living in poverty following decades of neglect... [Unfortunately,] these concessions sparked fears in Loyalist areas about the future of the link with Britain."[9] This situation drove Loyalists both within and outside government to act in fear of violence and relative loss of status.

Catholic protest expanded in 1968 and 1969, and by the end of the decade, Catholic protestors were met by an increasingly repressive Ulster government. The RUC responded to non-violent civil rights marchers with violent crackdowns. After days of violent rioting and with the RUC forces exhausted, "Britain deployed regular Army troops to the province's streets, ostensibly to protect the Catholic minority,"[10] and separate the two sectarian sides. Unaddressed grievances and fears on both sides of the dispute would fuel violence from that time forward and mark the establishment of the PIRA in December 1969.

Some former members of the IRA and new recruits generated from the Ulster government's response to civil rights protests supported violence as a means to establish their ultimate goal—the revived call for independence of all 32 counties of Ireland. This nucleus formed the PIRA and split from the Republican movement, leaving behind the old "official" IRA that was "more interested in exploring the political, socialist path than continuing with the armed struggle."[11] Meanwhile, the conflict devolved to a cycle of violence.

---

9   Jane's Provisional IRA, "Groups - Europe - Dormant, United Kingdom: Provisional IRA (PIRA)." Jane's Terrorism and Insurgency Centre

10   ). Kathryn Gregory. "Provisional Irish Republican Army (IRA) (Aka, PIRA, "the Provos," Óglaigh Na hÉireann) (UK Separatists)." Washington, D.C.: *Council on Foreign Relations*, 2010.

11   Rogelio Alonso. "The Modernization in Irish Republican Thinking Toward the Utility of Violence." *Studies in Conflict & Terrorism* 24, no. 2 (2001): 131-144,

In an attempt to restore security and at the request of the government of Northern Ireland, the British Army deployed to an unenviable position: directly in the middle of sectarian violence. Both sides of the Republican-Loyalist conflict used terrorism and intimidation tactics, although the PIRA was far more active and potent with its terrorist actions. Radio and television broadcasts provided news coverage framing the British Army within its historical role as an occupying force. Catholics residing in Ireland won support from coreligionists around the globe who identified with the repressed minority and, in some cases, provided material support to the PIRA.

Considering the level and nature of violence employed by both sides of the conflict, it is easy to understand the aggressive posture taken by the British Army upon its arrival in Northern Ireland. Two factors likely drove aggressive military actions: 1) the violence and intimidation perpetrated by the PIRA obligated the United Kingdom to provide security for its citizens, and 2) due to the Ulster government's disregard and the heavy-handed tactics employed by the RUC and the British Army, an effective intelligence base did not exist. Thus, U.K. forces could not identify potential allies, PIRA terrorists, or centers of influence with whom they could negotiate. An advanced intelligence base might have allowed the British to employ a more refined approach, but under the existing circumstances, the British government saw little choice other than brute force to bring order to the province as quickly as possible. The British Army therefore retaliated against PIRA attacks and used coercive techniques to procure information about the terrorist group. From the British perspective, extreme methods were necessary because the threat of violence was immediate and ever-increasing.

Unlike the Ulster government, the U.K. issued new laws to legitimize tactics that were sometimes harsh. Military actions were taken within legal framework that provided the necessary tools to collect intelligence and disrupt terrorist operations in these exigent circumstances. The provisions also set legal boundaries for the application of these powers. The 1973 Northern Ireland (Emergency Provisions) Act (EPA) established special criminal processes that included broad search and seizure authority, warrantless arrests and detention without trial. The Prevention of Violence (Temporary Provisions) Act (PVA) expired in 1973 but was reintroduced following a spate of bombings in 1974 as the Prevention of Terrorism (Temporary Provisions) Act (PTA). Under these laws "preventative detention was allowed for 48 hours without a warrant, and an additional five days could be authorized by the Home Secretary."[12] The new measures allowed British forces to disrupt terrorist attacks, but mass arrests without a transparent judicial process—which were condoned by the laws—adversely affected the relationship between the government and the Catholic citizens of Northern Ireland.

The PIRA then embarked on a campaign of dramatic violence that regularly resulted in civilian deaths, despite PIRA claims that the attacks targeted the British and Ulster governments. The two cases below represent a small sample of the 2,671 attacks committed by the PIRA and its affiliates between 1970 and 1998, as well as PIRA's obvious disregard for innocent life:

- On July 21, 1972, the PIRA's Belfast Brigade planted at least 20 bombs in the city center without prior warning. Nine people died, and more than 130 were injured. This attack became known as "Bloody Friday."[13]

- On November 21, 1974, the PIRA planted explosive devices in several pubs in Birmingham, on the British mainland. A total of 21 people were killed, and over 162 were injured. This attack expanded terrorist operations outside Northern Ireland and created a new paradigm for British security services.[14]

INTERNAL REVIEW AND STRATEGIC CHANGE

By 1975, the predominately Loyalist Stormont government in Northern Ireland had been abandoned and Northern Ireland was subjected to rule directly from London. It was evident to the U.K. that a new strategy to resolve the conflict would be required. Understanding that the conflict had produced multiple generations who viewed the British government as an occupying power, the British shifted strategies by adapting elements of the "hearts and minds" campaigns that had proved successful in fighting counterinsurgencies in Cyprus, Malaya and Kenya. The U.K. refined its approach to counterinsurgency to also counter terrorist activity at home.

The new strategy combined forensic police investigation with massive surveillance of terrorist suspects and was aimed at denying the terrorists popular support. Adapted for the domestic environment, the new strategy substituted massive physical, human, and electronic surveillance for the physical separation of insurgent and mass population in foreign

---

12   Laura K. Donohoe, "Britain's Counterterrorism Policy," *How States Fight Terrorism: Policy Dynamics in the West*, edited by Doron Zimmerman and Andreas Wenger,. Colorado: Lynne Reinner Publishers, Inc, 2007, 20.

13   "Bloody Friday: What Happened." BBC News,World Edition, 2002.

14   Kevin Toolis. "When British Justice Failed." Magazine ed. New York: New York Times, 1990.

counterinsurgencies.[15] The U.K. began to treat terrorism as a crime, rather than an act of war. This new way of doing things established, or perhaps reinforced, the legitimacy of government action, and in turn increased citizens' trust in the governing authority. As in Cyprus, Malaya and Kenya, the strategy proved effective when the government actions were devised to attract the public rather than just retaliate against the opponent.

With the PVA and PTA in effect, the U.K. continuously reviewed the application of counterterrorism strategies and corresponding laws to gauge their efficacy and identify operational gaps and necessary changes. For instance, in 1983, laws were changed to address "exclusion" and the deportation of travelers to and within the U.K. as a way to preclude radicalizing influences and operational cells from entering England.[16] The regular and objective review of policy revealed further gaps in the U.K. strategy, such as threats from external locals (i.e., Irish visiting England), making it possible to create and enforce laws that diminished the PIRA's ability to conduct attacks in England. Simply put, the British excluded travelers to the U.K. who were associated with terrorists. These tactics also aligned with the counterinsurgency concept of separating terrorists from the mass population in order to protect citizens and deny the terrorists opportunities to recruit operatives or raise funds.

The "criminalization" of terrorism lent credibility to the U.K. government's actions because of the transparent legal process. Additionally, criminal violations provided the British a broader array of tools to keep civilians safe. For many, the status of convicted PIRA members was altered. The PIRA's mythic appeal was tarnished when those perceived as a band of underdogs fighting a repressive establishment were revealed as an organization of calculating murderers and criminals. But from the perspective of those sympathetic to the PIRA, the U.K. continued its punitive and deterrent strategies, squelching citizens' freedom to constructively express opposition to ruling the governments on either side of the partition.

With Ireland politically divided and the Northern Irish economy in tatters, Catholics in Northern Ireland were unable to constructively communicate the root causes of the conflict and resulting social unrest. As a result, the Ulster government was incapable of addressing those grievances in a way

---

15   Geraghty, *The Irish War: The Hidden Conflict between the IRA and British Intelligence*, 74.

16   C.P. Walker, "The Jellicoe Report on the Prevention of Terrorism (Temporary Provisions) Act 1976." *The Modern Law Review* 46, no. 4 (Jul., 1983): 484-492

that could increase the public's trust and loyalty —even if it had been inclined to do so. Resistance to British rule remained high in some segments of the society.

Meanwhile, the PIRA faced challenges of its own. The terrorist organization was forced to contend with a public relations dilemma engendered by the legal process: to appeal to its base of support, PIRA would have to both convey the image of a morally righteous movement and account for its actions publically. For example, Gerry Adams, the President of the PIRA's political Sinn Féin, the political wing of the Provisional Irish Republican Army, "told The Irish Times that 'non-combatants' should not be acceptable as targets but equally," he said, "Sinn Féin recognised the right of Irish people to engage in armed struggle in pursuit of Irish independence."[17] Adams was forced to walk a fine line as the leader of a terrorist organization that sought political legitimacy. He had to avoid alienating his core base of support—fellow PIRA members closely associated with violent attacks—without alienating the larger Irish Catholic community on which the PIRA depended for support. It is likely that comments such as these won little favor with the growing numbers of Catholic families and associates of those "non-combatants" the PIRA killed with bombs and stray bullets.

The PIRA terrorists remained fixed to an identity associated with previous generations of Irish Republicans and their vision of an Ireland united through the violent ousting of the British. Claims made by their leadership cadre continued to justify violence as the only way forward: "Armed struggle is a necessary and morally correct form of resistance in the six counties against a government whose presence is rejected by the vast majority of the Irish people."[18] But for many Irish, both Catholic and Protestant, the PIRA's narrative was countered by legitimate and legal British actions and illusions of strong support for the PIRA proved false.

---

17   Gerry Moriarty, "Statements of Regret Over Deaths do Not Signal IRA Desire to End Campaign for Every Person Killed by the IRA, Republicans Cite a Corresponding Atrocity by the "Other Side", Making an End to the Terrorist Campaign as Elusive as Ever." *The IrishTimes*, 03/25/1993, 1993

18   Brenden O'Brien, *The Long War: The IRA and 1985 to Today*. Syracuse, NY: Syracuse University Press, 1999, 116. Attributed to Gerry Adams.

IMPACT

The PIRA's campaign of violence and bombs continued its spiraling course. Indiscriminate targeting—and the fact that the PIRA and its affiliates killed more Catholics than the British security services, the Royal Ulster Constabulary, and Protestant terrorist groups combined—undermined the message PIRA sought to communicate. Instead of being embraced by as liberators, the PIRA was perceived more frequently as a band of criminals and murderous thugs. As the cumulative death toll of PIRA victims increased to at least 3,168 in 1994,[19] the public wearied of violence and the moral appeal of political violence declined. With diminished appeal, PIRA hardliners lost public support. This effect was demonstrated in Adams' public statements, as well as the tactics employed by PIRA: on August 31, 1994, PIRA announced a cease-fire that distanced itself from terrorist attacks and focused more on political negotiation. The cessation of violence was welcomed "in West Belfast's mostly Catholic neighborhoods...the news brought vast crowds of people into the streets to wave Irish flags, honk horns and dance jigs."[20] PIRA's willingness to commit violent acts is demonstrated graphically below. The graph depicts violent acts that can be traced directly to the PIRA. This data may also indicate PIRA's assessment of public support for its terror tactics[21]:

---

19   John Darnton, (1994, Aug 31). I.R.A. said to be close to truce to end violent Ulster campaign. New York Times, pp. A.1-A.1. Retrieved from

20   William E. Schmidt, "I.R.A. Declares Cease-Fire, Seeing 'New Opportunity' to Negotiate Irish Peace." The New York Times, September 1, 1994, 1994, sec. International

21   "RAND Database of Worldwide Terrorism Incidents." RAND.

PIRA Violence 1973-2000

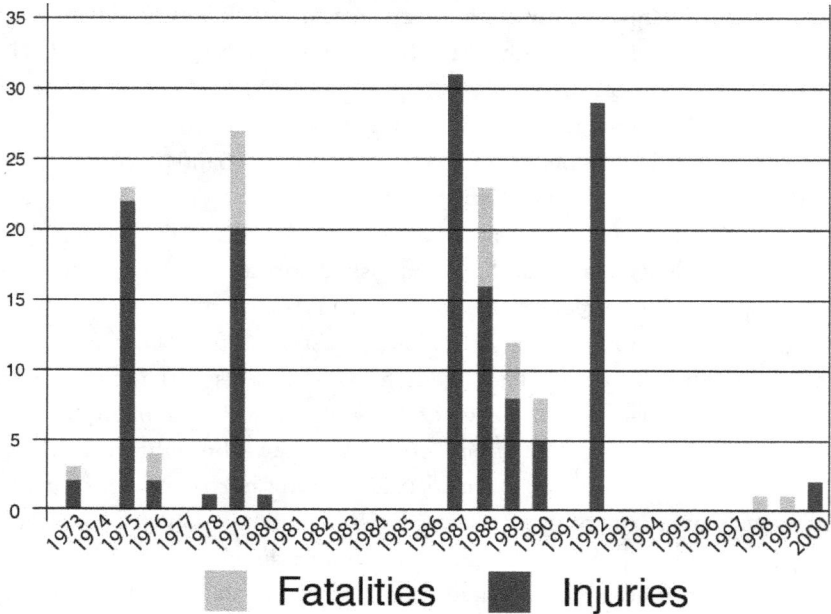

In contrast with PIRA, the Crown gained credibility with the same audience by demonstrating a long-standing interest in both peaceably resolving the conflict and increased investment in Irish infrastructure and the economy. Shifting public sentiment brought with it enhanced cooperation from the public, an increase in information volunteered by the public and more success in recruiting informants. Intelligence collection improved dramatically, and in turn, so did governance and tactical operations. It is now clear that "some very centrally placed Republicans" were enlisted to that end.[22]

The British adopted a holistic approach to address grievances. Contributions and compromises were required from both the Unionists and the Catholic minority's leadership. After three decades of violence, with all sides bloodied, Protestants, Catholics, and the British government all desired peace. In order to accomplish this goal, the government and the population were compelled to work together to maximize mutual benefit. The British strategy rendered legitimate authority to the leadership of competing parties

---

22   Brice Dickson, "Counter-Insurgency and Human Rights in Northern Ireland." Journal of Strategic Studies 32, no. 3 (2009): 475

and supported those who demonstrated both the ability to influence action on the ground and the willingness to address legitimate grievances without resorting to violence. Engagement was particularly important because, as some analysts contend, "the biggest problem [in uniting Northern Ireland] was the lack of trust between the Democratic Unionist Party and Sinn Féin."[23] Purposeful meetings, meaningful dialogue and the resulting joint initiatives facilitated by the Community Relations Council resulted in independent work by community-based groups.[24] Collaborative economic interests, community based drug initiatives, women's rights issues and integrated educational opportunities for youth provided the opportunity to accomplish superordinate goals—common objectives for competing parties, which required collaboration to attain. The value of pursuing such activities is well established, as the introduction of superordinate goals has proven to be the most successful mechanisms for reducing conflict between competing groups.[25]

The sincere efforts on the part of the British to develop cooperation between the Protestant and Catholic communities paid off. The Irish population began to see two ideologies emerge: one promised continued violence and indiscriminate killing, while the British counter-narrative offered hope for peaceful coexistence, a path to independence and improved quality of life.

As support for violence diminished, Sinn Féin, the political branch of the PIRA (which by now began to consider, or at least pay lip service to, political solutions) gained traction with Irish Catholics and legitimacy within the international community. The U.K. counterterrorism strategy had gained sufficient influence to attract most of the Irish population's support away from PIRA:

> ...At the peak of its campaign in the 1970s and 1980s the group enjoyed considerable support from these communities, and this was reflected in the fact that, following the end of the conflict, Sinn Féin became the largest party on the nationalist/Republican side in the Northern Ireland Assembly following the March 2007 elections. However, in the 2007 general election, Sinn Féin was

---

23   Kristin Archick, *Europe and Counterterrorism: Strengthening Police and Judicial Cooperation.* Washington, D.C.: Congressional Research Service, 2003

24   John Clark. (2008). Northern Ireland: A balanced approach to amnesty, reconciliation, and reintegration. *Military Review*, 88(1), 37-37-49. Retrieved from

25   J Hunger, J. David and Louis W. Stern. "An Assessment of the Functionality of the Superordinate Goal in Reducing Conflict." *Academy of Management Journal (Pre-1986)* 19, no. 000004 (Dec, 1976; 1976): 591-605

returned with only four of the 166 seats in the Dail (parliament). As such, despite the fact that PIRA purported to conduct its armed campaign in the name of the Irish people, the vast majority of people on the island of Ireland, north and south, voted for parties that rejected the violence of PIRA, an illegal organization in both jurisdictions.[26]

The PIRA splintered repeatedly as dissident factions refused to reconcile with Protestants and the Crown. These outliers left the group, and eventually the Good Friday peace agreement was signed on April 10, 1998. The agreement called for devolved government—the transfer of power from London to Belfast—with a Northern Ireland assembly and executive committee in which Unionist and nationalist parties would share power. The agreement also included a commitment by PIRA to disarm, a compromise that die-hard republicans would not accept. Shortly after the Good Friday Agreements, on August 15, 1998, one of the die-hard republican groups announced its opposition to this compromise. Historian Robgelio Alonso described how the opposition was announced this way:

> 29 people were killed by a car bomb planted in the packed town center of Omagh. The attack was claimed by the 'Real IRA…a non-reformist republicanism that finds its legitimization in…the use of force as the main and uncompromising method to achieve [its] republican goals…a 'necessary form of resistance' also provides them with the 'right to murder in the name of Ireland.'[27]

The U.K.'s principled and legal actions in the fight against terrorism contrasted sharply with the terrorists' portrayal of themselves as warriors fighting an occupying force. The dichotomy was so clear to the residents of Northern Ireland that even Gerry Adams, a 30-year PIRA veteran and suspected member of the Provisional Army Council finally denounced republican violence in the wake of the Omagh attack. Alonso noted,

> Omagh's atrocity was followed by Gerry Adams's first… condemnation of an attack carried out by republican activists. In the last three decades the IRA had perpetrated similar actions, though none of them had ever been condemned by any of its leaders.[28]

---

26   Jane's Provisional IRA. "Groups - Europe - Dormant, United Kingdom: Provisional IRA (PIRA)." Jane's Terrorism and Insurgency Centre.

27   Alonso. "The Modernization in Irish Republican Thinking Toward the Utility of Violence." *Studies in Conflict & Terrorism* 24, no. 2 (2001): 131,

28   Ibid.

Interestingly, Adams, who had already emerged as a political leader of the PIRA at the time of his statement, might have had ulterior motives for doing so. The Omagh attack may have been intended not only to express opposition to the agreement, but also may have been an attempt by his internal political rivals to undermine Adams' power and authority within PIRA. Alternatively, the attack may have been an attempt by the "Real IRA," a splinter faction within the PIRA, to win influence with those who were convinced that continued violence was in their best interest. One thing, though, was sure: The ingroup/outgroup dynamic within PIRA and potential internal competition and instrumental motivations signaled that, while the mass Catholic population had become "de-radicalized," an enduring, peaceful harmony in Northern Ireland would linger out of reach.

The U.K. government's willingness to address legitimate grievances of the population proved beneficial, especially as tensions remained between Irish republicans and the majority Protestants in Northern Ireland. Soft power tactics allowed or encouraged a leader like Gerry Adams, the same IRA leader who legitimized violence in 1993,[29] to engage in negotiations with the British government and the government in Ulster. Adams described why the new British policy was effective: "In the past I have defended the right of the IRA to engage in armed struggle...Now there is an alternative."[30] While the terrorists' message had promised continuing violence, legitimate actions by the U.K. posited a future that resonated even with those hardened by years of political violence. In this way, the U.K. strategy countered the terrorists' ideological narrative, even if it did not offer a panacea.

The Troubles in Ireland continue at a subdued rate, with spikes in activity from dissident republicans that cost lives, even today. Nevertheless, the British government met its principle goal for the threat posed by terrorism, and the risk of Irish terrorism has been "reduced sufficiently so that people can go about their lives freely and with confidence."[31] Notably, the British have remained steadfast to this goal throughout their strategy documents for at least the last decade.

---

29   Moriarty. As provided Gerry Moriarty in his 1993 article published in the *The Irish Times* article cited above.

30   Verbatim. *Time Magazine,* April 11, 2005, 2005.

31   United Kingdom. Home Office (Countering International Terrorism). *The United Kingdom's Strategy for Countering International Terrorism. 2009* Crown ed. London: Prime Minister and the Secretary of State for the Home Department, 2009

THE NETHERLANDS' MALUCCAN PROBLEM

During the same approximate timeframe as the Irish Troubles, the Netherlands also encountered a dramatic wave of terrorism. During the 1970s, Dutch-Moluccan nationalists—Indonesian exiles and their children—lived in the Netherlands while maintaining close affinity and historical roots in the Moluccas Islands, part of the colonial Dutch East Indies. These Dutch-Moluccans formed a government in exile that was committed to regain control of their homeland, and sought Dutch support for their cause. Some of these refugees determined violent political action was necessary in order to bring attention to their cause.

Former soldiers of the Royal Netherlands Indies Army (KNIL) the Dutch Moluccans led the fight against Indonesian independence on behalf of the Dutch from 1945–49. Displaced from their homeland where they had enjoyed high social status based on their association with the colonial power, the former KNIL soldiers migrated to the Netherlands when Indonesia won its independence and the Dutch government was obligated to demobilize its 4,000 KNIL troops. After relocation to the Netherlands, the former KNIL soldiers and their families sought and expected to quickly return to the Moluccas. The Dutch also anticipated expedient repatriation of the KNIL troops, but this repatriation never came.

Since both the Dutch and the exiles expected the refugees to return, Dutch Moluccans were not afforded citizenship or legal status that might have facilitated assimilation. Instead, this first wave of Dutch-Moluccans was treated poorly by the Dutch government and never fully integrated into Dutch society.[32] The "temporary resident" status of hopeful Dutch-Moluccans severely limited their opportunities for integration in to Dutch society and adversely affected the way they perceived themselves and the Netherlands. On one hand, the former KNIL soldiers admired Dutch society enough to have served the country loyally in combat. On the other, they were aggrieved by their diminished social status and mistreatment at the hands of their Dutch hosts. This love-hate relationship played itself out in Dutch-Moluccan identity and shaped actions on both sides of the ensuing conflict.

---

32   Carl H. Yaeger, "Menia Muria: The South Moluccans Fight in Holland." *Studies in Conflict & Terrorism*, 13, no. 3 (1990): 215

On their native islands, the former KNIL soldiers had once comprised the social elite,[33] but in the Netherlands, the exiles were discouraged from work, "forced to idleness, isolated in their camps [many were housed in WWII concentration camps], robbed of their military status, confronted another climate, [and struggled to learn the Dutch language]."[34] Thus, the Dutch-Moluccan population lived in isolation from the rest of Dutch society until it became clear at the end of the decade that their residence in the Netherlands would be permanent.[35] Despite gradually improving conditions, Dutch-Moluccan resentment grew regarding their treatment, relative shifts in social status, and perceived betrayal of their loyalty to the Netherlands. The emotional and social impact of real and perceived mistreatment ran deep in the community of exiles.[36]

The community became incensed by its perception of unfair treatment by the Netherlands. Through Moluccan eyes, the Netherlands applied its foreign policy inconsistently across its former colonies: on the one hand, the Dutch supported independence for Suriname, but on the other, they had denied support for Malucca's independent rule (both states were part of the Dutch colonial empire until 1949). When second-generation Dutch-Moluccans came of age, they closely identified with the cause of their parents, possibly because of the alienation they and their parents had experienced in the Netherlands and nostalgic recollections of the lifestyles their parents enjoyed. The second generation found itself unwelcome and unsupported by its government, and thus had no basis for affinity to the Netherlands. In retrospect, these underlying circumstances make it possible to understand why second and third generations of Dutch Moluccans clung to the nationalist cause of independence for the homeland of their parents and grandparents rather than embrace the Dutch culture into which they were born.[37] New generations of Dutch-Moluccans found themselves in a position where they were neither

---

33   Olenka Frenkiel. "Dutch Malaccans Appeal for Solidarity." BBS News, March 8, 2001.

34   Shelia Rule. "Vught Journal; Remember the Moluccans? is this a Last Stand?" *New York Times,* June 9, 1989, 1989,

35   Ronald Janse. "Fighting Terrorism in the Netherlands; a Historical Perspective." *Urecht Law Review* 1, no. 1 (2005).

36   Marina Brouwer. "the Moluccan Dream – Still Alive at 60." *Radio Netherlands Worldwide,* April 26, 2010

37   Ton Van Naerssen. "Title: Migration Associations and Multi-Local Politics: Rethinking the Case of Migrants from Indonesia in the Netherlands." The Hague, Netherlands, Institute of Social Studies The Netherlands, August 30-31, 2007

fully accepted by the population of the Netherlands, the nation in which they were born, nor in Molucca, the idealized country of their forefathers that was currently "occupied" by the predominately Muslim nation of Indonesia.

The result of the Dutch-Moluccans' identification with their families abroad, paired with local isolation and legitimate local grievances, manifested in eight dramatic terrorist attacks or attempted attacks over an eight-year period. These attacks included an attempted assassination of the royal family, hijackings, murder and the mass hostage taking of schoolchildren.[38] With the exception of the final attack in 1978 (a train hijacking), these terrorist attacks garnered broad support from the Dutch-Moluccan community.

In 1970, Dutch-Moluccans took hostages at the Indonesian ambassador's residence in Wassenaar, killing a police officer in the process. The short-term response by the Dutch security services to these violent acts was aggressive and repressive. The Prime Minister of Justice

> ...ordered a major raid on the Moluccas' camp, Ijsseloord, as a show of force and to arrest suspected extremists. One thousand soldiers and special police forces, backed up with helicopters and tanks entered the camp, hermetically sealed it and patrolled in armored vehicles.[39]

This extremist action by the government caused further resentment and anger from the mass population, and increased support for the terrorists' cause –a point reinforced by the disrupted attempt by 13 Dutch-Moluccans to kidnap Queen Juliana only four months later.[40]

INTERNAL REVIEW AND STRATEGIC ADJUSTMENT

Considering the very personal nature of the attempt on the nation's royal family and the continuing vitriol from the Dutch-Moluccan community, it might have been understandable for the Dutch government to pursue a retaliatory program. Other nations might have created new laws, or reorganized the security services to deal explicitly with the obvious "Moluccan problem." Instead, the Dutch government and security services addressed the hostage-taking and subsequent deadly attacks in accordance with established criminal

38   Global Terrorism Database, National Consortium for the Study of Terrorism and Responses to Terrorism (START). (accessed 08/07/2010, 2010).

39   Martin Rassner. "The Dutch Response to Moluccan Terrorism, 1970-1978." *Studies in Conflict and Terrorism* 28, no. 6 (2005)

40   TERRORISM: Murder on the Milk Train. *Time Magazine*, December 15, 1975.

laws. These organizations sought to understand and address the underlying circumstances that had resulted in terrorism in order to diminish the likelihood of attacks in the future.

Rather than enhancing sentences for political crimes and creating new laws to address violent political acts, the Dutch court recognized the legitimacy of some Moluccan grievances. The court that tried the takeover of the Indonesian embassy case concluded that the Dutch government ought to reflect on its obligations toward the people of the South Moluccas over the previous 20 years and that the Dutch government must engage in dialogue with the Dutch-Moluccan community.[41] With these considerations in mind, the court assigned only one year in prison to each of the hostage-takers.[42] This very public demonstration of Dutch intent to understand and subsequently address the causes of terrorism would serve as a foundation for a new aspect of the Netherlands' approach to national security. Application of Soft Power would serve as a vehicle for the government to regain credibility with the Moluccan population. The strategy evolved, and continuing assessments by the government contributed to more efficient application of resources and refined applications of military and police actions to address terrorism.

The Dutch appear to have taken a long-term, strategic position with the intent to prevent future terrorist acts. The government was willing to consider Moluccan concerns in its domestic policies, despite attacks from radical elements of the community. This was an important and politically risky venture for the Dutch, since the Dutch-Moluccan terrorists were by far the most damaging of terrorist groups to Dutch society; the public verged on severe polarization in reaction to the attacks.[43] The Dutch government faced the challenge of the general public's demand for aggressive tactics to confront violent acts of terrorism that targeted not only government officials and edifices, but also schoolchildren and mass transit.

The Dutch government honed its tactical response to crimes of violence and simultaneously adhered to a long-term strategy aimed at addressing the messages that those acts communicated. The Dutch never hesitated to use

---

41   Janse, "Fighting Terrorism in the Netherlands; a Historical Perspective,"62.

42   Rassner. "The Dutch Response to Moluccan Terrorism, 1970-1978."

43   The Provisional Irish Republican Army was more lethal in the Netherlands than Malaccan terrorists during the 1980s but the terror instilled by the Malaccans was more damaging to the social fabric of the Netherlands. The PIRA targeted British nationals with surgical precision (principally British government officials, including the British ambassador), whereas Dutch Malaccans tended to attack "soft" targets like transit systems and schoolchildren.

force to address violent acts, but they did increase their precision in applying force. Thinking strategically, the Dutch recognized that to stop the flow of new generations of terrorists, it would be necessary to address social factors that contributed to the radicalization process and sought to understand and address the social and cultural grievances of the Moluccan nationalists. The Dutch government demonstrated its willingness to consider the social impact of its policies and their long-term implications for domestic security without compromising established foreign policy. And, the government's efforts to attract the loyalty of the Dutch-Moluccan minority opened a door to communication because the government's overtures were credible.

The Netherlands' recognition of the need for engagement did not translate immediately to effective programs, however. Despite acknowledging the need to develop more preventative and holistic tactics as early as 1971, successful implementation of strategies to counter the homegrown threat was delayed for more than half a decade. Some attribute the delay explicitly to "tensions between the various governmental offices."[44] Domestic politics within the government would have to be overcome in order to fully implement a strategy that included both Hard and Soft Power.

IMPACT

In 1976, a panel of Dutch-Moluccans was established to advise the government on social and cultural conditions of that population. One of the more progressive developments was the formation of "a triad of government agencies, nongovernment organizations and advocacy groups" that cooperated on improving relations.[45] These efforts not only ensured dialogue between the Dutch government and the Dutch-Moluccan community, they also provided a platform to air concerns and to create projects that required mutual contributions—for instance, the construction of a Moluccan Historical Museum to educate the public on the experiences of Dutch-Moluccans. This symbolic act was important because it recognized Dutch-Moluccans as an important part of the national "ingroup" and acknowledged Dutch-Moluccan contributions to Dutch society.

As in the British experience with the IRA, the results of the Soft Power approach were not immediately apparent. In some quarters of the Dutch-Moluccan community, cultural and familial ties run deep, and some still long

---

44   Janse, Ronald. "Fighting Terrorism in the Netherlands; a Historical Perspective."
45   Rassner. "The Dutch Response to Moluccan Terrorism, 1970-1978."

passionately for independence of the Moluccas Islands. The impact of the Soft Power strategy is evident, though. The last terrorist attack by Dutch-Moluccans was in 1978, and the violent nationalists' passionate ideology no longer resonates strongly. As the current president of the exiled Moluccan government in the Netherlands recently pointed out, "We're living in different times now. We believe that to achieve our aim—the establishment of an independent state—we don't need to use violence. It's better to choose a path of dialogue, lobbying and all that. That way, we'll actually achieve more."[46]

COMMON THEMES OF BRITISH AND DUTCH STRATEGY ADJUSTMENTS

In between target and terrorist lies a segment of the community that the government cannot afford to alienate: the mass base, or "fence-sitters," who naturally share some similarity or alignment with terrorist grievances. This community should be sought by the government as a pool of potential allies because they, as part of the ingroup, have more credibility than government officials who are often considered inherently outsiders. If the trust and cooperation of the mass base can be earned by the government, these people have the capacity to directly influence the ideological battle via a credible counter-narrative. On the other hand, if the mass base exhibits apathy, the result is a populous that will neither confront terrorist ideology nor support government efforts to address it. The net result is that suspicious activities go unreported. In a war of ideas, an apathetic response to terrorist ideologies by the public has the same practical effect as condoning terrorism.

Therefore when conditions exist wherein cooperation is gauged to be low, it is the responsibility of leaders from both sides to ask why. It is equally their responsibility to change the circumstances that prevent cooperation. The obligation applies to both community and government leaders because the constituencies of both suffer under these circumstances.

The mass base also represents a potential recruiting pool for terrorists. Leaders within any community have a unique ability to diminish the social status of terrorists, thereby reducing the appeal of terrorist groups and their ability to recruit new terrorists. Of course, if government actions are perceived by ingroup members to be discriminatory and unjust, one might expect support for terrorist groups to increase. The British experienced this reality in Northern Ireland, and the condition is all too common today in

---

46   Brouwer. "the Moluccan Dream – Still Alive at 60."

the United States. This is an important point for consideration, particularly when influential, national-level non-government agencies actively advocate withholding cooperation with law enforcement.[47]

In foreign theaters, the effort to attract the mass population away from terrorist groups is a preeminent concern and Soft Power is the prescribed method for dealing with this category of community members. As evidence, the Defense Department's Counterinsurgency Strategy, adopted in December 2006, states clearly that in considering the strategic implication of counterinsurgent targeting:

> Lethal targets are best addressed with operations to capture or kill; nonlethal targets are best engaged with [civil-military operations] CMO, [information operations] IO, negotiation, political programs, economic programs, social programs and other noncombat methods. Nonlethal targets are usually more important than lethal targets in COIN; they are never less important.[48]

The implications of counterinsurgency strategy are relevant here only in terms of their philosophical conclusion. The mass population is always as, and sometimes more, important than those who would conduct or support terrorist attacks. If counterterrorists alienate or make enemies of the mass population, it becomes easier for terrorist groups to recruit more terrorists. As we have seen in the British and Dutch examples, both nations employed coercive tactics in their initial response to the threat of terrorism, as did the United States in military operations overseas. All three shifted their strategies to incorporate Soft Power.

Hard Power tactics are a normal and, some might say, expected, government response to attacks on the civilian population. The Catholic population in Northern Ireland suffered acutely prejudiced treatment at the hands of the Protestant government, then violent repression. When the British Army arrived to quell violence, the coercive tactics it employed likely exacerbated the mistrust of government that existed for many Catholics who had thus far opposed violence. This left the majority of the Catholic community with no way to legitimately voice its grievances. The Catholics in Northern Ireland were also faced with severe repercussions from PIRA for cooperating with the British "enemy." Irish Catholics were caught in the middle, a figurative purgatory.

---

47   Eileen Sullivan and Chris Hawley. "Angry Over Spying, Muslims Say: ' Don't Call NYPD'." *The Associated Press,* November 14, 2011, sec. Domestic news,

48   United States Army. *FM 3-24.2: Tactics in Counterinsurgency.* Washington, DC: Department of the Army, 2009

Similarly, when Dutch troops surrounded Moluccan communities with tanks to establish control and apprehend terrorists, the general, non-Moluccan, population likely felt more secure. The fence-sitting population inside the cordon, however, had an entirely different experience. In retrospect, the Dutch government recognized that "retaliation" against entire communities inflamed, rather than extinguished, radicalization in vulnerable populations. In these experiences with homegrown terrorism, the British and Dutch learned that reactionary, sloppily-executed strategies that consisted only of Hard Power tactics contributed to an increased threat of homegrown terrorism.

The government has a fundamental need to understand the dynamics that contribute to "security" for the communities it governs. The quality of human intelligence available to the British and Dutch in these circumstances limited the tactical options available to them. Sound intelligence consists of both overt and covert sources of information, and both of these elements can be dramatically enhanced through positive interaction between government agents and the community. A poor understanding of potential threats and their underlying drivers allowed legitimate grievances to fester in populations, in turn producing violent responses. The British, for example, might have incorporated the perspectives of Open Source Intelligence from Republican-leaning news media and public speeches into their assessment of the security situation in Northern Ireland. Similarly, the Dutch might have considered demographic data that would have indicated severe deficiencies in housing conditions, literacy and economic status between the Dutch-Moluccan and the general population. In response to violent protest, the British and Dutch security forces responded in ways that squelched the immediate threat but eroded the legitimacy of the government perceived to be deaf to the protesting voices of these communities. Ultimately government responses led to increased isolation, the inability and unwillingness of the aggrieved populous to communicate with government and, as a result, to more bad decisions by the governments. Effective HUMINT collection from overt and covert sources would have afforded these governments the opportunity to make better-informed decisions about the need to address fundamental challenges, how to respond to protest and allowed for a precise rather than blunt response to violence.

The disastrous outcome of poor intelligence was exemplified in the case of Northern Ireland in 1969. The Ulster government misinterpreted Catholic protests, which resulted in the RUC's disproportionately violent reaction to civil disobedience. This tragedy occurred precisely because of classic ingroup/outgroup dynamics, at least partly based on social identity. The social division and repressive governance of the majority (Protestant) government drove a wedge between the security services and the Catholic population. The police were neither respected nor trusted to be honest brokers in disputes. Thus, positive interaction between the security services and the population was severely limited, and the resulting decisions were disastrous.

The British faced a series of dilemmas when they arrived in Northern Ireland: the U.K.'s military forces were so handicapped by a lack of local intelligence that they were compelled to resort to extreme tactics to restore order. Their tactics, however, did little to increase the public's sense of security. Harsh tactics undermined the British military's ability to win public trust. Since the population feared both the PIRA and the British military neither overt, volunteered information, nor reliable human intelligence provided the ability to understand and address Catholic grievances, which were very real. The fundamental need for good human intelligence went unmet because the British military did not have the trust of the local populace.

Similarly, the Dutch Moluccans had legitimately experienced prejudice and isolation from the Dutch population. Like the Irish, the Dutch Moluccan community was frustrated in its attempts to voice community grievances. As suggested by the Dutch court, a whole-government approach was adopted to better serve its citizens, and efforts were made to integrate the Dutch Moluccan community in to mainstream Dutch society. The government acknowledged Dutch Moluccan grievances and addressed them through negotiation. This provided legitimacy and relevance to a community whose identity had been stripped via its refugee experience. Once empowered, the government relied on the Dutch Moluccan community leaders to influence the threat within their local communities.

Despite the tactical competency of the British services, it was not until the U.K. government incorporated methods of building trust between the Northern Irish communities that real progress was made. Likewise, in the Netherlands, direct engagement with centers of influence contributed to a more granulated understanding the threat and the Dutch Moluccan community grievances. Only when these nations dedicated resources to engage with at-risk populations did terrorism diminish and negotiations take place. Engagement created a context wherein the underlying motivators that had resulted in a cycle of violent conflict could be resolved, or at least diminished.

Looking to the future, both the British and the Dutch would come to the conclusion that a strategy consisting of both Hard and Soft Power was necessary to defeat the terrorists' ideology, and that the middle ground, where fence-sitters reside, would be the battle-space in future ideological conflicts.

This is an important consideration for the homeland security apparatus in the United States, as well. Domestic counterterrorist efforts have, in some cases, been perceived as discriminatory and made the American Muslim community feel unsafe in their own country and communities. The result of such actions played out on the national stage, as the Associated Press reported:

> Fed up with a decade of the police spying on the innocuous details of the daily lives of Muslims, activists in New York are discouraging people from going directly to the police with their concerns about terrorism, a campaign that is certain to further strain relations between the two groups.[49]

Clearly, it is imperative that the United States find a better way of conducting its counterterrorism mission.

---

49   Sullivan and Hawley. "Angry Over Spying, Muslims Say: ' Don't Call NYPD'."

CHAPTER 3

PREVENTION AND THE LONG WAR

STRATEGIES THAT ALIGN WITH THE THREAT

"Experience teaches us that it is much easier to prevent an enemy from posting themselves than it is to dislodge them after they have got possession."

–George Washington

For the U.K. and the Netherlands, like most of the Western world, the emergence of the Salafi-jihadi threat presented challenges not previously faced. The PIRA, for instance, articulated limited goals–political independence from Protestant rule and British occupation. In the Netherlands, the Dutch-Moluccan community sought support for its ethno-nationalist goals and recognized Dutch support was essential to attaining that goal. Al Qaeda, however, set forth ever-increasing foreign policy demands, sought political domination across a vast region and the religious conversion of its enemies. For Islamists, the underlying Salafi-jihadi narrative exposed the West as an existential enemy and called on "true believers" in Islam, regardless of their geography, to take up arms against Western oppressors. Salafist-jihadis perceive the secular-Western world to be bent on the religious and cultural annihilation of Muslims. With organizations like al Qaeda, negotiation is not feasible.

While shocked by the attacks on the United States of September 11, 2001, neither the British nor the Dutch made dramatic changes in their counterterrorism policies until al Qaeda-inspired terrorism was recognized as a threat in their own territories. At the cost of lives, both nations were late to act on social polarization between their traditional majority Christian/secular population and growing minority populations that were Muslim.

To be sure, the threat of terrorism in the United Kingdom was complex in the new millennium. On the one hand, the British had been engaged in a conflict with one of the world's most sophisticated and long-lasting terrorist organizations, the PIRA, and its offshoots since 1969. Only recently had a threat from al Qaeda and like-minded Salafi-jihadi terrorists reached British shores. But much of the threat in England was not imported—it was resident in the U.K. already. Why did the Salafi-jihadi narrative appeal to British

Muslims? To try to understand the Salfi-jihadi threat in the U.K., it is useful to explore the context of Muslim-majority relations in the spring of 2001 in Britain. During that period,

> ...spasmodic rioting skipped between towns in the north of England ... white and Asian youths fought each other and the police. In Bradford, cars were torched, businesses were firebombed and, on July 7th alone, 164 police officers were injured.[1]

This turmoil, occurred prior to September 11, 2001, and foreshadowed the depths of social division that would follow. Radicalization that led to violence would increase in Britain's Muslim communities.

With the March 2003 invasion of Iraq, the threat increased exponentially. As provided by Eliza Manningham-Buller, the former head of MI5, the U.K. "involvement in Iraq radicalized a whole generation of young people who saw [the U.K.'s] role in Iraq and Afghanistan as an attack on Islam."[2] The U.K.'s close alignment with the United States changed Britain's status in the "global jihad" from support base to target.

British security services consistently assessed that the global jihadist threat emanates both from terrorists guided by core al Qaida leadership, as well as self-radicalizing actors who are "autonomous and take their lead from radical propaganda shared via the internet and other channels."[3] MI5 subsequently concluded that Islamic terrorists draw their inspiration from al Qaeda's global message: the West represents a threat to Islam, loyalty to religion and democratic institutions is impossible, and violence is the only proper response.[4]

This Salafi-jihadi ideology may resonate with some British Muslims because many perceive themselves as a disadvantaged minority. In fact, this perception is supported by socioeconomic metrics: Muslims in the U.K.

---

1   The Economist London. "Britain: Alone, Together." *The Economist.* London 360, no. 8230 (July, 14, 2001, 2001): 53.

2   Chris Hughes. "Iraq War 'Caused Terrorism in U.K.'; Says Ex-Boss of Mi5." *The Mirror,* July 21, 2010, sec. NEWS."

3   MI5. "Security Service MI5."

4   Ibid.

are the least likely of religious groups to own their own homes or hold professional jobs, and the most likely to be unemployed.[5] But socioeconomic motivations alone have not proven to be a key indicator for radicalization.[6]

Many of the U.K.'s immigrant Muslims relocated to the U.K. from regions of conflict (particularly Kashmir) where tribal and clan affiliations had great influence on daily life and social norms. For instance, most women in Muslim countries do not work outside the home. In the U.K., where the cost of living is very high and most women in the general population do work outside the home, the cultural proclivity for a wife to abstain from outside employment reduces the household income below the average. A similar pattern emerges when one considers that the average number of children born to Muslims in the Europe is three times that of non-Muslims.[7]

Reasons for polarization can be complex. For instance, Gallup polling data of Muslims in London indicated that they were "less likely than the general public to say they would prefer to live in a neighborhood made up mostly of people who share their religious or ethnic background (25% versus 35%)."[8] Contrasting with this articulated desire, the cultural tradition and economic conditions of many Muslim immigrants compel multiple generations to live in the same home. Most homes in the U.K. are small, making this type of arrangement difficult. The obvious alternative for children is to buy a home close to other family members. This course of action seems to resolve the cultural preference, but to other British citizens in the neighborhood, it might appear that the immigrant population is buying up local properties with intent to form a political block. This is one example of how the majority population of a local area might sense a threat to its long-held and deeply rooted identity. In such circumstances, the failure of individuals to engage with one another can cause social polarization—similar to the circumstances of Catholic and Protestants in Ireland in 1969.

5   The Economist. "Special Report: The Enemy within - Muslim Extremism in Europe." *The Economist* 376, no. 8435 (Jul 16, 2005): 24,

6   Jeff Victoroff. "The Mind of the Terrorist: A Review and Critique of Psychological Approaches." *The Journal of Conflict Resolution* 49, no. 1 (Feb 2005, 2005): 3-42

7   Omer Taspinar. Europe's Muslim Street. Washington, D.C.: Brookings Institute, 2003,.

8   Dalia Mogahed. Beyond Multiculturalism Vs. Assimilation. Princeton, New Jersey: The Gallup Organization, 2007

Understanding that ascribed identities like ethnicity and religious beliefs are fundamental drivers for ingroup/outgroup alienation,[9] and in the context of an already polarizing society, it is easy to see why British Muslims were emotionally impacted by U.K. military actions against coreligionists and extended family abroad. Some British Muslims suffered the predictable outcomes of these circumstances—cognitive dissonance and crisis of identity. The result for some British Muslims was increased hostility toward the government, its population and relatively high levels of domestic radicalization in the British-Muslim community.

ADDRESSING DOMESTIC RADICALIZATION

The terrorist attacks of September 11, 2001, the allied invasion of Iraq on March 20, 2003 and the al Qaeda attack on the London railway system of July 7, 2005 exacerbated polarization of British society. The British acknowledged that underlying social conditions and intergroup conflict between the United Kingdom's Muslim and non-Muslim populations were brewing well before any of these events. Accordingly, the U.K. set out to address the threat to its national security on multiple fronts with a new strategy in 2003[10].

As a result of the circumstances described above, regardless of the one's perception of the validity of British Muslim grievances, much of Britain's Muslim population felt alienated from the majority population. The British determined that these circumstances must be dealt with effectively to prevent further social polarization and increased violence over the long term. Based on past experiences in Northern Ireland, the British developed a strategy adapted to al Qaeda's ideology and an environment changed by globalization. To implement the strategy, new structures, doctrine and tools would have to be applied.

First, and at a strategic level, the U.K. approached national security in an academic and intelligence-minded way. The riots in Bradford and elsewhere were investigated not just as crimes, but also in a way that could inform government policies that might impact security. Even before the attacks on Washington and New York on September 11, and while strategically focused on the Irish "Troubles," the Home Office became concerned with the obvious risk of escalating violence between British Muslims and other segments of

---

9   Pew Global Attitudes Project. *Global Public Opinion in the Bush Years (2001-2008)*. Washington, D.C.: Pew Research Center, 2008

10 Project CONTEST: The Government's CounterTerrorism Strategy. London: United Kingdon. House of Commons, 2009.

society. Key to preventing violence would be an increased understanding of the factors that might fuel inter-ethnic and religious violence. The Home Office commissioned Ted Cantle to lead an investigation to assess why the rioting occurred, and he came to the following conclusion:

> Whilst the physical segregation of housing estates and inner city areas came as no surprise, the team was particularly struck by the depth of polarisation of our towns and cities. The extent to which these physical divisions were compounded by so many other aspects of our daily lives, was very evident. Separate educational arrangements, community and voluntary bodies, employment, places of worship, language, social and cultural networks, means that many communities operate on the basis of a series of parallel lives. These lives often do not seem to touch at any point, let alone overlap and promote any meaningful interchanges.[11]

The underlying polarization of British society was assessed to indicate the possibility of continuing violence, in direct parallel to the polarization between Protestants and Catholics in Northern Ireland thirty years before.

By 2003 it was obvious that Salafi-jihadi ideology represented not just a threat from abroad, but also from within a British Muslim population that maintained familial and ideological links to regions where the U.K. and its allies were engaged in military operations. Facing the prospect of internal political, religious and ethnic conflict, the British government devised a "long-war" strategy for the new threat, a balanced approach incorporating both Hard and Soft Power. While the British employed aggressive military action against terrorists overseas, domestic policing and intelligence collection were focused on disrupting terrorist operations in the U.K. British security services also recognized the urgent need to pair these tactics with engagement strategies designed to stop the flow of new recruits to Salafi-jihadi terrorism and cut off support for terrorist organizations. The resulting holistic, government-wide strategy to counter terrorism was titled "CONTEST."

In CONTEST's development, British security services recognized that this "new terrorism" and the conditions allowing it to develop contrasted sharply with the Irish threat. PIRA's "terrorism was domestic, operatives used bombs and bullets and aimed to avoid capture, and there was an end goal that could potentially be reached through negotiation."[12]

---

11   Ted Cantle. Community Cohesion: A Report of the Independent Review Team Chaired by Ted Cantle (Cantle Report). London: U.K.: Home Office, 2001.

12   Rosenau, William, Bruce Hoffman, Andrew J. Curiel, and Doron Zimmerman. "Mike Whine, Community Security Trust Terrorism and Diasporas in the UK." RAND Corporation, 2007

In contrast, Salafi-jihadi ideologies presented a more complex challenge that required immediate steps to address the long-term threat. With the reference of historical and ongoing "hearts and minds" campaigns, the services considered Soft Power approaches to address threats from Salafi-jihadi ideology—not just Hard Power tactics to disrupt imminent threats of attack. This approach was important because of the particular challenge that Salafi-jihadi ideology poses, as it is exceptionally violent and has potentially unlimited reach:

> Where the Irish pursued a limited and defined political agenda, al Qaeda and similarly motivated groups are "global in origin, global in ambition and global in reach…[with] an ambition to kill as many people as possible."[13]

COUNTERTERRORISM STRATEGY IN THE UNITED KINGDOM

The United Kingdom grounded its strategy on clearly defined terms. In 2000, the U.K. defined terrorism as:

> …the use or threatened use of violence, designed to influence the government or an international governmental organization or to intimidate the public or a section of the public for the purpose of advancing a political, religious or ideological cause.[14]

This definition remained consistent throughout the decade and is recognized across the entire government—a circumstance enabled by the U.K. structure, which will be addressed later. This definition also enabled broad measures to be taken to address the roots of terrorism outside the sphere of law enforcement, opening the door to government inquiry into religion and ideology.

The U.K. developed a comprehensive counterterrorism strategy that included projects extending into both foreign and domestic activities. The strategy, the CONTEST strategy mentioned in the prior section, is arranged into four components:

1. **Pursue:** i.e., stopping terrorist attacks;

2. **Prevent:** i.e., stopping people from becoming terrorists or supporting violent extremism;

3. **Protect:** i.e., strengthening protection against attack; and

---

13   O'Neill, Sean. "Special Branch Absorbed into Counter-Terror Unit." *The Times,* 2006.

14   *Terrorism Act 2006.* London: UK Home Office, 2006

4. **Prepare:** i.e., mitigating the impact of attacks.[15]

Of these four components, only the Prevent strategy (hereafter referred to as "Prevent") will be discussed in detail because Prevent is an attempt to counter terrorist ideology and is particularly relevant in the domestic environment. As such, Prevent is intended to provide long-term solutions to national security concerns. It aims to counter the appeal of extremists' narratives locally, and recognizes that such appeals may vary from community to community and individual to individual. The Prevent strategy promotes a joint effort between government and community to decrease terrorism by acting along five main axes[16]:

1. Challenge violent extremist ideologies and support mainstream ideology;

2. Disrupt those who promote violent extremism and support the institutions that are victim to such voices;

3. Support individuals who are being or have been recruited to the cause of violent extremism;

4. Increase the resilience of communities to violent extremism; and

5. Address the grievances that ideologues are exploiting.[17]

According to Marc Sageman's testimony before the 9/11 Commission, bin Laden and like-minded extremists adhere to a "global Salafi jihadist" ideology that is an ultra-conservative form of Islam, which subverts the ideology of "peaceful fundamentalist Muslim groups ... [that might] ... promote a peaceful message and repudiate terrorist violence."[18]

Therefore, the "peaceful fundamentalist Muslim groups" described by Sageman represent the mass base—a recruiting pool for both terrorists and the government. Engagement and partnership with that mass base was, and is, central to the U.K. strategy. Communities are expected to play an active role in countering radicalization by developing support functions that provide positive options to those who may be vulnerable to recruitment by

---

15 United Kingdom. Home Office (Countering International Terrorism). *The United Kingdom's Strategy for Countering International Terrorism. 2009* Crown ed. London: Prime Minister and the Secretary of State for the Home Department, 2009.

16 United Kingdom. Home Office (Prevent). "Prevent."..

17 United Kingdom. Home Office. Prevent.

18 National Commission on Terrorist Attacks Upon the United States. *Statement of Marc Sageman to the National Commission on Terrorist Attacks upon the United States July 9, 2003 the Global Salafi Jihad.* 2003

terrorists. Such individuals regularly come into contact with government officials (including, but not limited to, law enforcement, community workers or religious figures).

Disrupting the propagandists and recruiters for al Qaeda and like-minded extremists is the underlying intent of the Prevent strategy. U.K. laws allow for arrest and prosecution of individuals who incite violence or provide justification for violent acts,[19] but the application of executive action by law enforcement officials is coordinated by police with local authorities. In turn, local authorities can begin addressing the ideological vacuum that might result from law enforcement action. Thus, the Prevent strategy recognizes the importance of consultation and coordination between agencies prior to law enforcement action in order to affect the community in a positive or least damaging way.

COUNTER TERRORISM STRUCTURE IN THE UNITED KINGDOM

To implement the strategy, a concerted effort across governmental departments was required. The United Kingdom's counterterrorism strategy emanates from the Home Office, which has overall responsibility for immigration and passports, drug policy, counterterrorism, and police.[20] The U.K. counterterrorism mission enjoys the advantages of a unified command under Home Office because each officer in the security apparatus can trace missions and guidance to a common source. Overarching policing policies and philosophy are set by the central government, which also establishes strategy, develops training and provides funding related to these functions. This framework ensures a common sense of mission, a common language and an intelligence-minded culture for the counterterrorism community.

The Office for Security and Counter-Terrorism (OSCT) was established as part of the Home Office "to give strategic direction to the U.K.'s work to counter the threat from international terrorism." [21]The OSCT reports to both the secretary of the Home Office and the undersecretary for Security and Counterterrorism, and is directly responsible for implementing and coordinating efforts across the "whole of government" for the execution of the CONTEST strategy. The overarching responsibility of the OSCT ensures a broad-lens view of the terrorism challenge and common doctrine.

---

19   *Racial and Religious Hatred Act 2006*

20   United Kingdom. Home Office. 2010. Current threat level.

21   "about the Office for Security and Counter-Terrorism." United Kingdom, Home Office,

This multidimensional perspective informs recommendations for legislation, guidance, and funding to set a "strategic government" response. OSCT ensures that the counterterrorism effort is addressed through collective effort.[22]

The Research, Information and Communications Unit (RICU) of the OSCT was created in 2007, to ensure consistent counterterrorism "messaging" across all levels of government. Like the OSCT, RICU is responsible to key leaders within the Home Office, the Foreign and Commonwealth Office and the Department for Communities and Local Government. CONTEST communications strategies are developed by RICU, which assists local governments to communicate more effectively regarding CONTEST. The U.K.'s Home Office is attuned to "short-term opportunities and developing longer-term communications projects, to weaken terrorist ideologies and strengthen credible alternatives to them." Informed by a deep understanding of the complex systems that result in terrorism, RICU plays an invaluable role in the "battle of ideas."

The U.K. staffs RICU with experts from a spectrum of fields, including intelligence officers, anthropologists, and educators. These "academic practitioners" conduct research and analysis to ensure that decision makers across government speak with consistency regarding policy matters and government actions.[23]

This is not to say, however, that all counterterrorism operations are strictly directed from London. Until March 2011, as a way of ensuring coordination at local levels, Government Offices (GOs) formed multiagency regional resilience forums. The GOs convened in each English region to coordinate wide-area planning. GOs also acted as a bridge between central government and the local response: many of the outreach and partnering functions previously conducted by GOs are now conducted by local authorities, which are encouraged to develop strategies to address threats in the local context.[24]

22   United Kingdom. "Home Office: Office for Security and Counter Terrorism." U.K. National Archive.

23   United Kingdom. Home Office. "Office for Security and Counter-Terrorism, about RICU." U.K. National Archives.

24   United Kingdom. Government Office Network, 2011

As evidenced in government restructuring and Prevent adaptations, the U.K. recognized the dynamics that fuel terrorist threats vary, and that tactics employed in one region may not work in another. Therefore, GOs coordinated "best practices" within and between regions.[25]

Joint-service counterradicalization efforts like those described above are still coordinated at regional and local levels. The U.K.'s flexible structure, designed to address local needs, enhances the potential for success. Local governments and remaining GOs have the capacity to provide "full-service" responses to local grievances and have been fully integrated into the U.K.'s counterterrorism strategy. This allows the a concerted effort to:

- Foster partnership of police and citizens to involve the whole community in strategies to promote greater public safety;

- Take a problem-solving approach to identify and effectively address the underlying conditions that give rise to crime and disorder;

- Transform the government to respond to community needs more effectively;

- Enhance the understanding of interdisciplinary capabilities between government agencies.

The U.K. model demonstrates that joint-agency coordination at regional and local levels can ensure that national strategies are correctly resourced and prioritized where it counts—in regular interaction with the public. In turn, coordinated local efforts ensure that the central government is informed regarding the intricacies of the region. When information from various cities and localities is consolidated, a national threat picture can be developed with sufficient specificity to materially affect strategic planning. A further advantage of joint service is that some government officers, including selected MI5 personnel, are required to serve three-year tours outside central headquarters. This facilitates the transmission of fresh ideas back to London and a better understanding of interdisciplinary capabilities for developing leaders. Rotation of mangers outside of headquarters also provides central headquarters with an improved understanding of localized dynamics.[26]

---

25 *Preventing Violent Extremism: Next Steps for Communities.* Rotherham, UK: Communities and Local Government Publications, 2008

26 United Kingdom. Security Service. "Security Service MI5: Your Career."

The challenge for the British government is to disrupt and discredit the Islamist message without alienating the mass base (British Muslims in general, and especially peaceful fundamentalist British Muslims) or the general population. A further challenge is to avoid focusing so many resources on the Muslim community that other underprivileged minorities are alienated.

Civil libertarians and free-speech advocates voiced opposition to the Prevent program:

> The atmosphere promoted by Prevent is one in which to make radical criticism of the government is to risk losing funding and face isolation as an 'extremist.'...Depoliticizing young people and restricting radical dissent is actually counterproductive.[27]

The British have also been criticized for engaging principally with moderates within the Muslim community. Nick Chatrath, of Oxford's faculty of Oriental Studies, for instance, criticized the Muslim Council of Britain (MCB), declaring that the MCB's effectiveness in countering radicalization was hampered by its unwillingness to confront more extreme members of the Muslim community. Chatrath put forth that,

> ...in the face of growing radicalisation in Britain, Muslim leaders are ignoring extremists' points of view and glossing over some of the more unsavoury parts of Islam's ancient texts... This attitude must change, as the best way to extinguish extremist arguments is to deal with them out in the open, not just sweep them under the carpet and hope for the best.[28]

Competition within the Muslim community was also evident. It is possible that these critics were concerned that their particular community did not receive commensurate financial support and attention from the government. Some Muslim communities decried discrimination as they sought to gain advantage for their own subgroup, based on the perception that the government is sponsoring Muslim organizations on the basis of theological criteria —for example holding Sufis to be intrinsically more moderate than Salafis. [29]

It appears, however, that many in the Muslim world understood the intent of the Prevent strategy, even in Saudi Arabia, where one might expect substantial objection:

27　Arun Kundnani. *Spooked! how Not to Prevent Violent Extremism.* London: Institute for Race Relations, 2009.

28　Ruth Gledhill. "Muslim Leaders 'Failing to Tackle Extremists'." *Times Online,* March 30, 2010

29　*Preventing Violent Extremism: Next Steps for Communities.* Rotherham

> "If...the policy is applied sensitively and Muslims are supported
> in their disgust at terrorism, rather than challenged over their
> loyalty to the U.K., then [the Prevent strategy] may be a useful
> contribution to combating the men of violence.[30]

Despite criticism, placing a high priority on engagement with British Salafist
communities and supporting their counter-radicalization efforts with
commensurate resources was consistent with the British policing model. The
UK employs resources based upon the level of perceived threat, with the
highest threats receiving the most resources. The intelligence-led policing
(ILP)[31] model in the U.K.is described by Jerry Ratcliffe, writing for the
Australian Institute of Criminology below:

> ...the U.K. National Intelligence Model emphasizes that crime is
> not randomly distributed, with the corollary that identification of
> hotspots of criminal activity is a worthwhile pursuit. It recognizes
> the importance of working with partnerships to achieve crime
> prevention, and finally that there should be a spotlight on targeting
> the criminal and not a focus on the crime.[32]

In accordance with the ILP model, the U.K. initially focused its efforts on
the ideological group it perceived to be particularly vulnerable to recruitment
by al Qaeda. The keys to Prevent's success appeared to be the ability to
ensure a correct balance of resources and continual objective evaluation
of the program's effectiveness. Unfortunately, robust spending for Prevent
programs was poorly tracked, and Prevent was subject to mixed reviews by
both Muslims and the British Parliament. The effectiveness and efficiency of

---

30 Arab News.com. "'Prevent' Strategy:The UK's "Prevent" Strategy to Target Young
British Muslims Who might be Susceptible to Radicalization and Recruitment by Al-
Qaeda is Fraught with Dangers." *Arab* News.Com, March 20, 2010.

31 According to Ratcliffe, "The aim of intelligence-led policing can be interpreted from the
tactical tasking priorities of the U.K. National Intelligence Model, as disseminated by
the National Criminal Intelligence Service (NCIS). The four elements concentrate on:
targeting offenders (especially the targeting of active criminals through overt and covert
means); the management of crime and disorder hotspots; the investigation of linked
series of crimes and incidents; and the application of preventative measures, including
working with local partnerships to reduce crime and disorder."

32 Jerry H. Ratcliffe. *Intelligence-Led Policing.* Canberra, Australia: Australian institute of
Criminology, 2003.

the Prevent strategy was brought under government scrutiny in keeping with British tradition and doctrine,[33] and a formal review of the Prevent strategy ensued in July 2010.

COUNTERTERRORISM TOOLS IN THE UNITED KINGDOM

Alternatives to the coercive power of traditional law enforcement action are available to the government through the Prevent framework. In many instances, the government may be able to facilitate intervention by the community at a point in the radicalization process prior to an act of violence. Rather than enforce petty criminal offenses, local government authorities, including police, community leaders and intelligence services, may instead choose to support community groups or leaders who are willing to intervene to disrupt the radicalization process through a variety of non-judicial techniques. This manner of disrupting the radicalization process surrenders nothing from the government. The de-radicalization effort increases opportunities to collect information on radicalizing influences, might de-legitimize claims of entrapment and charges can always be pursued at a time of the government's choosing if de-radicalization efforts fail. Rather than an ILP approach, Prevent represents a community-oriented policing model. De-radicalization efforts also present opportunities develop trust between the government and community partners. Increased levels of trust are likely to enhance collaboration and diminish the risk of perpetuating the West-versus-Islam narrative.

Building trusting relationships with the community can assist in understanding grievances. If the government can address grievances positively, it gains credibility with the public. In the United Kingdom, actions along this axis include creating safe venues for debate and a space to discuss extremism—a place where grievances can be aired and Salafi-jihadi ideology can be confronted.[34] These venues also allow for community leaders to challenge calls to violence and recognize when mistakes are made.

---

33   For an example related to the Northern Ireland conflict, refer to the 1973 Northern Ireland (Emergency Provisions) Act (EPA), which established special criminal processes that included broad search and seizure authority, warrantless arrests, and detention without trial. This Act was allowed to expire in 1973 but its authorities were reintroduced in 1974 as the Prevention of Terrorism (Temporary Provisions) Act (PTA) when the threat level increased.

34   National Commission on Terrorist Attacks Upon the United States. Statement of Marc Sageman.

The government, and particularly the police force, works directly with community leaders and activists to build strong community leadership and increase the community's ability to "self help" by providing social services and positive alternatives to violent expression for the community at large. In order to increase the capacity of communities to resist violent extremism, police services adhere to community policing models, including civilian police community support officers (PCSOs) specifically designed to serve as a bridge between police and the public.[35] This strand of the Prevent strategy involves direct, grassroots involvement with Muslim communities and their leaders through forums, town-hall meetings, research and focus groups, and educational services.

In one example, the Kent Constabulary has developed the "Partners and Community Together" (PACT) program, where police work alongside elected, religious, and neighborhood leaders to address community needs, be they increased patrols or facilitating neighborhood cleanups. The local police are dedicated to providing accessible and visible policing teams that respond to the needs of local communities.[36] This type of collaboration brings together members of the government and community who, working together, exert a positive influence on the environment that is much greater than the influence they might generate working on separate, parallel paths.

The Prevent program also supports nongovernment organizations and educators to build the society's resilience to violent extremism through a wide array of activities. The Creativity, Culture and Education (CCE) program is aimed at exposing children to different cultures and to encouraging critical thought and shared identities as British citizens. CCE is responsible for developing a range of programs in collaboration with local communities. The programs vary; from efforts like "Spirit of Hyndburn," a photography project that "encapsulates the diversity" of the township, "Not in My Name," an interactive theatre project that "boldly and unreservedly explores issues around religious extremism and terrorism," and "London Tigers," a community-led sports and youth charity that aims to build leadership and provide a positive environment to explore religion and good citizenship.[37]

---

35   United Kingdom. Metropolitan Police. "Metropolitan Police: Police Community Support Officers."

36   United Kingdom. Kent Constabulary. "Neighbourhood Policing: Visible, Accessible, Responsive."

37   United Kingdom. (2010). Create/participate (Brochure. London: Creativity, Culture and Education. Retrieved October 12, 2010.

Within the Prevent framework, the "Channel" program, is designed to provide "a mechanism for assessing and supporting people who may be targeted by violent extremists or drawn in to violent extremism."[38] Channel is administered by a local Channel coordinator and includes the participation of a panel of representatives from government, nongovernment organizations, and community leaders. This panel meets regularly to discuss with great specificity individual cases of radicalization, and to develop local strategies to address the threat. In cases where an individual is believed to have begun the radicalization process, panel members devise a strategy suited to the particular individual. Actions necessarily vary by individual, but prescribed actions might include religious counseling from a perspective that does not condone terrorist violence in order to impact the subject on a theological framework, direct communication with family members of the subject, or in more serious instances, removing a child from foster care and resettling the child with other foster parents. This program has been controversial due to its focus on Salafi orientations and concerns over privacy matters.[39]

RECENT ADJUSTMENTS

In February 2011, the Prime Minister David Cameron weighed in regarding the perceived threat to national security and set the groundwork for a revised version of the strategy to stop British citizens from being recruited to terrorist groups. The revised strategy (hereafter referred to as Prevent 2.0) was expanded to include right-wing extremists, but makes clear that the U.K. considers the domestic Islamist threat its prime concern:

> [t]he biggest threat that we face comes from terrorist attacks, some of which are, sadly, carried out by our own citizens. It is important to stress that terrorism is not linked exclusively to any one religion or ethnic group... the United Kingdom still faces threats from dissident republicans in Northern Ireland... Nevertheless, we should acknowledge that this threat comes in Europe overwhelmingly from young men who follow a completely perverse, warped interpretation of Islam, and who are prepared to blow themselves up and kill their fellow citizens."[40]

---

38   United Kingdom. Home Office: Office for Security and Counterterrorism (OSCT). Channel: Supporting Individuals Vulnerable to Recruitment by Violent Extremists: Home Office: Office for Security and Counterterrorism, 2010.

39   Alarabiya.net. "UK Police Probe Muslim Youth for Radical Views." Alarabiya.Net, March 29, 2009

40   U.K.. HM Government (2011). PM's speech at Munich Security Conference

This statement made it immediately apparent that the philosophy behind Prevent revisions (Prevent 2.0) means the U.K.'s war on terrorism will not just be fought overseas. Salafi-jihadi ideology is to be viewed as the principal opposition. Prevent is based on the premise that "extremism breeds terrorism."[41] [42] According to the Prime Minister, the revisions are expected to have long-term benefits beyond security. He speculated that conflict prevention would be much less expensive than exorbitant amounts of money spent on counterterrorism investigations and recovery efforts in the wake of a terrorist attack.[43]

On April 1, 2011, British Security Minister Baroness Pauline Neville Jones hinted at some of the expected refinements of Prevent at a symposium on U.K. and U.S. approaches in countering radicalization. According to Jones, the keynote speaker, the revised British strategy would be more narrowly focused "on violent extremism and the pathways that lead to [the] espousal of violence." Central to the new strategy would be the 'three I's": ideology, institutions, and individuals" that promote values in conflict with those identified as central to "British identity."[44]

Prevent 2.0 took is a more aggressive approach than its predecessor. In refiguring its counterradicalization strategy, the U.K. studied and assessed the impact of Prevent on the security of its citizens. The British government turned introspective, ultimately determined it necessary to define itself more clearly. The counterterrorism effort would proceed based on the "British" core values and national identity; in turn, Prevent 2.0 would be more broadly aimed at "Extremism," rather than "violent extremism."

Extremist ideology, which the strategy describes as "vocal or active opposition to fundamental British values, including democracy, the rule of law, individual liberty and mutual respect and tolerance of different faiths and beliefs" is clearly defined as the target of Prevent 2.0. [45] The strategy recognizes the imperative for government to avoid meddling with religion,

---

41   Carlile, Alex. *Report to the Home Secretary of Independent Oversight of Prevent Review and Strategy (also Referred to as the Lord Carlile Report), as Provided in Prevent 2011.*: United Kingdom. The Stationery Office Limited on behalf of the Controller of Her Majesty's Stationery Office, 2011. Also referred to as the Lord Carlile Report.

42   United Kingdom. HM Government. PREVENT (2011), Annex A, Published by the Stationary Office,

43   U.K.. HM Government (2011). PM's speech at Munich Security Conference.

44   "UK and U.S. Approaches in Countering Radicalization: Intelligence, Communities, and the Internet: British Security Minister Outlines Key Elements of New Prevent Agenda." Washington, DC, Federal News Service, April 1, 2011, 2011.

45   U.K.. HM Government (2011) Prevent Strategy (Prevent 2.0), Glossary, 107.

but recognizes the intent of Salafi-jihadist to intertwine religion and politics. Prevent 2.0 addressed this issue and the challenge it presents for counter-terrorists: "that the line between extremism and terrorism is often blurred; and that what appear at first sight to be non-violent extremist ideologies are drawn upon by terrorists to justify violence."[46]

Prevent 2.0 clearly states that the government "will support the efforts of theologians, academics and communities by providing information on the texts which are being used to radicalise people in this country... [with an intent to] to ensure that counter-narrative work is widely circulated and in a form that reaches as many people as possible."[47] For many, particularly those who view politics is an extension of religion, this tact may cause recoil, but to effectively hold to British values the differentiation is critical.

The U.K. is currently in the process of decentralization, closing down Government Offices and empowering local authorities. During the assessment process of 2010,

> respondents clearly saw the benefits that localism could bring to Prevent. It was seen first and foremost as an opportunity to use the knowledge, access and influence of people and communities to challenge extremist and terrorist ideology. Respondents also noted that communities very often had the best understanding of how and with whom Prevent could best be delivered.[48]

Government Offices have been disbanded in order to reduce the bureaucratic burden placed on local governments through a top-down government process. The Home Office announced it will "bring about a power shift, taking power away from Whitehall and putting it into the hands of people and communities, and a horizon shift, making the decisions that will equip Britain for long-term success."[49] However, because counterterrorism efforts are recognized as a national-level priority, project management for Prevent 2.0 holds to the established centralized structure. The Home Office will develop overarching Prevent strategies and support and fund their implementation. This allows for localized implementations of the strategy that emanates

---

46 Carlile, Report to the Home Secretary of Independent Oversight of Prevent Review and Strategy.

47 U.K.. HM Government. Prevent Strategy 2011 (Prevent 2.0), p.52.

48 U.K.. Home Office (2011). Prevent Strategy,(Prevent 2.0) p. 33.

49 "Business Plan 2011-2015." Home Office

from the Home Office, based on local contexts. Decentralization means that local authorities will have more control –and responsibility—for serving the citizens of their local communities.[50]

Since Prevent Coordination positions have been disbanded (like other positions in the regionally based GOs), a network of up to 25 Prevent Coordinators will work with police who are dedicated to Prevent programs at local levels. The Prevent Coordinators will monitor local governments' compliance with the national strategy and facilitate engagement across a broad range of partners from both within and outside the government. This realignment is important because it means that Prevent 2.0 will permeate local government structures rather than be imposed by central government offices. Prevent Coordinators will still report to national level authorities, but they will be compelled to work with and advise local services and deal directly with local communities.

The de-centralized structure and overarching mission are intended to result in a unified effort across national and local level government agencies, even if the techniques applied locally vary. This structure should assist local governments in strategic decision-making by making sure local leaders understand the objectives of Prevent 2.0 and how local decisions play into the overall strategy. Likewise, local Prevent Coordinators might support the Home Office through increased "connectivity" with local governments and communities.[51] Prevent Coordinators' advice and commentary should provide a realistic rather than hypothetical understanding of local threat dynamics, and create a platform for sharing of "Best Practices" that might be customized in other localities.

The new government structure and revised strategy thus go a long way toward empowering local communities to work alongside Prevent 2.0. As in the initial rendition of Prevent, the Channel Program will play a significant role in Prevent 2.0, focusing on individuals. As Minister Neville-Jones stated, the "importance of community empowerment and engagement...

---

50   U.K.. Communities and Local Government (2011)

51   Carnes Lord. " Reorganizing for Public Diplomacy." In *Information Strategy and Warfare: A Guide to Theory and Practice*, edited by John Arquilla and Douglas A. Boxer, 118. New York: Routeldge, 2007, 118. Arquilla and Boxer Douglas A (Ed). Routeldge, New York. Carnes writes in detail with a prescription for re-organizing the US Department of State to counter messages propagated by al Qaeda. Here, his observance that local "connectivity" is critical to effective educational and cultural public diplomacy. In a domestic environment, local governments provide services and messaging that are akin to DOS efforts to support U.S. interests in other nations. There is currently no US domestic equivalent to the U.K.'s Home Office, which provides overarching strategy and resources for local communities in the U.K. as well as the domestic intelligence service.

preventing vulnerable individuals from becoming terrorists… is enormously more cost effective than maintaining an MI5 investigation or dealing with the consequences of a successful attack."[52]

Multi-agency partnerships will be led by Channel Coordinators to evaluate individuals "at risk of being drawn into terrorism, and work alongside safeguarding partnerships and crime reduction panels to provide tailored support" to the vulnerable.[53] This holistic approach provides a wide variety of tools that will be applied by local governments. Social services, policing, children's services, youth services, U.K. Border Agency, representatives from further and higher education, probation services, schools, local prisons, and public health providers are all identified as contributors to delivery of Prevent 2.0.[54]

In addition to trying to keep good citizens from going bad, the U.K. also intends to take active measure to keep out individuals who visit the country with the intent of subverting British values. Prevent 2.0 reiterates measures established under the PVTA and reaffirmed in 2005:

> [W]here propagandists break the law in encouraging or approving terrorism it must also mean arrest and law enforcement action.… where people seek to enter this country from overseas to engage in activity in support of extremist and terrorist groups we will also use the Home Secretary's power to exclude them.[55]

The Home Office took seriously the criticism of the first version of Prevent and solicited input from a broad spectrum of partners, including "delivery partners, opinion formers, community and faith groups and members of the public."[56] Respondents contributed via on-line surveys, e-mail, through regional meetings and in focus groups. These contributions revealed that most respondents recognized the long-term benefits of a pro-active and preventative strategy. The U.K. took from this input that Prevent 2.0 should:

- Focus on all threats of violence, not just those from Al Qa'ida;

- Increase community resilience and cohesion as part of a long-term approach to defeating terrorism and extremism

---

52 International Centre for the Study of Radicalization (Blog) (2011). British Security Minister Outlines Key Elements of New Prevent Agenda.

53 U.K.. Home Office (2011). Prevent Strategy,(Prevent 2.0) p. 101.

54 U.K.. Home Office (2011). Prevent Strategy,(Prevent 2.0) p. 33.

55 Ibid, 50.

56 U.K.. HM Government (2011) Prevent Review: Summary of Responses to the Consultation, p. 4. June 11, 2011.

- Be run in parallel with tighter controls on, for example, immigration and better use of existing regulations and penalties to undermine radicalisers;

- Focus on working in schools and with faith institutions; and

- Include a more effective communication strategy aimed more widely at the entire country and not just certain communities.[57]

This consultation process was a wise step for the Home Office because it encouraged cooperation between the national government, local government and local communities in order to adjust conditions in a way that benefited all, thereby creating a superordinate goal. In accordance with the government's position, "the two tasks of fighting terrorism and creating a more integrated and cohesive society were [viewed as] inseparable."[58] Further, the consultation process itself contributed to increased trust between government and potential fence sitters and enhanced government credibility.

The new structure and continuing consultation process is likely to lend fresh ideas to British counterterrorism strategy. The Home Office indicated such malleability was highly desirable when Prevent 2.0 was delivered:

> I hope that whatever Government is in office, they will be as flexible as circumstances suggest. In CT work, in order to protect citizens, the State pits itself against extremist and often heretical ideologies and their sometimes cruel manifestations. Such ideologies are often best challenged by the dynamic use of ideas, rather than by opposing ideologies.[59]

At the time of writing, Prevent 2.0 is merely a few months month old—as such, it is impossible to predict its effectiveness. Will the new, broader focus on "extremism" serve as a mechanism for increased intrusion on British freedoms, or will the government avoid crossing the "blurred lines" of religious and political ideologies? Local approaches, facilitated by Prevent Coordinators seem poised to assist in maintaining compliance to British Law, but the jury of public opinion remains out. It will truly require a national effort to avoid further exacerbating the divided population, an effort that will be affected by not only the British government:

> There is a great responsibility on all, especially respected senior figures, to emphasise the benefits of the cohesiveness of Britain, and to heal divisions where they exist. This applies equally to politicians, commentators and others who, even accidentally,

---

57   Ibid., p.5.

58   Internation Centre for the Study of Radicalization (Blog) (2011). British Security Minister Outlines Key Elements of New Prevent Agenda.

59   U.K.. HM Government (2011). PM's speech at Munich Security Conference.

demonise Muslims or others, as this feeds prejudice, and undermines Prevent and other activities designed with a healing purpose.[60]

One thing is certain, the U.K. has adopted an SIT approach: "Even if we sorted out all of the problems…there would still be this terrorism. I believe the root lies in the existence of this extremist ideology. I would argue an important reason so many young Muslims are drawn to it comes down to a question of identity."[61] But ultimately, Prevent 2.0's effectiveness will depend on its implementation and the government's ability to balance Hard and Soft Power.

BACKGROUND AND CONTEXT IN THE NETHERLANDS

Like the U.K., the Netherlands recognizes a multidimensional threat to national security: both internal and external drivers are judged to foment violence. And, also like the British, the threat posed by Islamist ideology is considered by the Dutch to be dissimilar to previous experiences with terrorism. "The complexity of [the threat] prompts us to give up our usual perceptions and to translate the new approach into policy measures."[62]

Indications of radicalization in Dutch society became evident shortly after the September 11 attacks in Washington and New York, when two Dutch citizens of Moroccan descent were killed by the Indian army in Kashmir. Soon thereafter, Dutch authorities publicly acknowledged that a network of Islamic militants was recruiting Dutch citizens for jihad.[63]

At that time in the Netherlands "there was a tendency to downplay the problem…Even if Dutch Muslims were being recruited for the jihad, they were choosing to seek martyrdom elsewhere…The risk that these young radicals could bring jihad to Western Europe, even to the Netherlands was conceivable but thought at the time to be minimal."[64] Dutch optimism was based on observations that radical Islamists were recruiting for

---

60 Ibid.

61 U.K. HM Government (2011). PM's speech at Munich Security Conference.

62 *From Dawa to Jihad: The various Threats from Radical Islam to the Democratic Legal Order.* Netherlands Ministry of the Interior and Kingdom Relations, 2004.

63 Marlise Simons. "Militants Recruiting Young Dutch Muslims for Foreign War." *New York Times,* May 31, 2002.

64 U.S. Senate Homeland Security and Governmental Affairs Committee. *Homegrown Terrorism and Radicalization in the Netherlands: Experiences, Explanations and Approaches: Testimony by Lidewijde Ongering, Deputy National Coordinator for Counterterrorism.* Violent Islamist extremism: the European experience sess., June 27, 2007.

foreign battlegrounds in places like Kashmir, Pakistan, and Afghanistan. Unfortunately, that paradigm would soon change. The Dutch security service had misjudged the salience of European nationalism for Salafi-jihadists.

The sense of relative security throughout Europe was shattered when the Madrid rail system became a target for al Qaeda's bombs on March 11, 2004. In April of the same year, the Dutch Minister of Justice conducted a review of the Netherland's counterterrorism apparatus. The findings of this research called for a central point of coordination for the counterterrorism mission. As a result, the office of the National Coordinator for Counterterrorism (NCTb) was created (The structure of the Dutch counterterrorism effort will be discussed in more detail later in this chapter).

COUNTERTERRORISM STRATEGY IN THE NETHERLANDS

Soon after the creation of NCTb, in June and July 2004, Dutch police acted on information provided by the intelligence service. Five Islamic militants who were believed to be plotting terrorist attacks against the country's only nuclear power plant, Schiphol airport, the Dutch Parliament, the Defense Ministry and other public buildings were arrested.[65] Only a few months later, the NCTb faced the first lethal case of homegrown Salafi-jihadi terrorism in the Netherlands. Theo van Gogh, an internationally renowned filmmaker and outspoken opponent of Islamic extremism, was murdered on November 2, 2004. In dramatic form, a "note, stuck to the body of Theo van Gogh with a knife, contained a 'direct warning' to the screenwriter, Ayaan Hirsi Ali, a Somali-born member of Dutch Parliament who has enraged fellow Muslims by criticizing Islamic customs and the failure of Muslim families to adopt Dutch ways."[66]

Rather than issue orders for dramatic change, the Netherlands responded pragmatically. Similar to its measured response to attacks by Dutch-Moluccan terrorists, the Netherlands opted to study the problem of Salafi-jihadist radicalization in detail, in a way that emphasized academic research. The NCTb was thus commissioned to assess counterterrorism strategies employed by other Western nations in order to determine the best way forward for the Dutch government. The Dutch would draw from not just

---

65   Marlise Simons. "A Van Gogh Suspect is Linked to Islamists ; 8 More are Arrested by Dutch Police." *The International Herald Tribune*, November 4, 2004.

66   "Note Pinned to Body Threatened Dutch MP." *The Globe and Mail (Canada)*, November 5, 2004, sec. INTERNATIONAL NEWS; World in Brief.

their own experiences with Moluccan nationalists but also from best practices of other nations to formulate new policies—which resulted in a solidly based and defendable strategic approach.

One might expect that a comprehensive and detailed national strategy resulted from the academic study. This did not happen initially. Rather than a comprehensive strategy, the Dutch took on the task piece by piece. In fact, the Netherlands did not have a formal counterterrorism doctrine at all until 2011. A compilation of policy papers and letters defining Dutch efforts to combat counterinsurgency and terrorists reveal an approach that paid great attention to the impact of policing efforts on communities and gaining community cooperation. Dutch machinations were based on previous experience with homegrown and international terrorism, as well as scholarly review of the policies and approaches of other governments.[67]

The policies devised by the Netherlands have at their base a definition of terrorism that acknowledges terrorism is an ideologically motivated act. The Dutch define terrorism as " threatening, making preparations for or perpetrating, for ideological reasons, acts of serious violence directed at people or other acts intended to cause property damage that could spark social change, creating a climate of fear among the general public, or influencing political decision-making."[68]

With this clearly defined vision of terrorism, a vision of Dutch counterterrorism strategy was set forth in 2005, even if not codified in a formal strategy:

> Firstly, to strengthen the ties within Dutch society, especially by groups open to radical ideas. Secondly, to empower society, i.e. increase its defenses, so that individuals as well as communities may oppose the extremism that affects them or tries to recruit them. Thirdly, to intervene actively through the creative use of existing judicial and administrative measures—both by central and municipal governments—and through the development of a limited number of new measures. These include making the glorification of violence a criminal offence and measures against terrorist statements and sowing hatred on the Internet.[69]

---

67   Netherlands. Hague Centre for Strategic Studies. "Counterinsurgency and Counterterrorism." The Hague Centre for Strategic Studies.

68   Netherlands. NCTb (What?). "NCTb: Themes; what is Terrorism?.".

69   Netherlands Ministry of Justice. *Broad Government Anti-Radicalism and Radicalisation Approach.* The Hague: Netherlands Ministry of Justice, 2005.

The NCTb observed in 2005 that the jihadist threat was "inextricably linked with international developments...such as the deployment of Dutch [military] units in Afghanistan and the growing international interest in interethnic relationships in the Netherlands."[70] But the Dutch analysis went well beyond the obvious physical threat to national security (attacks on critical infrastructure, assassination, mass killing or threats thereof) in its assessment. The Dutch view it as a constitutional obligation to protect its society against any who would seek to undermine its "democratic legal order" with violence. The Netherlands considered the implications of an ideological struggle and the threat that radical Islam posed to Dutch society. The implications of Salafi-jihadi ideology are viewed as threats to the codified "vertical relationships" between government and its citizens, as well as the more ephemeral "horizontal relationships" between citizens or groups of citizens.

The Dutch consider that democratic legal order is compromised when (undefined) amounts of social trust, social cohesion, solidarity, active citizenship and loyalty do not meet adequate levels.[71] The Netherlands, generally accepted to be one of the most liberal nations in Europe, perceived that the nation might be negatively affected by a social chasm between ultraconservative Muslims who deny the authority of "man-made laws" and the rest of the Dutch population. To the Dutch government, societal cohesiveness is a fundamental national security concern and therefore, the ability to maintain democratic legal order is a fundamental responsibility of the national government.

The NCTb considers terrorism "the ultimate consequence of a development starting with radicalization processes. ... [and that]... Combating terrorism starts with combating the radicalization processes."[72] For this reason, radicalization –early in the progression toward violent extremism –is the preferred intervention point for the Netherlands to address the threat. From the Dutch perspective, it is better to prevent terrorism on the front end than to risk physical threats and interethnic and interreligious conflict. The government believes that it must act against radicalism under two conditions:

---

70   Netherlands. National anti-terrorism coordinator. *Second Anti-Terrorism Progress Report.* The Hague: National anti-terrorism coordinator, 2005.

71   For a detailed discussion of the concept of "democratic legal order and its role in the assessment of the Islamist threat to the Netherlands, see "From Dawa to Jihad," p. 6–16 (Netherlands, NCTb 2004).

72   Here the U.K.'s Prevent 2.0 also closely resembles the Dutch "Broad Approach."

1. When such radicalism directly results in violence or other criminal activity;

2. When a form of radicalism that rejects the democratic rule of law gathers a large following.[73]

After the attacks in 2004, the Netherlands developed new laws that enhanced state powers toward the counterradicalization goal and did so in collaboration with fellow members of the European Union (EU). The EU agreed on a strategy framework to combat terrorism and established a universal baseline response for member states.[74]

The common strategy framework was based on four pillars: "Prevent, Protect, Pursue and Respond." [75] [76] For instance, it is now a crime to recruit on behalf a designated terrorist organization. But "most EU-wide results have been obtained in the 'Protect' strand, where the European Commission is a leading actor, and in 'Pursue', where the member states' vital interests are at stake and close cross-border cooperation is vital. Less progress has been recorded in 'Prevent' and 'Respond.'"[77] Along the "prevent" pillar, the Dutch have far exceeded the baseline performance of other EU countries.

The Netherlands enhanced state powers with new legislation like Dutch Act on the Extension of the Scope for Investigation and Prosecution of Terrorist Crimes (ESIPTC). The purpose of ESIPTC was "to enable the police and the public prosecution service to initiate criminal proceedings as early as possible in order to prevent terrorist attacks from taking place."[78] Some of the provisions of this act were dramatic and indicate how seriously the Netherlands considers the threat of radicalization. The ESIPTC act made it possible for an individual suspected of being involved in a terrorist crime

---

73   European Union. Action Plan. . EU Plan of Action on Combating Terrorism. Brussels: Council of the European Union, 2004.

74   Ibid.

75   Ibid.

76   European Union. *Council Framework Decision of 13 June 2002 on Combating Terrorism.* Luxembourg: Publications Office of the European Union, 2002. The EU counterterrorism strategy builds on preliminary steps that are articulated in the Council Framework Decision of June 13, 2002, on combating terrorism. This decision neatly captures specific steps agreed to by European Council member nations to combat terrorism.

77   Rik Coolsaet. "EU Counterterrorism Strategy: Value Added Or Chimera?" *International Affairs* 86, no. 4 (2010): 857, 865.

78   C. J. Poot,, R. J. de Bokhorst, W. H. Smeenk, and R. F. Kouwenberg. *The Act on the Extension of the Scope for Investigation and Prosecution of Terrorist Crimes.* The Hague: WODC Wetenschappelijk Onderzoek- en Documentatiecentrum(translated Research and Documentation Centre), 2008.

to be arrested without meeting the legal threshold of "probable cause," and it delayed the moment at which the suspect of a terrorist crime is allowed to inspect all court documents. Under ESIPTC, the maximum pretrial detention period can continue for in excess of two years.

Another significant change in policy came in the form of the Aliens Act.[79] The Aliens Act allows for expedited removal of aliens who are judged by the AIVD to be a threat to national security or "public order." The Aliens Act also allows for "a recommendation to refuse entry, cancellation of a residence permit, removal from the Netherlands, declaring a person to be an undesirable alien, placing them on an alert list and refusing to grant Dutch nationality (or withdrawing citizenship if it has already been granted).[80] These measures enable the national security apparatus to physically separate radicalizers from the potential recruiting pool. Removal actions can be expedited, which means radicalizers are simply and efficiently removed from the country. Streamlining this procedure dampens the radicalizer or terrorist supporter's ability to inflame sympathizers' sentiments and mitigates the potential for the radicalizer to gain public support in the domestic environment.

The above measures reflect a continuing willingness to apply Hard Power to address the counterterrorism mission. The Dutch posit that recruitment by Islamist terrorists "demonstrates the fact that the fight against Islamist terrorism does not only require great effort on the part of intelligence and security services, police and judicial authorities, but also permanent alertness in other policy areas, like immigration and aliens' policy and integration."[81]

With Hard Power tools secured the Netherlands was prepared to face the challenge of finding the right balance between confronting violent extremism and the Salafi-jihadist narrative while simultaneously fostering diversity. In other terms, the Dutch recognized the importance of preventing the development of more terrorists than their policies created. As a solution, the Dutch determined to employ an equally aggressive application of "soft power." The Netherlands elected to engage and partner directly with its Muslim community to develop a de-radicalization capacity. To orchestrate such a holistic and broad based approach, a new security structure was required.

---

79   Netherlands. *Aliens Act, Published 01/05/2007* (01/05/2007, 2007).

80   Ibid.

81   Akerboom, E. S. M. "Counter-Terrorism in the Netherlands." *Tijdschrift Voor De Politie (Police Magazine)* no. June (2003).

COUNTERTERRORISM STRUCTURE IN THE NETHERLANDS

The Dutch developed a centralized coordinating component, the NCTb to administer counterterrorism priorities. Like the U.K.'s Prevent and Prevent 2.0, the NCTb has a dual reporting stream. NCTb reports to both the Minister of Justice and the Minister of Internal Affairs and Kingdom Relations, sitting at the apex of counterterrorism operations for the country while managing components of approximately 20 agencies. In this capacity, the NCTb was designed to address critical needs through the following means:

- A single joint strategic conceptual counterterrorism framework, to include international concerns, to be used to determine priorities in policy and action;

- A single central institution to organize the required higher level of collaboration, leadership, and perseverance, like a spider with its web;

- The collation, assessment and use of information collected by third parties;

- An administrative and statutory structure, appropriate to the gravity of the situation, setting out the requisite powers in connection with counterterrorism.[82]

In practice, the NCTb is responsible for:

- Analysis of intelligence and other information;

- Policy development;

- Coordination of anti-terrorist measures.

By coordinating these tasks at a central point, agencies work less often at cross-purposes and function in support of a strategy designed by the national government, rather than through internal strategies that may overlap or conflict. Fulfilling the role of a single strategic coordination point, NCTb increases the effectiveness of the government's efforts to combat terrorism and ensures these efforts are conducted in concert with one another. None of the component agencies holds counterterrorism as its principal reason for existence: terrorism is but one of many matters that each of these agencies address. For this reason, the NCTb's role as a coordination point was deemed essential to the Dutch counterterrorism effort.[83]

---

82 Netherlands. NCTb (Mission). "Mission of the NCTb.".

83 Netherlands. Ministers of Justice and Internal Affairs & Kingdom Relations (Letter No.1). *Counterterrorism Policy10-09-2004* . The Hague: National Coordinator for Counterterrorism, 2004.

The NCTb's counterterrorism doctrine calls for municipalities to work directly with communities to develop localized strategies. In example, Amsterdam supplements the efforts of the NCTb by:

- Focusing on the long-term sustainability of the inclusive, pluralist society in which Islam has an accepted place;

- Building resilience among and with the Muslim communities so that an alternative can be provided to radical ideologies through specific prevention; and

- Investing in formal and informal networks that can report early warning signals as well as intervene as early as possible in individual cases of actual radicalization.[84]

REGIONAL AND MUNICIPAL BOARDS

At a regional level, the General Intelligence and Security Service of the Netherlands (AIVD), a civilian intelligence service responsible for national security threats, works with the Dutch national police from 25 regional service offices. These regional police forces are governed by regional police boards, consisting of mayors and a chief public prosecutor.[85] The regional police boards maintain horizontal coordination through parallel "national police" in other regions of the country, vertical integration via AIVD reports and analysis that is integrated with regional partners. The result is a networked structure that allows for an:

> up-to-date picture…within the municipal authority of the situation as regards integration and radicalisation. Indications of any threat that young men or others (girls or women) might be likely to turn against society or towards radicalism might first be noted by employees of the local authority, or by Muslim communities, the police, schools, social services…housing corporations or community centres and clubs.[86]

84　Colin Mellis. *Amsterdam and Radicalization the Municipal Approach*. The Hague: National Coordinator for Counterterrorism, 2007.

85　The Organization for Security and Co-operation in Europe (OSCE). *POLIS - Policing OnLine Information System: Policing Profiles of Participating and Partner States-Netherlands*. The Organization for Security and Co-operation in Europe, 2009.

86　Remkes, J. W. and J. P. H. Donner. *Addressing Radicalism and Radicalisation at Local and Judicial Levels*. The Hague: House of Representatives of the States General (Netherlands), 2005.

Thus AIVD can identify, advise, and mobilize regional and local leadership to independently reduce the risk of terrorism in the framework of national security policies.[87]

With only about 80 personnel, the NCTb serves as a strong strategic guide for the AIVD and the police who, on the basis of the Intelligence and Security Services Act 2002, play the largest governmental roles in the counterterrorism mission.[88] In this way, police boards can enjoy the benefit of intelligence with a national level perspective as provided by the NCTb, as well as AVID and police analysis at the regional and local levels. Police boards are further informed by community contacts with both law enforcement and nongovernment entities. This vast array of information inputs affords local governments the opportunity to reduce radicalization through a variety of means, not just law enforcement action.

The direct engagement of local political leaders in this process is clearly critical to the success of national counterterrorism objectives.[89] This relationship tends to ensure that the government, at all levels, is accountable for engagement with the public. It also verifies that leadership of regional counterterrorism efforts is attuned to local factors that may influence radicalization.

The regional structure supports an "intelligence mindset" of the police and a culture of alertness to local indicators that could signify radicalization because local policies are directly impacted by the local governments' ability to gauge community needs and grievances. At the same time, the collaborative environment increases critical evaluation of intelligence and information reports, which encourages refined analysis. This capacity for refined analysis is essential to the Dutch approach, as behaviors that are alarming in one location may be completely normal in another context. The General Intelligence and Security Service's (AIVD) national and regional assessments led to changes in structure, policy, new laws, and more specific terminology that lay the framework for the new "broad approach" to counterterrorism.

---

87   Netherlands. Algemen Inlichtingen-en Veilighdsdienst (AIVD). "The Mission of the AIVD." The Netherlands.

88   E. S. M. Akerboom Akerboom, E. S. M. "Counter-Terrorism in the Netherlands." *Tijdschrift Voor De Politie (Police Magazine)* no. June (2003)

89   Note that the U.K.'s Prevent 2.0 and its general government decentralization efforts result in a structure where representatives of the national government are embedded in local governments. This structure is the functional equivalent of the Dutch structure.

COUNTERTERRORISM TOOLS IN THE NETHERLANDS

The willingness to engage with potential recruits to violent extremism, paired with a regionalized structure and a detailed understanding of local influences resulted in a very progressive and nuanced approach to counterterrorism, and even counterradicalization, in the Netherlands. In fact, since 2006, "the focus of official counterterrorism efforts fell increasingly on deradicalization, with 'repressive' counterterrorism taking a back seat."[90] Amsterdam, the largest city in its municipal region, pursues counterradicalization at the individual level.[91] This process is developed, informed, and executed by "an intricate web of ministries, governmental agencies, local authorities, social services, educational facilities, think tanks, religious institutions and freelance consultants."[92] The central government provides a large part of the funding, training, and overarching strategy for the counterradicalization effort. Local authorities, through the components described above, coordinate and execute local strategies to support the larger picture. These strategies are mostly based on the Amsterdam model that defines the radicalization processes and a model for deradicalization, created by Colin Mellis,[93] the Amsterdam municipal government's policy advisor for counterterrorism. Mellis described radicalization in this way:

---

90   Froukje Demant and Beatrice De Graaf. "How to Counter Radical Narratives in the Case of Molaccan and Islamic Radicals." *Studies in Conflict and Terrorism* 33, (2010): 408,

91   Froukje Demant, Marieke Slootman, Frank Buijs, and Jean Tillie. *Decline and Disengagement: An Analysis of Processes Of Deradicalization.* Amsterdam, NL: Institute for Migration and Ethnic Studies (IMES), University of Amsterdam, 2008

92   Lorenzo Vindino. "A Preliminary Assessment of Counter-Radicalization in the Netherlands." *CTC Sentinel* 1, no. 9 (2008): 12

93   Mellis. *Amsterdam and Radicalization the Municipal Approach.*

Explaining Radicalization

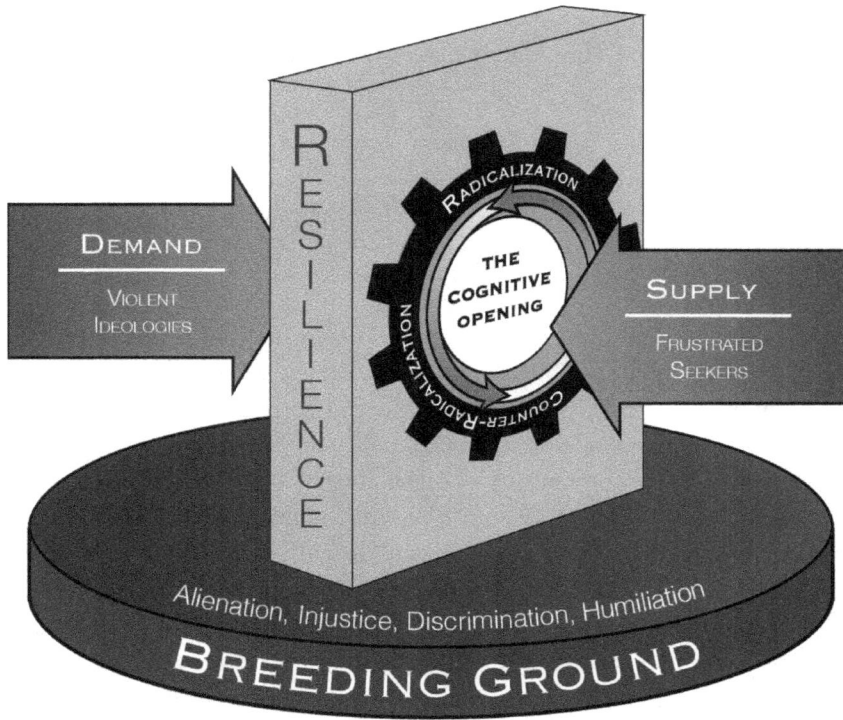

Figure 1. Adapted from, Recognising and Responding to Radicalisation Considerations for policy and practice through the eyes of street level workers - Yousiff Meah and Colin Mellis

Breeding ground: The breeding ground consists of the societal context that is experienced by the individual. According to Mellis, the breeding ground frustrations for Muslims living in the West might include experiences of discrimination, the depravity and immorality they perceive in Western culture, or social injustice that conflicts with the individual Muslim's belief system. As Muslims living in the West, some (and particularly young "seekers") may withdraw from the mainstream and become less resilient to extremism. This vulnerability is particularly evident when the potential recruit experiences a personal crisis or "cognitive opening" that "shakes the certainty of previously held beliefs and renders individuals receptive to alternative perspectives.[94]

---

94 Mellis, *Amsterdam and Radicalization the Municipal Approach*, 42.

Demand: Mellis asserts that demand is increasing in the Netherlands, particularly from young generations who experience a crisis of identity. These individuals are embroiled in psychological conflicts between "Westernization" and "Muslim" identities. Conflicted individuals may seek to expand their knowledge of Islam. With limited knowledge of the religion, those seeking a more positive identity may be susceptible to negative influences.

Supply: Radical ideologies that encourage violent extremism are abundant on the Internet, through traveling imams and radical individuals that the potential recruit might encounter in daily life. Suppliers of the "global jihadi" narrative actively seek to influence the recruiting pool to adopt ingroup/ outgroup perspectives.

Though not specifically addressed by Mellis in the model above, his recommendations support an SIT approach. One might describe "resilience" as the home of counterterrorists. In between recruit and recruiter, salient identities can be developed to encourage the rejection of violent ideologies. The impact of family members, collaboration with community leaders and centers of influence serve to diminish the credibility of radicalizing influences and provide alternatives to help subjects develop positive identities in the Amsterdam model. Hard Power is employed judiciously by government and the community to disrupt activities of those who propose violent political action. And, interactions with the "other" that contradict stereotypes propagated by radical influences serve to diminish the radicalizer's narrative.

Mellis proposed a two-pronged approach to combat radicalization: Intervention with individuals to attract or bind the individuals to Dutch identity and disruption in the form of judicial process. Broadly speaking, the Amsterdam model that Mellis developed is locally focused. The policy is "aimed at individuals, and not the radical movement as a whole."[95] The deradicalization strategy is derived from a concept that argues, "...the decline of a radical movement can only be indirectly influenced, by "stealing away" members from that organization. No influence is exerted on radical ideology, its legends, nor on persons that are susceptible to Islamic radicalism or are already involved in a process of radicalization"[96] This is an entirely different approach from "preventing a terrorist attack or "protecting from a

---

95   Demant, and Beatrice De Graaf. "How to Counter Radical Narratives in the Case of Molaccan and Islamic Radicals," 420.

96   Ibid.

terrorist attack." Guided by recommendations from a study by the University of Amsterdam's Institute for Migration and Ethnic Studies (IMES),[97] the Amsterdam municipality has taken steps to:

1. Increase societal trust;

2. Increase political confidence;

3. Increase religious defensibility;

4. Find ways of contacting radical youngsters; and

5. Provide assistance to mosques in countering radicalization.

Outreach efforts are intended to support the "binding" of an individual to social networks that engage in and support democratic society. When individuals are assessed to be at risk of radicalization, the government apparatus makes sure to support those in the individual's life who actively counter the West versus Islam narrative.

While the Dutch hold that "tackling polarization and radicalization is primarily a matter for local governments,"[98] there is a clear delineation between counterradicalization and counterterrorism efforts; as such, the subject's behaviors dictate which organization is the lead. For the Dutch, "A distinction has been made between 'thinking' and 'acting'. The moment there are indications of preparatory action(s)…the case becomes the responsibility of the police."[99]

As a conceptual framework, Amsterdam's counterradicalization model assigns responsibilities to the community (social network), religious leaders, and the government:

- Those involved in the lives of at-risk youth increase resilience in at risk-youth by nurturing confidence in an "inclusive democratic narrative and emphasizing potential and empowerment" despite obstacles;

- Religious communities are actively encouraged and supported by the government to provide diverse and active alternative ideologies; and

- Interconnected, formal, and informal networks positively address circumstances that result in frustration and anger.[100]

---

97 European Union. Transnational Terrorism and the Rule of Law. *The EU Counterradicalization Strategy: Evaluating EU Policies Concerning Causes of Radicalization (EU Counter-Radicalization Strategy)*. Luxembourg: Publications Office of the European Union, 2008.

98 Mellis, *Amsterdam and Radicalization*, 43.

99 Ibid., 43-45.

100 Ibid.,43-44.

Providing yet more specificity, Mellis describes how deradicalization is tailored to individual cases with a separate model that has been adopted throughout the Netherlands:

> When individuals observe changes in an associate and decide to report the "signal," the reporter seeks assistance from the Information House—a non-law enforcement collaborative body that works through dedicated case management teams (CMT) to analyze and assess the circumstances around the person at risk of radicalization[101].

The CMT then draws from an established network of counter-radicalization partners to change the context of the at-risk subject. Early in the process, this may mean that the CMT identifies and facilitates employment or educational opportunities or positive group activity that exposes the at-risk person to broader world views and alternative perspectives that counter Islamist narratives.

When the at-risk person has progressed further in the process, CMTs may instead call on religious experts—also within the trusted network—to attempt "ideological intervention." Depending on how much the at-risk individual has internalized the violent extremist narrative, key figures may be introduced with varying knowledge bases. In moderate cases, "key figures … will need some knowledge of Islamic theology and democratic society, but those intervening later in the later stages of radicalization will need to be theological experts of some stature… The real challenge [of the CMT] is finding these figures and forging lasting alliances with them."[102] This is a formidable task in contexts where levels of trust are low between the government and the Muslim community and impossible where engagement is not purposeful.

---

101 Mellis. Amsterdam and Radicalization the Municipal Approach. The Hague: National Coordinator for Counterterrorism, 2007, 7.

102 Yousiff Meah and Colin Mellis. "Recognising and Responding to Radicalisation: Considerations for Policy and Practice through the Eyes of Street Level Workers." Amsterdam, Netherlands, EU Project Recognising Radicalisation, November 27-28, 2008..

The Case Process

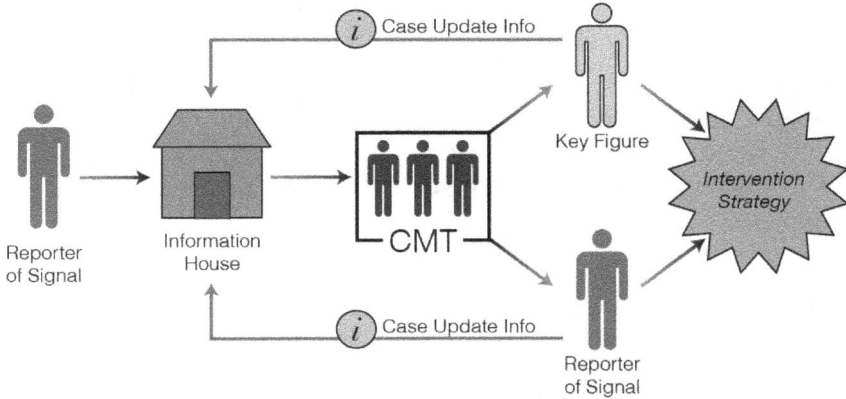

Figure 2. Adapted from, Recognising and Responding to Radicalisation Considerations for policy and practice through the eyes of street level workers - Yousiff Meah and Colin Mellis

Trusting relationships between government, nongovernment, and religious partners in the counter-radicalization network are therefore crucial to successful intervention strategies. Low levels of trust between network members can delay or forestall the decision to report concerning behavior at any stage of the deradicalization process, which in turn provides the opportunity for a "jihadist identity" to be adopted by the vulnerable subject. In order to be most effective, these strategies should be applied as early as possible in the radicalization process.

RECENT ADJUSTMENTS

The NCTb held to its quarterly review protocols and semi-annual reports to the central government regarding the terrorist threat to the Netherlands. In December 2010, NCTb assessed that despite "a limited number of violent extremist incidents... resistance of the Dutch population against violence based on ideological motives remained high in general."[103] Continuing and independent study by the University of Amsterdam into Salafism in the

---

103 Netherlands. National Coordinator for Counterterrorism (2011). Thirteenth Progress Report on Counterterrorism

Netherlands supported that conclusion.[104] The study confirmed the view of the General Intelligence and Security Service and the National Coordinator for Counterterrorism that the Salafist community in the Netherlands does not constitute a breeding ground for jihadist terrorism.[105]

On June 11, 2011, the NCTb affirmed these conclusions. The greatest terrorism threat to the Netherlands generated abroad and the threat of domestic radicalization remains low,[106] "principally because the threat posed by jihadist networks in the Netherlands itself is small...[and]... due to the fact that resistance against violent radicalism, extremism, and terrorism has remained high."[107]

Also in 2011, after completing a review of counterterrorism efforts during the last decade, the Netherlands produced its first national counterterrorism strategy. The strategy was designed to promote unity of effort across national and regional governments in order to realize an integrated approach. Not surprisingly, the "foundation of the national counterterrorism strategy remains a broad-based approach that involves identifying the risks of terrorism at the earliest possible stage and tackling them with a combination of preventive and punitive measures."[108]

The Dutch thus presented to the nation a comprehensive strategy that captures the balanced and pragmatic approach previously employed through policies rather than formal doctrine. The "five pillars of Dutch national strategy" would remain constant: gathering information, preventing attacks and violent extremism, defending vital objects, services and people, preparing for a possible attack and its consequences, and prosecuting those suspected of terrorist offences had proven effective during the last decade.[109]

Reflecting the emphasis on and pride in the refined approach taken by the Netherlands, the Dutch Ministry of Security and Justice described its constantly evolving strategy this way in 2011:

---

104 *Institute for Migration and Ethnic Studies (IMES) Research: Strictly Orthodox Muslims Pose no Threat to Dutch Democracy.* Amsterdam, Netherlands: University of Amsterdam, 2010

105 Netherlands. National Coordinator for Counterterrorism (2011). Thirteenth Progress Report on Counterterrorism

106 Netherlands. National Coordinator for Counterterrorism (2011). Presentation of the Summary of the 24th Terrorist Threat Assessment.03/18/2011

107 Netherlands. National Coordinator for Counterterrorism (2011). Fourteenth Progress Report on Counterterrorism.

108 Netherlands. National Coordinator for Counterterrorism (2011). 04/19/2011. Government presents National Counterterrorism Strategy for 2011-2015.

109 Ibid.

Dutch counterterrorism measures are characterised by customisation. The Dutch approach to terrorism develops in line with the development of the phenomenon, learns from practical lessons and judicial review, and is open to criticism from society. It is sound, proper and not cast in stone.[110]

IMPACT OF BRITISH AND DUTCH APPROACHES TO HOMEGROWN COUNTERTERRORISM

It is difficult to conclusively evaluate the impact of the U.K. strategy, and at the time of writing, the results of Prevent 2.0 remain to be seen. The current threat assessment for the U.K. remains heightened, at the "severe" level, which means an attack is officially considered "very likely."[111] The Prevent strategy is subject to mixed results, and it may be premature to make a definitive call as to the strategy's effectiveness; this is certainly the case in regard to Prevent 2.0. It can be logically inferred from the British experience with the "Troubles" that domestic tranquility is, realistically, a long way off. The British government is truly in a battle to win the "hearts and minds" of a rising generation of British Muslims. It is encouraging though, that through Prevent 2.0, the government is correctly aligned to this goal.

Anecdotally, there is evidence of increased cooperation in some arenas. For example, Andrew Ibrahim, a Muslim convert, was reported to a police community relations officer when he discussed suicide bombing. According to the senior investigating officer, "He [Ibrahim] was unknown to us, the first thing we knew about his device was from the Muslim community. All of Bristol should be grateful to them for providing information. Without a doubt they saved people from serious injury and worse."[112] This is exactly the end that Prevent aims to achieve—an alert community that is willing to cooperate with government authorities.

Polling data, too, indicates positive movement toward coexistence. British Muslims rejected moral justification for attacks on civilian targets at a slightly higher rate (3%) than in 2006–2007 polling.[113] While the rate of

---

110 "Dutch Policy on Terrorism to be Shaped More Soundly." Netherlands. Ministry of Security and Justice

111 United Kingdom. Home Office. "Current Threat Level."

112 Gardham, Duncan. "Terrorist Andrew Ibrahim was Turned in by the Muslim Community." Telegraph.Co.Uk, July 18, 2009

113 Muslim West Facts. *The Gallup Coexist Index 2009: A Global Study of Interfaith Relations With an in-Depth Analysis of Muslim Integration in France, Germany, and the United Kingdom.* London: Gallup Incorporated, 2009

condemnation changed very little, it is important to note that those able to morally justify a violent attack on a civilian target fell from two percent to less than one-half percent. It would appear that Prevent is, at least, positively influencing the most radical of British Muslims. The British strategy appears to be on the right track.

In the Netherlands, results are more clear. Based on its continuing assessment of the threat situation, the Netherlands reduced its national "threat level" in December 2009 to a condition that recognized the possibility of a terrorist attack but considers an attack unlikely. The assessment was based on a diminished threat from core al Qaeda and a Muslim population that overwhelmingly rejects violence. The Dutch considered that al Qaeda was largely on the defensive due to international pressure in places like Pakistan and Afghanistan and that the domestic policies discussed above had succeeded in increasing the resilience of the Dutch Muslim population to violent Salafi-jihadi ideology. Salafi-jihadi groups present the Netherlands lack coherent leadership, an impact that can be directly related to Dutch counterterrorism strategy. The Netherlands was in a position to conclude that

> Terrorist attacks in the Netherlands have been able to be prevented, thanks to the efforts of the intelligence and security services, the police ... and many other services and organizations, but also as a result of the vigilance of ordinary citizens. Important in this context was society's growing resilience, especially that of the Muslim communities, against radicalization. All of the above means that the group of radicals in our country, who are prepared to further their political or religious goals by means of violence, has steadily decreased in size, and more has become known about the operation and modus operandi of this group.[114]

Based on Dutch experiences with counter- and deradicalization efforts in the case of both Moluccans and Islamist terrorists, it appears that "not only government interventions, but also the discourse that is produced or reinforced through these interventions, have profound effect on the processes of de-radicalization [because] combating terrorism is itself a form of communication, just as terrorism itself is." [115]

---

114 Netherlands. NCTb. *11th Progress Report*. The Hague: National Coordinator for Counterterrorism, 2009

115 Froukje Demant and Beatrice De Graaf. "How to Counter Radical Narratives in the Case of Moluccan and Islamic Radicals." *Studies in Conflict and Terrorism* 33, (2010): 408

It may also be that the flexibility inherent in the Dutch approach provides both "repressive" tools to deal with the "doers" and a curative approach for "thinkers" that demonstrates government credibility and inclusiveness to the broader population.[116] What is undeniable is that the balanced-power strategy provides more tools to deal with radicalization in a way that can be tailored to local contexts than can be found in a hard power only strategy—and that the Dutch model has been effective.

---

116 Vindino. "A Preliminary Assessment of Counter-Radicalization in the Netherlands," 12.

CHAPTER 4

SMARTER, NOT HARDER

LESSONS FROM THE BRITISH AND DUTCH

"If everything is well considered, it will not be difficult for a wise prince to keep the minds of his citizens steadfast from first to last, when he does not fail to support and defend them."

-Niccolo Machiavelli

Past experience and thorough study by the United Kingdom and the Netherlands, resulted significant changes to their respective security strategies when these nations confronted (or were confronted by) the Salafi-jihadist threat. Consistently reviewed and continuously evolving, British and Dutch counterterrorism policies provide useful insight as to how Western liberal democracies might best develop strategies of their own. The U.K. and the Netherlands achieved unity of command for the counterterrorism mission; adopted flexible, learning, and networked structures; enhanced quality intelligence for decision makers; and separated radicalizing influences from the mass population. They also developed short- and long-term strategies to address counterterrorism, created structures to ensure the strategies permeated the counterterrorism effort and empowered community-based networks to influence the contexts surrounding communities at risk of radicalization. Elements of British and Dutch strategies should therefore be explored for common themes that might inform counterterrorism strategy and policies in the United States. Set against the four parameters identified in Chapter One (Structure, Strategy, Tools for Fighting a War of Ideas, and Impact of the doctrine) for analysis, it is apparent that the British and Dutch governments reached similar conclusions about how a battle of ideas should be fought in their domestic environments. Here, we visit their common smart practices.

SMART STRATEGIES

Salafi-jihadist terrorism is particularly threatening to liberal Western democracies, and not just because they employ tactics aimed at killing as many people as possible. The outcomes these groups propose for the West would require subjugation to their archaic religious and societal norms. These are much broader aims than either PIRA or Moluccan terrorists. The goals of al Qaeda and its associated groups are non-negotiable and unrealistic. As delineated in Chapter three, the British and the Dutch recognize that the physical threat of terrorism is intended to advance "religious or ideological cause" or "spark social change." For this reason, they approach terrorism, and especially Salafi-jihadist terrorism, along two coordinated fronts: terrorist plots are confronted aggressively by strong law enforcement powers, and underlying social problems are addressed with a "whole government" response.

Both governments developed components of their strategy that: 1) impede the spread of violent Islamist messages, and 2) support those who actively counter the violent Islamist narrative. While methods of propagating Islamist ideologies are not always criminal in nature, British and Dutch approaches to counterterrorism recognize a long-term danger of polarization within their societies. As a result, these governments take active steps to address grievances of minority groups, actively counter terrorist messaging and promote an "inclusive" national identity that can provide security over the long haul.

The U.K. and the Netherlands provide "some of the most developed programmes for outreach and dialogue with the Muslim community, including co-ordinating councils with government officials and clergy, youth outreach, women's outreach, social cohesion and dialogue programmes or events to support moderation and tolerance, and anti-discrimination efforts."[1] Their efforts are not based on liberal philosophy, a search for self-blame, or altruism. Instead, objective analysis of past victories and failures in asymmetrical conflict allowed these learning organizations to apply the strategic lessons from these conflicts in ways that confront Salafi-jihadists' most critical vulnerability: ideology.

The British and Dutch made efforts to attract the mass population away from violent extremism and accepted the prospect of a generations-long conflict for the hearts and minds of their own populations. Both the United Kingdom and the Netherlands have successfully migrated balanced power strategies across religious, ethnic, and political contexts. From the actions of the United Kingdom and the Netherlands, the United States might glean

---

1   Jane's Islamic Affairs Analyst, "Europe's Emerging Solutions to Radical Islam," Jane's. http://search.janes.com

a framework for a successful national counterterrorism strategy, one that includes state, local, and nongovernment partners and introduces Soft Power strategies.

The United Kingdom and the Netherlands pursue strategies that incorporate aggressive law enforcement to disrupt terrorist attacks, but they also target the radicalization process. British and Dutch counterterrorism orientations evolved from a reactive "response" framework in the 1970's to one that proactively addresses the causal factors of terrorist attacks today. These nations viewed their homegrown terrorist threats as something more meaningful than individual attacks conducted by "the other." Current British and Dutch approaches express strategic goals to minimize the polarization of their societies through both Hard and Soft Power tactics. These governments recognized that in order to truly prevent terrorism they first had to understand both the grievances of the mass base and the way preemptive and retaliatory measures can impact the community vulnerable to recruitment by terrorists.

The British and the Dutch determined it necessary to view counterterrorism as "system management," and to develop localized strategies to influence the radicalizing context that impacts individuals. Both nations realized open an ongoing dialogue with the community vulnerable to recruitment was a critical component of their long-term strategies. This recognition logically leads to a unified, "whole of government" approach that might be managed and supported at a national level but must be implemented more locally. The goal of these nations seems to have been akin to the concept of "deep security" described by Joshua Cooper Ramo in his book *The Age of the Unthinkable*. Ramo used this term to describe a state's "ability to manipulate environmental factors rather than be surprised by their impact, thus ensuring resilience to unexpected changes".[2]

---

2   Joshua Cooper Ramo. *The Age of the Unthinkable*. 2010 ed. New York: Back Bay Books, 2009. Comparing homeland security to the "sandpile physics" of Danish Physicist Per Bak, Ramo suggested that as "complex behavior in nature reflects the tendency of large systems to evolve into a poised 'critical' state, way out of balance, where minor disturbances may lead to changing events, called avalanches, of all sizes." Similarly, homeland security faces slow-moving environmental factors in society—like polarization—that underlie major social changes—like revolution.

SMART DEFINITIONS OF THE THREAT

British and Dutch governments consider that violent extremist ideologies to be existential threats: that is, threats to the very existence of their nation.[3] Both nations consider that "new terrorism" spawns from Islamism (or "political Islam"), a worldview that places Islam "at the centre of an individual's identity, as either the overriding or the only source of that identity... [and] essentially divides the world into two distinct spheres: 'Muslims' and 'the rest.'"[4] This is the previously described Huntington-Qutbian perspective, an ingroup/outgroup mental construct that negatively impacts security for both those in the Muslim community and those in the West.

The British and Dutch governments understand that Salafi-jihadists represent an extreme fringe of Islamist philosophy that aims to impose social constructs that would fundamentally alter democratic government. Both the U.K. and the Netherlands have come to the conclusion that the propagation of this form of violent and repressive ideology—for instance through the glorification of martyrdom and the promotion of Islamic courts that might supersede the established judicial process—functions in parallel to the state's authority and constitutes an ideological attack on their pluralist societies. For the British and Dutch governments, Salafi-jihadi ideology is itself considered a threat.

But both the U.K. and the Netherlands differentiate between Salfi-jihadists who encourage or engage in violence and the non-violent Islamists at the other end of the threat spectrum, who constitute less of a threat. Salafi-jihadists are considered to be an inherent danger to the state and its citizens. Islamists who pursue a "Dawa" or proselytizing strategy on the other hand, seek to continuously influence the mass population toward

---

3   Kapitan, Tomis. "Can Terrorism be Justified?" 1-18, 7-8. Kapitan describes the clearest form of "existential threat", as an "attempted extermination" of a community or nation, but includes other forms of existential threat as "enslavement or forced conversions of its members, destruction of its vital institutions (economic, agricultural, political, and cultural), appropriation of its natural resources, seizure of its territory and dispersion of its members." According to Kapitan," Nowhere is the justice of collective self-defense more manifest when a community faces an aggressive threat to its very existence." Both British and Dutch government definitions of terrorism seem to consider Salafi-jihadi ideology as an existential threat to national identity..

4   Shiraz Maher and Martyn Frampton, *Choosing our Friends Wisely: Criteria for Engagement with Muslim Groups*, (London: Policy Exchange, 2009), 18

...extreme puritanical, intolerant and anti-Western ideas. They want Muslims in the West to reject Western values and standards, propagating extreme isolation from Western society and often intolerance towards other groups in society.[5]

Discerning the nature of these threats allows for different approaches. Salfi-jihadists are targeted by coercive tactics, non-violent Islamists are afforded the same free-speech rights and responsibilities that the general public enjoys. The British and Dutch employ a values-based approach, which demonstrates confidence in pluralistic values; The British and Dutch governments developed their balanced–power approaches from a position of moral strength and confidence rather than fear or intimidation. The values-based approach to counterterrorism strategy affords British and Dutch governments the ability to delineate policies according to clear legal principles, and provides justification for the support of Muslim communities that challenge Salafi-jihadist ideologies, even when these communities adhere to Islamist (but non-violent) principles.

For example, the desire of many Muslim communities in the West to have a religiously based jurisprudence system is subject to much publicized opposition by majority populations. The opposition to the prospect of Islamic courts in the West is understandable because, unlike rabbinical courts in the U.K. that address civil matters, many Islamic courts in Muslim countries receive severe criticism from the international community, which decries the unequal treatment of women and inhumane punishments. [6] When the topic was considered in the United Kingdom, for instance, "the Archbishop of Canterbury, was pilloried for suggesting that the establishment of sharia in the future 'seems unavoidable' in Britain."[7]

The responses of the British and Dutch governments to this issue yield insight to their values-driven strategies and how the government's reaction can shape the population's response. In recognition of the rights of association and freedom of religion, the U.K. and the Netherlands adopted long-term strategies intended to attract Muslim citizens to Western forms of democratic rule and integrate Muslim citizens into "mainstream" society. Both the U.K. and the Netherlands allow moderate forms of sharia as a mechanism for

---

5   Netherlands. NCTb. *From Dawa to Jihad: The various Threats from Radical Islam to the Democratic Legal Order*, 7.

6   Noah Feldman, "Why Shariah?" *New York Times*, March 16, 2008.

7   Abul Taher, "Revealed: UK's First Official Sharia Courts," *The Sunday Times*, September 14, 2008, 1.

mediation in some civil matters.[8] [9] From an SIT perspective, allowing forms of Islamic jurisprudence in civil matters (like marriage and divorce) might be expected to undermine arguments that Islam and democracy are entirely incompatible. Further countering the Islamist narrative, British and Dutch governments support those who promote ideals consistent with British and Dutch values, yet these governments are not shy about withholding support from those who oppose democratic principles. In so doing, The British and Dutch sacrifice nothing, but stand to gain credibility in the eyes of the disaffected by applying jurisprudence equally to all religious groups and in a manner consistent with articulated values.

INCORPORATION OF IDENTITY APPROACHES

The concept that "understanding the enemy" enhances a government's ability to successfully defeat it is perhaps as old as military philosophy. But strategies that employ Social Identity Theory (SIT) concepts go beyond the necessity of seeing through enemy eyes. SIT requires one to understand how the enemy is affected by surrounding contexts and the way individuals within a group might be influenced by personal stressors and social dynamics. And importantly, an SIT approach encourages the direct and indirect support and influence by counterterrorists on the environment—the creation of circumstances across a number of fields to change the context that foments violence and the ability to shift tactics appropriately to exploit opportunities that result from contextual shifts.

For example, the Dutch and Ulster governments were initially unprepared for an SIT approach because these governments had policies and social structures that impeded integration and assimilation. Moreover, the Dutch-Moluccan refugee population was physically isolated from the rest of Dutch society and discouraged from integration because it was expected that the entire population would be repatriated to its native islands. Both governments lacked awareness of the coalescing threat because it was disengaged from the minority population. The Dutch did not understand that their Moluccan refugee population might view the lack of support for Moluccan independence as a betrayal, and perhaps an existential threat. Until the Dutch

---

8   Matthew Hickley. "Islamic Sharia Courts in Britain are Now 'Legally Binding'." Daily Mail, September 15, 2008, sec. Mail Online, 1.

9   Netherlands, Research and Documentation Centre (WODC). *Investigation: No Sharia Courts in the Netherlands*, The Hague: NL Ministry of Justice, 2010, 1.

developed tools that recognized the cultural legacy of the Moluccans and assisted the Moluccan exiles with integration into Dutch society, the threat continued to grow, exacerbated by repressive tactics.

Similarly, the Irish Catholic population was effectively barred from the democratic political process before the Good Friday Agreement of 1998 by gerrymandering of political boundaries put in place by the Protestant majority and discriminatory policies of local governments (which precipitated direct rule by the British). Much, if not most, of the Irish Catholic population believed it was subject to exploitation and discrimination by the Protestant "others." Catholics in southern Ireland had succeeded in establishing independence decades earlier, yet the independence they enjoyed was not similarly shared by their co-religionists, just across the political border in Northern Ireland. In these circumstances, the rational choice for Irish Catholics was to protest their condition. But when Irish Catholics employed tactics similar to those used by African Americans in the United States, they were met with violence by the government. Unsurprisingly, Catholics in Northern Ireland responded in kind. Then, when British troops were deployed to restore security in Northern Ireland, British military forces were perceived by Catholics to act on the side of the Loyalist Protestants.

Both British and Dutch governments ultimately were compelled to address the underlying grievances of these populations. Had they taken an SIT-informed approach sooner, government authorities might have diminished violence from disenfranchised second and third generations; perhaps dramatic levels of violence would never have occurred. Neither the Dutch nor the British acted out of weakness to meet terrorist demands, and neither made significant concessions on issues that impacted their national security. They did, however, make logical changes that might have been considered "good government," had they understood the identity conflicts existing within their societies.

SECOND AND THIRD IMMIGRANT GENERATIONS

It is notable that in both the historical examples described just above, it was neither the first generation of Irish Catholics in Northern Ireland nor the generation of Moluccan exiles from which the threat developed. Instead, the second and third generations of these aggrieved populations constituted the groups "radicalized" to violence.

In terms of the Salafi-jihadi threat, we again see groups that are (or perceive themselves to be) socially isolated in Britain and the Netherlands; in this iteration of terrorist threat, the "aggrieved" groups that are inclined toward violence are mainly composed of second- and third-generation Muslim immigrants. Social polarization resulted in large and violent demonstrations against these governments well before catalyzing incidents like U.S. military strikes in Afghanistan and, especially, the U.S. invasion of Iraq. Whereas most of the world understood the compelling argument to deny al Qaeda a safe haven in Afghanistan, the U.S. invasion of Iraq seemed to corroborate the Islamist narrative of a Western world bent on destroying Islam. In nations like the U.K. and the Netherlands, where second and third generations of Muslim immigrants already felt isolated and repressed, the "West versus Islam" narrative resonated profoundly and reinforced that mental construct. Because immigrant populations failed to integrate into broader society (or because nations failed to welcome them to the mainstream), immigrant populations held strong affinity for their cultural, religious, and familial roots.

Second- and third-generation Muslims may have identified more closely with those with whom they shared ethnic and religious ingroup status than those with whom they shared only nationality. According to SIT, this situation might be exacerbated if the second and third generations assessed they were not welcome or mistreated by their fellow countrymen because of characteristics which were difficult or impossible to change. This type of cognitive dissonance provides an opening for radicalization and recruitment.

SMART STRUCTURES

The role of the U.K.'s Home Office is neatly summarized in a single sentence at the top of its web page: "The Home Office is responsible for keeping the U.K. safe from the threat posed by terrorism."[10] The NCTb is assigned two tasks: to "minimize the risk and fear of terrorist attacks in the Netherlands and to take prior measures to limit the potential impact of terrorist acts."[11] The Home Office and the NCTb guide counterterrorism operations across either country's respective government, and will continue to inform local strategies subsequent to each government's ongoing restructuring. This allows the Home Office's Office for Security and Counter-Terrorism OSCT and NCTb to tailor solutions based on regional needs.

---

10   United Kingdom. Home office: Counter-terrorism.

11   Netherlands. NCTb. Mission of the NCTb. Retrieved October 13, 2010,

The OSCT and the NCTb can quickly adjust enforcement, support, and messaging strategies in ways that are responsive to local, regional, and national requirements. No department of the British or Dutch governments devotes all or even most of its resources to counterterrorism, therefore each department has only a limited interest in the counterterrorism mission. The Home Office's OSCT and the NCTb allow for certain elements or activities within larger government departments to focus exclusively on counterterrorism. The centralized, national counterterrorism component reduces interagency competition and conflicting intra-agency mission priorities because operational control of dedicated resources lies within the authority of the OSCT and the NCTb.

WHOLE-GOVERNMENT APPROACHES

The United Kingdom and the Netherlands developed holistic counterradicalization strategies that align directly with the ideological threat. Current British and Dutch strategies evolved from the nations' experiences with homegrown separatist and ethno-nationalist terrorist groups—terrorism motivated by limited goals that allow for the possibility of negotiation. Both countries recognize that Salafi-jihadi terrorism presents a challenge that requires counterradicalization tactics designed to impact the social context of potential recruits across a variety of axes. These factors are seen to combine in complex ways, leading communities toward or away from radicalization; they therefore require a multidimensional approach from policymakers wishing to affect them. The British Office for Security and Counter-Terrorism (OSCT) and the Netherlands' National Coordinator for Counterterrorism (NCTb) address terrorism as a "system" of complex and interconnected factors, acting as a single entity within the government serves as a coordination point for a broad array of activities.

LOCAL INTEGRATION OF INTELLIGENCE, OPERATIONS AND POLICIES

Beyond the ever-present need for traditional human intelligence, the government's ability to understand all source intelligence in the context of local community needs and grievances is critical. This contextualization has direct bearing on the effectiveness of government action to address those concerns and may increase development of collaborative relationships. Used constructively, good intelligence can make government more effective and efficient. Regional hubs for government counterterrorism efforts increase the continuity and translation of national objectives to local government.

Likewise, regional hubs secure the ability of local government and communities to "send up the chain" messages that may inform the national government of the effect of its policies on domestic security matters.

IDEOLOGY CHALLENGED IN REGIONAL AND LOCAL CONTEXTS

To counter the terrorists' narrative, the British and Dutch governments actively target and counter ideologies that support violent action to achieve political or religious aims, and they encourage mainstream citizens to do the same. This involves debate, coordinated messaging, and government agencies that have sufficient authority to take action that is both strong and empathetic to community concerns. To be effective, government personnel must be strategically placed, have a detailed understanding of local dynamics and be informed by a unified strategy—needs that cannot be easily met by a centralized authority. Strategies can be devised at the national level, but they are always implemented locally. Local contexts may differ from national conditions, which are necessarily less refined.

Through joint service centers like government offices (GOs) in the U.K. and municipal police boards in the Netherlands, the British and the Dutch empower all levels of government to act within the bounds of national strategy while providing "full-service" to local communities (The U.K.'s 2011 structural adjustments resulted in embedded national security representation at the local government level, a move that parallels the Dutch approach.) These joint, networked structures enable counterterrorism practitioners to improve their overall capacity to reduce radicalization and increase security.[12] When local governments work with communities to diminish radicalization, social status is enhanced for community partners who confront influences that are considered to be negative by the local community.

INTEGRATED LEADERSHIP DEVELOPMENT

Through their regional, networked structures, the U.K. and the Netherlands have "bureaucratized" the exercise of imagination in their counterterrorism community. They have developed an ability to manipulate the environment surrounding vulnerable communities. Thus, these governments have developed the ability to decrease (if not eliminate) radicalization toward

---

12   Mathieu C. Scheider, Robert F. Chapman, and Michael F. Seelman, "Connecting the Dots for a Proactive Approach. United States," 2003. Washington, DC: Office of Justice Programs National Criminal Justice Reference Service, 2003

violence and increase resilience to Salafi-jihadist messages. Regional hubs of
the counterterrorism effort in both the U.K. and the Netherlands tailor local
strategies and tactics to local challenges, inform national policy makers of
emerging domestic threats, and share best practices through a networked
structure. This process enhances both regional capabilities and organizational
adaptability.

The regular rotation of developing leaders through these joint-service
regional offices ensures that fresh ideas reach national counterterrorism
leadership, and creates a culture of "jointness." As officers progress through
their careers, they are exposed, individually, to a variety of circumstances,
tools and outcomes that shape their decision-making. As they mature
professionally, the national-level leadership, collectively, benefits from a
broad base of experienced officers. These structures and processes may tend
to immunize the U.K. and the Netherlands from "failures of imagination,
policy, capabilities and management," the four underlying conditions that
the 9/11 Commission described as the fundamental failures that resulted
in the terrorist attacks of September 11, 2001.[13] This approach to strategy
and leadership development has enabled the British and Dutch security
services to adjust quickly to environmental changes. The U.K. and Dutch
counterterrorism apparatuses have become complex adaptive systems.[14]

SMART TOOLS FOR FIGHTING A WAR OF IDEAS

Prosecuting a "battle of ideas" requires an overarching vision of the end
result. The Provisional Irish republican Army (PIRA) and Moluccan
separatists were able to clearly articulate their long-term goals: a united
and independent Ireland and an independent Moluccan state supported by
the Netherlands, respectively. These ideas probably appealed to their core
audiences—Irish Catholics who were subject to discrimination in Northern
Ireland and Moluccan refugees living in the Netherlands—because the mass
base viewed itself a disadvantaged outgroup in relation to the larger society
and believed that actualization of the terrorists' goals would improve the

---

13   National Commission on Terrorist Attacks upon the United States, Thomas H. Kean,
      and Lee Hamilton. *The 911 Commission Report: Final Report of the National Commission on
      Terrorist Attacks upon the United States.* Official government ed. Washington, DC: U.S.
      Government Printing Office, 2004, 339.

14   Ramo, 49.

condition of their groups. Regardless of whether community perceptions of unfair treatment are valid, the government must address perceptions to avoid social polarization.

ENGAGEMENT WITH CENTERS OF INFLUENCE AND SUBSEQUENT EXPANSION OF ENGAGEMENT EFFORTS

The British and Dutch were successful in the Troubles and during the Moluccan Problem only when these governments entered into negotiations with dissidents. The British and Dutch governments were able to garner influence with fence sitters and the mass population by partnering with individuals within the minority groups who were inclined to wage peace. This highlights the importance of engagement with centers of influence in vulnerable communities and is consistent with the concept that social categorization is critical to social influence.[15] As a practical example, if the British had decapitated PIRA by assassinating Gerry Adams, with whom might the Brits have negotiated? Adam's credibility with his own ingroup provided built-in support when he shifted tactics from violence to arbitration.

Government must offer a viable alternative to violent recourse that allows those who feel disenfranchised to positively change their situation. Unlike dealings with PIRA and Dutch Moluccans, Salafi-jihadi terrorism does not offer national-level leadership or structure with which to engage because the Salafi-jihadi mindset obligates each individual to fight the forces opposing "true Islam." This presents a particular challenge for a bureaucracy because the local approaches and empowerment are essential to devising local negotiation strategies. Clearly, a cookie-cutter approach will not best serve the counterterrorism effort.

The British and Dutch focus on building trusting relationships with influential members of groups; they also aim to influence the mass population and provide high-status alternatives to those vulnerable to radicalization. Even those highly critical of the government can be valuable partners so long as they hold to the premises of a democratic society and nonviolent

---

15   Dominic Abrams, Margaret Wetherell, Sandra Cochrane, Michael A. Hogg, and John C. Turner, "Knowing What to Think by Knowing Who You Are: Self-Categorization and the Nature of Norm Formation, Conformity and Group Polarization," *Intergroup Relations: Essential Readings*, edited by Michael A. Hogg and Dominic Abrams (Ann Arbor, Michigan: Edwards Brothers, 2001), 270-288, 286.

protest. In some cases, these individuals may actually be more valuable than "mainstream" Muslims because they are identified more closely with the subgroups most susceptible to radicalization.

CREATION OF SAFE SPACE FOR FRANK DIALOGUE

The British ultimately won the "hearts and minds" of the mass population by providing Catholics, even some who were engaged in the terrorist campaign, a venue for dialogue where grievances could be openly discussed. Similarly, the Netherlands opened dialogue with Moluccan leaders even while violence persisted. The British and Dutch governments communicated simultaneously complete intolerance for violent extremism and a vision of peaceful coexistence. This message resonated with the population at large because so many had been affected by violence during 30 years of conflict. This strategic position shift by the U.K. provided a sharp contrast to the PIRA. Similarly, when the Dutch government opened communication channels with Moluccan separatists, who had increasingly used indiscriminate violence, many in the Moluccan community recognized that with little support for self-rule from those residing in the Molucca Islands, the government in exile had no realistic chance to attain its goal. Terrorist actions thus became self-limiting because of their diminished ability to recruit new terrorists.

APPLICATION OF FLEXIBLE TACTICS, IN CONTEXT

The threat of an imminent terrorist attack warrants an aggressive tactical response to save lives and deny terrorists an opportunity to bring attention to their cause. Effective and efficient application of overwhelming force may serve to instill a sense of futility related to violent tactics. Most importantly, rapid responses are necessary to save lives, particularly in hostage situations or in order to disrupt other various terrorist operations. These points are well-established and particularly important when facing an enemy that is determined to kill as many people as possible and is willing to die as part of what it views as a "martyrdom" operation. In scenarios such as these, such responses to tactical threats are appropriate.

British experience with Catholic civil-rights protests in Northern Ireland and military-supported fugitive searches of Dutch-Moluccan villages taught the U.K. and the Netherlands that the use of force that is perceived to be discriminatory or disproportional to the threat can fuel "ingroup/outgroup" resentment. Ingroup/outgroup polarization can fuel further polarization and isolation, and thus may increase radicalization and diminish the mass population's trust of government.

Good intelligence and partners within the community, however, can make the government aware of emerging threats as they develop, providing alternatives to law enforcement action. "Rapid response" might not always mean SWAT operations, and it is effective intelligence and community collaboration that enables a different, more favorable type of government response:

> [T]he key to a successful domestic counterterrorism strategy is actually identifying the terrorist as early as possible ('Left of Boom'). Once found, the nation's domestic intelligence gathering techniques can then be fully deployed to identify linkages to other terrorist networks at home and overseas, to develop a comprehensive evidential case and to effect arrests without causing alienation within the community where the terrorist cell resides.[16]

On some (or most) occasions, it might be better to gain the cooperation of a suspect in such an investigation rather than prosecute him. Under appropriate circumstances, community partners might intervene to dissuade the subject based on theological grounds, aided by a credibility that a government agent can never have. When this type of cooperation occurs, the government gains trust with the Muslim community and intelligence related to the threat. As a result, the community becomes safer and the government can more effectively demonstrate that to the community that they do not simply assume Muslims to be terrorists.

BUILDING TRUST

Community policing programs introduce the opportunity for community groups to work with government officials to achieve "superordinate goals,"[17] with tangible results that are desirable by both groups' standards. Superordinate goals tend to build cohesion and cooperation between groups, which could benefit the community with enhanced responsiveness to grievances and the government with increased cooperation and security. Positive relationships with community leaders should be pursued because government-community partnerships can result in three main benefits:

---

16 Paul Smith, "A Critical Assessment of the US National Strategy for Counterterrorism: A Missed Opportunity? (ARI)," Real Instituto Elcano.

17 Abrams et al., "Knowing What to Think by Knowing Who You Are," 64–70.

- Information about community reactions and perceptions may identify emerging trends;

- The feeling of consultation and partnership gives minorities the assurance that the government targets terrorists, not ethnicities or religions. It might also enlist community leaders in individual and collective efforts to counter terrorist narratives; and

- Trusting relationships would reassure the community that the police will aggressively respond to threats against the community.[18]

REFINED COLLECTION AND ANALYSIS

In order to shape the ideological battlefield, the government must have or develop a strong intelligence base, consisting of technical, liaison, and human collectors. Poor intelligence leads give military and police forces little alternative but the use of coercive power to ensure the security of the civilian population from terrorists. As the British experience at the beginning of the Troubles demonstrated, when coercive power was used too broadly, or in a way that could be perceived to be discriminatory, it alienated the very hearts and minds that the government needed for support. As a result, the majority of the Catholic population in Ireland became more isolated and moral support for the terrorists increased. In the early years of the Troubles, heavy-handed tactics used by the Royal Ulster Constabulary (RUC) and the British Army contributed to a feedback loop that actually increased the level of violence. Similarly, in the Netherlands, cordon and search operations against Moluccan villages produced an attempt at violent retort.

INCLUSION OF NON-TRADITIONAL PARTNERS

Both British and Dutch security services recognized nongovernment agencies and community leaders as important parts of their counter-radicalization strategies. It is exceptionally difficult to disrupt the radicalization process once an individual has committed to Islamist ideology. Credible voices are required to intervene with a religiously motivated recruit to terrorism. It is more likely that a radicalized subject would respond positively to someone who can speak with religious authority and with whom he or she shares a common background than with a government agent who represents the "evil" that the subject might be radicalized against.

18　Johnathan Paris, "Discussion Paper on Approaches to Anti-Radicalization and Community Policing in the Transatlantic Space," Washington, DC, June 27-28, 2007, 14

Positive relationships with community leaders should result in media coverage that establishes a "mainstream" interpretation of Islam that rejects violence as a means of achieving political goals. Indications of support from the community abound anecdotally,[19] although Muslim rejection of terrorism rarely receives national media coverage. A communications strategy that incorporates coordinated messaging between government and Muslim partners might ensure increased media coverage of positive news stories. For instance, government agencies might carry stories on official websites that highlight community outreach efforts, laud community organizations for their cooperation, and publicize upcoming outreach efforts rather than carrying only stories about arrests of prosecutions. Immediately upon conducting an arrest of terrorist subjects, the government should immediately make available the charging documents and "push" the information to local centers of influence—this information would assist community partners in shaping their response. In the current paradigm, and considering the speed of the internet, the government almost immediately finds itself defending its investigative techniques, rather than lauding community contributions to the successful operation.

Community organizations engaged in counter-radicalization work have a parallel role. The U.K.'s Prevent strategy calls directly on community leaders to actively counter the Islamist narrative. British programs support a variety of initiatives that are intended to assimilate Muslim youth into British culture. Likewise, other government-supported programs provide platforms for communities to explore diverse cultures and perspectives. This may tend to diminish religious and cultural isolation, which in turn may reduce the likelihood of prejudice and isolation on a societal level.

SEPARATION OF TERRORISTS AND RADICALIZERS FROM THE POPULATION

The separation of mainstream community from extremist messages need not be literal. The U.K.'s Channel Program and the Netherlands' Information House function as barriers to Salafi-jihadi ideology. By supporting voices in the community who oppose violence and denounce terrorism, the government can diminish the credibility of the global jihadist's message. Both the British and Dutch create safe platforms for public discussion and accept criticism, making changes to policy where appropriate and feasible. These platforms for dialogue provide a mechanism for grievances to be consolidated and

---

19   Shelia Musaji, "North American Muslims Determined to Counter Violence and Terrorism: The American Muslim," 2010

voiced as regional concerns, which likely carries more influence than those presented by individual citizens or special interest groups. By creating a political path for nonviolent Islamists, the U.K. and the Netherlands provide a legitimate alternative to violent expression.

When separation strategies are applied literally by arresting or deporting radicalizers, the intent of such action by the British and Dutch governments is to remove the individual(s) from communication with society as quickly as possible and for an extended period (in the case of criminal proceedings) or permanently (through deportation). Thus, the radicalizer's ability to communicate violent ideology to the public is inhibited.

Fast-tracking judicial action also obligates the government to make public any criminal charges against the radicalizer. The British and the Dutch governments consider criminal activity is a violation of the state's trust by the visa holder and might undermine the visiting radicalizer's moral authority. Public platforms, as described above, allow a venue for the government to describe the reasons for its actions in an environment that promotes objective evaluation. Public debate might be enhanced by follow-on discussions via an interconnected and expanded network of associates that do not directly involve the government but can understand and articulate the government's perspective.

The British and Dutch found that when judicial removals are delayed, the government is precluded from commenting publicly on the details of a case for fear of prejudicing jury pools. Once speedy trials and processes were implemented, the amount of time a subject had to portray himself or herself as a martyr diminished, thus removing a cancer from society in its early stages. These governments also aggressively distribute information that is available to the public through its informal networks. By making the facts of the case known through a liaison platform and making counter-radicalization partners aware of press releases and where to find public indictments, much of the rumor of conspiracy can be mitigated.

On a less formal basis, both government officials and local counterradicalization partners aggressively inform community representatives about the charges against a subject when the local community might be affected by the arrest or removal. Ideally, a strong counterradicalization network might distribute such information informally, by interpersonal contact and social media, and more quickly and effectively than mainstream media.

CHAPTER 5

FUEL FOR THE FIRE

COUNTERTERRORISM IN THE UNITED STATES

"Everything that we are making, we are making more and more complex."

–Kevin Kelly

The effort of the United States government to address terrorism is fundamentally shaped by the complex nature of a changing enemy. This chapter is intended to explain the changing structure of the United States counterterrorism effort in the context of the nation's threat posture after the death of Osama bin Laden. The United States' approach will be analyzed based on the smart practices of the British and the Dutch. Social Identity Theory, of course, will necessarily be imbedded in this discussion.

BACKGROUND AND CONTEXT IN THE UNITED STATES

The announcement that bin Laden was killed on May 11, 20011, delivered an audible sigh of relief from the American homeland, and a degree of closure for the American public. Young and old alike gathered spontaneously to celebrate his death. For a moment, the nation shared an unrealistic vision of a world without terrorism. Almost immediately, media commentators and some politicians called for expedited troop withdraws from foreign conflict zones, "the blood on the corpse was barely dry before calls began for American withdrawal from Afghanistan: the risk of going to war over a symbol."[1] One must wonder how the death of al Qaeda's leader—more icon than operational planner—will affect the continuing threat. Unlike wars between princely states where a king's death would indicate defeat and subjugation of his kingdom, the death of al Qaeda's leader does not connote immediately increased security for the rest of the world. Core al Qaeda is no doubt diminished by his absence, mostly because of his heroic appeal to Salafi-jihadists. The continuing threat posed by Salafi-jihadi ideology to our national security, however, remains.

---

1   Burden of Victory: It's the Finest Moment of Obama's presidency—but it also Raises Uncomfortable Moral Questions. *Newsweek*, 05/21/2011, 2011.

This is true because the essence of the threat to the American homeland changed immediately when al Qaeda's leadership cadre lost its safe haven in Afghanistan. The shifting nature of the threat was not unanticipated:

> [a] group of diplomats and MI6 officers met their American counterparts [soon after the attacks of September 11, 2001]... inquiring what the CIA was going to do once the US had 'hit the mercury with the hammer in Afghanistan and the al-Qaida cadre has spread all over the world'.[2]

This rhetorical question indicates the British recognized the challenge that lay ahead and that the nature of the conflict with al Qaeda would change. The obituary statement by Ayman Zawahiri, following bin Laden's death confirmed the perspective of Salafi-jihadists on the impact of bin Laden's demise. In the vview of al Qaeda, those who practice "true Islam" were not inspired by just bin Laden, but by a sense of Islamic nationalism that transcends borders:

> ...The Sheikh [bin Laden] has departed... to his God as a martyr, and we must continue on his path of jihad to expel the invaders from the land of Muslims and to purify it from injustice... and thanks be to God, America is not facing an individual or a group... but a rebelling nation which has awoken from its sleep in a jihadist renaissance challenging it wherever it is.[3]

A month after this obituary statement, U.S. Defense Secretary Leon Panetta assessed that "Al-Qaida's defeat is 'within reach,' ... as few as 10 of the group's top figures could cripple its ability to strike the West."[4]

These starkly contrasting perspectives reflect the ephemeral nature of al Qaeda and its capabilities. When looked at in relation to one another, these statements also demonstrate how differently the essence of the conflict is viewed by some of its most prominent leaders –and, perhaps, how much propaganda plays a part in the battle of ideas. For many outside the movement, al Qaeda *was* bin Laden, in much the same way as Nazi Germany *was* Adolf Hitler. It is less clear that bin Laden's charismatic leadership was the essential element for al Qaeda's survival, its center of gravity. But then, regardless of what bin Laden was, what *is* al Qaeda today?

---

2   Richard Norton-Taylor. " The Calamity of Disregard: It is Now Chillingly Clear: MI6's Pre-Iraq Warnings were Swept Aside by an Obsessed White House." *The Guardian*, 08/04/2007, 2007

3   "Profile: Ayman Al-Zawahiri:Physician Considered to be the Brains Behind Al-Qaeda Began His Journey as a Dissident in Egypt." *Al Jazeera*, 06/16/2011, 2011

4   "Panetta: US within Reach of Defeating Al-Qaida." *Associated Press*, 07/09/2011, 2011

On May 2, 2011, Peter Bergren, writing for CNN, proclaimed "Killing bin Laden is the end of the war on terror. We can just sort of announce that right now,"[5] Undoubtedly he will be joined by others who will argue that the Salafi-jihadi threat will quickly dissipate now that bin Laden is gone.

Others might suggest the organization will splinter as affiliate groups and their leaders vie for status amongst their peers. If bin Laden was a figurehead, his demise will likely be inconsequential to the continuing threat,[6] and over the long haul, Salafi-jihadi terrorism will continue unabated because the real center of gravity was not bin Laden, but his ideology and the resonance of its West-versus-Islam narrative.

As previously noted, most analysts agree that today's terrorist threat changed dramatically in the years immediately following September 11, 2001, but experts have also disagreed about who and what constitutes the Salafi-jihadism posed by al Qaeda and its like-minded affiliates for a number of years.[7] The media has sometimes exaggerated disagreements regarding the nature of the threat, which in turn resulted in public debate related to al Qaeda and affiliate organizations. One side of the argument suggested that al Qaeda had survived the attempts of the United States to destroy or dismantle it and that al Qaeda continued to represent the principal, but not the only, threat to the United States. The Defense Secretary's assessment implies that he considers "al Qaeda" (the group) to be the strategic enemy, an organization that consists of a defined number of identifiable individuals. If this analysis is correct, when the 10 or so top al Qaeda leaders are gone—dead or imprisoned—so must be the threat they pose. The Global War on Terror will be complete.

The other position aligns with the "al Qaeda as a movement" concept. Proponents of this approach acknowledge that much of al Qaeda's core leadership cadre has been captured or killed; therefore, the threat from the organization itself has been curtailed, and the al Qaeda cadre in the Federally Administered Tribal Areas (FATA) of Pakistan is no longer the principal

---

5   Peter Bergen. "Bergen: Time to Move on from War on Terror." CNN.

6   Bob Clifford. "Kill a Leader, Murder a Movement? Leadership and Assassination in Social Movements." The American Behavioral Scientist 50, no. 10, (2007): 1370-1370-1375,1377-1394, 1390

7   Sciolino, Elaine and Schmitt, Eric. "A Not very Private Feud Over Terrorism." *The New York Times,* 06/08/2008, 2008, sec. The Nation

threat. Rather than emanating from the FATA, the main threat derives from relatively leaderless and self-generating terrorist cells that operate independently of al Qaeda direction.[8]

If the former position is correct, Western nations can expect a continuation of dramatic, internationally directed terrorist attacks that are sometimes years in planning, highly sophisticated, and strategically designed; however, if the core leadership of al Qaeda is hunted and killed, the threat will no longer exist. The implication of the latter position is that the United States can expect isolated cells and individuals with relatively less capability to launch sophisticated attacks. These less sophisticated terrorists will therefore act based on opportunity rather than a coordinated strategy. In this scenario, the Salafi-jihadi movement is likely to "spontaneously reconstitute itself,"[9] even in the face of major victories like the deaths of bin Laden and Awlaki. It may be that the suggested reconstitution of global Salafi-jihadi activism is realized in the form of homegrown terrorists.

The threat posed by these "wannabe terrorists" was poorly understood and perhaps underestimated until a spate of homegrown terrorist plots and two successful attacks between 2009 and 2011 made the growing threat obvious. The intelligence community's underestimation is evidenced in official threat assessments from that period[10]:

> Homegrown Muslim extremists who have little if any connection to known terrorist organizations have not launched a successful attack in the United States. The handful of homegrown extremists who have sought to strike within the Homeland since 9/11 have lacked the necessary tradecraft and capability to conduct or facilitate sophisticated attacks.[11]

---

8   For a concise summary of the debate, see Bruce Hoffman's review of Sageman's book, *Leaderless Jihad* (2008).

9   Marc Sageman. 2004. *Understanding Terror Networks*. Philadelphia: University of Pennsylvania Press.

10   To be fair, it should be understood that comprehensive threat assessments are generally based on intelligence that has accumulated over a period of time. Projective analysis is much more challenging when the structure, capabilities and intent of the enemy changes rapidly. Projective analysis – the kind that anticipates the enemy's future actions, is especially challenging in asymmetrical conflict. Unlike estimating the disposition of enemy ships, which are large and slow-moving, terrorists can move literally around the world in hours, transfer money in seconds and communicate in ways that require an extraordinary amount of resources to compromise. Therefore, strategic analysis almost inevitably will reflect what the threat *was*.

11   Leiter. "The Aspen Institute: The Terror Threat Picture and Counterterrorism Strategy." 3.

UNDERSTANDING THE HOMEGROWN THREAT IN THE UNITED STATES.

The counterterrorism community should recognize that today's threat from Salafi-jihadists was a long time in coming. Bin Laden began talking about his "beliefs, goals, and intentions" and speaking to journalists in 1993.[12] He declared war on the United States in 1996,[13] and in 1998 he delineated three basic grievances against the United States:

- The United States' occupation of Islamic holy lands,

- Americans' murderous humiliation of Muslims, and

- The United States' support for Israel.[14]

While many Americans would disagree with bin Laden's characterizations, argument is irrelevant: bin Laden made an emotional appeal simultaneously to Muslims, Arabs, and anti-Zionists, in a form true to the character of a Type-A terrorist, one who is uncompromising and to whom negotiation will not appeal.[15] The objective validity of his claims do not matter; what does matter is that Americans have increasingly identified with the construct bin Laden set forth.

Until the attacks of September 11, 2001, al Qaeda's efforts to coerce Western and Muslim-majority nations were mostly ineffective. Even when successful operationally, their attacks did not produce the influence they sought and were therefore considered both internally and externally as failures. For example, Senior al Qaeda operations planner Khalid Sheikh Mohammed (KSM) and his nephew Ramzi Yousef stumbled repeatedly. In 1993, Yousef successfully exploded a vehicle-borne bomb in the garage of the World Trade Towers. Despite successful detonation, the towers remained. The success was disappointingly impotent to many in al Qaeda, including Yousef himself. The attack killed six, but Yousef was later to have said " he had hoped to kill 250,000 people."[16]

12   Michael Scheuer. *Through our Enemies' Eyes : Osama Bin Laden, Radical Islam, and the Future of America*. Rev, 2 ed. Washington, D.C.: Potomac Books, Inc., 2006.

13   bin Laden, Usama. "Usama Bin Laden: "Declaration of War Against the Americans Occupying the Land of the Two Holy Places" August 1996." Nine Eleven Finding Answers (NEFA) Foundation

14   bin Laden, Usamah, al-Zawahiri, Ayman, Taha, Abu Y., Hamza, Mir and Rahman Fazlul. "Bin Laden, Others Sign Fatwa to "Kill Americans Everywhere"

15   Paul K. Davis and Michael J. Jenkins. *Deterrence and Influence in Counterterrorism: A Component in the War On al Qaeda*. Santa Monica, California: RAND, 2002

16   National Commission on Terrorist Attacks upon the United States, 72.

More humiliating were the "Bojinka" operation and plans to assassinate President Clinton when he visited Manila. KSM and Yousef developed the Bojinka plot to blow up 12 airliners as they traveled from Asia to the United States. This operation and the assassination attempt were compromised by Philippine investigators in the fall of 1994. Adding insult to injury, in 1995, Yousef was arrested by Pakistani authorities when an accomplice betrayed him. This enforcement action disrupted a plan he and KSM developed to blow up cargo aircraft bound for the United States.[17]

Subsequent to his arrest, Yousef was brought to trial and convicted in the United States for both the 1993 World Trade Center attack and the Bojinka plot. In court, Yousef spat words that lend insight to the West versus Islam narrative:

> Yes, I am a terrorist and I am proud of it. And I support terrorism so long as it was against the United States Government and against Israel, because you are more than terrorists; you are the one who invented terrorism and using it every day. You are butchers, liars and hypocrites.[18]

It might be argued that Yousef expressed pride in his actions because, from his perspective, he had enhanced his status and that of his group by striking out against those he viewed as oppressors. He may have seen himself as a soldier of the Salafi-jihadi nation, striking out against the evil colonial oppressor. Indeed, for bin Laden's audience, the September 11 attacks were a great and unique success. The attacks on New York and Washington, DC redeemed the organization's honor that had been soiled by the previously impotent performance of its premier operators.

In the years since the al Qaeda attacks on New York and Washington, DC, the West-versus-Islam ideology influenced many whom bin Laden sought to recruit. For those inclined to Salafi-jihadi ideology, joining al Qaeda represented an opportunity to become part of an "elite" organization that fought to avenge what many Muslims considered "violations of their rights and demands for expanded rights."[19] It is likely that this sense of injustice was pronounced among Muslims with familial and historical ties to Muslim-majority countries and those who already considered the policies of the United States to be "unjust" or who might come to feel so due to perceived

---

17   National Commission on Terrorist Attacks upon the United States, 145-148.

18   *New York Times*, Archives (1998). Excerpts from statements in court (01/09/1998).

19   Fathali Moghaddam. *Multiculturalism and Intergroup Relations : Psychological Implications for Democracy in Global Context.* 1st ed. Washington, DC: American Psychological Association, 2008, 122.

unfair treatment.[20] With bin Laden in the lead, the Islamists had finally begun to enhance the status of their ingroup, and the cause that resonated in bin Laden's 1998 manifesto.

STRATEGY

Before the United Kingdom developed Prevent and before the Dutch created its Information House, the United States' National Commission on Terrorist Attacks upon the United States (the 9/11 Commission) suggested the United States should adopt a "broad political-military strategy that rests on firm tripod of policies to":

- Attack terrorists and their organizations;

- Prevent the continued growth of Islamist terrorism; and

- Protect and prepare for terrorist attacks.[21]

Initial Counterterrorism efforts focused mainly on the first and third suggestions—matters that could be addressed in a clear-cut legal framework. Abroad, the nation aggressively pursued terrorists with a political-military approach—Hard Power (focused on sticks in the carrots and sticks approach).

Domestically, the government's response was based on the United States legal code, where terrorism is defined as

> ...activities [that] (A) involve violent acts or acts dangerous to human life that are a violation of the criminal laws of the United States or of any State, or that would be a criminal violation if committed within the jurisdiction of the United States or of any State; (B) and appear to be intended to intimidate or coerce a civilian population; to influence the policy of a government by intimidation or coercion; to affect the conduct of a government by mass destruction, assassination, or kidnapping.[22]

The Bush administration issued the National Strategy for Combating Terrorism (NSCT 2003) in February 2003, prior to the 9/11 Commission's report. This expansive and detailed prescription for the terrorism threat mostly focused on dismantling terrorist groups abroad and establishing

---

20   Kohut, Andrew. . *Anti-Americanism: Causes and Characteristics*. Washington, DC: Pew Research Center for People and the Press, 2003

21   National Commission on Terrorist Attacks upon the United States, 363. It is interesting to note that the steps described above pre-date and align directly with the "four 'P's" of the UK's Contest Strategy.

22   18 USC CHAPTER 113B - TERRORISM, (2010): 18 USC 2331 - Terrorism

domestic physical security defenses, not diminishing radicalization in the homeland. Heavy emphasis was placed on border control, aviation screening procedures and domestic intelligence collection, similar to the approaches taken by the British and Dutch in the 1970s. Some, however, suggest that the NSCT 2003 was not actually a strategy at all, but instead several disjointed ideas: "an approach to addressing a range of terrorist threats, a bureaucratic blueprint, a spending plan and a political statement."[23] Perhaps the most dramatic changes to the NSCT 2003 and contemporaneous directives brought forward was the re-alignment of the United States National Security structure. The depth and nature of change was unparalleled in U.S. history.

The Bush strategy was updated in 2006, in a document that described tangible progress toward a more effective national security apparatus. The amended strategy almost exclusively addressed the external terrorist threat, but did make an important contribution by acknowledging a domestic threat, a threat that had not yet fully developed. As articulated in the *National Strategy [updated 2006] for Combating Terrorism* (hereafter referred to as NSCT 2006), "in the War on Terror, there is also a need for all elements of our Nation—from Federal, State, and local governments to the private sector to local communities and individual citizens—to help create and share responsibilities."[24] This laid the groundwork for future strategies that would be necessary to counter growing radicalization in the homeland. In time, homegrown terrorism would come to represent a principal concern for the nation --and it would need to be addressed by full breadth of elements available.

Events since May 2009 have altered national threat assessments with an increased appreciation of the terrorist threat from both external and internal actors, as indicated by the director of the National Counterterrorism Center, Mike Leiter in April, 2010:

> During the past year our nation has dealt with the most significant developments in the terrorist threat to the homeland since 9/11... The range of al Qaeda core affiliated, allied, and inspired US citizens and residents plotting against the Homeland...

23   Goure, Daniel. "Homeland Security." In *Attacking Terrorism: Elements of a Grand Strategy*, edited by Audrey Kurth Cronin and James M. Ludes, 261. Washington, D.C.: Georgetown University Press, 2004.

24   National Strategy for Combating Terrorism (updated 2006].

has become more complex and underscores the challenges of identifying and countering a more diverse range of Homeland plotting.[25]

National Security Strategy 2010 held to the nation's course, maintaining

> …substantial continuity with the policies and philosophies adopted by the Bush administration in its final two years. The Obama administration built on [the Bush Administration's strategy and increased] efforts in a range of key areas: engagement, outreach and a rhetorical commitment to restoring the rule of law on the one hand, and on the other, escalated (though not publicly acknowledged) drone strikes and counterterrorism partnerships in the ungoverned spaces where al Qaeda and its affiliated movements thrived.[26]

Importantly, however, NSS 2010, was the first recognition of the changing nature of the Salafi-jihadi threat in the national security strategy since the 9/11 attacks. NSS 2010 made note of the homegrown threat and recognized that countering violent extremism (CVE) must be seen as a whole-government challenge.[27] But, like the Bush strategies, NSS 2010 did not empower a coordinating authority outside of Washington to ensure the strategy was implemented at regional and local levels, no resources were committed to CVE and no funding stream was associated with CVE matters.

More recent strategy documents indicate that the National Security Staff recognizes the Salafi-jihadi threat is bifurcated, emanating from external foreign powers like al Qaeda and other international terrorist groups, as well from some portion of Western population that identifies with and has proven susceptible to Salafi-jihadi ideology. It is likely that the threat will vary from region to region, nation to nation and state to state—and in some cases, from neighborhood to neighborhood. But before turning to the adjustments made in the summer of 2011, it is necessary to think more specifically about why the Salafi-jihadi narrative resonates with some, albeit very small percentage, American Muslims. It is also be useful to consider whether our current structure, strategy and tactics are aligned with the relatively new threat of homegrown terrorism.

25   Mike Leiter. "The Aspen Institute: The Terror Threat Picture and Counterterrorism Strategy." Aspen, Colorado, Federal News Service, 2010

26   Mark Lynch. (2011). Rhetoric and Reality: Countering terrorism in the age of Obama, p.3. Center for a New American Security, Washington, DC.

27   Obama Administration. *National Security Strategy 2010.* Washington, DC: Whitehouse.gov, 2010

STRUCTURE

When one considers the whole-government strategies executed by the British and the Dutch, inherent challenges for the United States' national security structure, and particularly the domestic counterterrorism effort are quickly revealed: DHS,[28] NCTC,[29] and the FBI,[30] all have legitimate and overlapping claims to primacy in "protecting the United States from terrorism." And notably, state and local governments are not integrated into, or necessarily informed by a national strategy. In foreign nations, United States' embassies serve to implement foreign policy. Domestically, there is no entity that coordinates federal actions, nor a structure that integrates federal with state and local missions. With these concerns in mind, we now turn to the current structure of the national counterterrorism apparatus, and we'll explore how its design affects the implementation of national counterterrorism strategies.

The Director of National Intelligence (DNI) and the Office of National Intelligence (ODNI) were codified by the Intelligence Reform and Terrorism Prevention Act (IRPTA) of 2004,[31] and "stood up" on April 21, 2005.[32] According to the IRPTA, the DNI serves as the head of the Intelligence Community (IC), and is responsible for direction and oversight of the National Intelligence Program. In this capacity, the DNI acts as the principal advisor to the President, the National Security Council, and the Homeland Security Council for intelligence matters related to national security; however, this role has been subject to dispute and periodic friction with the leadership of some of its component agencies. There are six departments and 16 different agencies. So what the Director of National Intelligence's role is, is an attempt to coordinate and integrate the activities of 16 different agencies toward some common purpose—obtaining information to protect the nation's

---

28   Department of Homeland Security. *One Team, One Mission, Securing our Homeland U.S. Department of Homeland Security Strategic Plan Fiscal Years 2008*. Washington, D.C.: Department of Homeland Security, 2008

29   United States National Counterterrorism Center. (2010). About the national counterterrorism center. Retrieved October 5, 2010

30   Federal Bureau of Investigation. (2010). The Federal Bureau of Investigation: Quick facts.

31   Masse, Todd M. *The National Counterterrorism Center: Implementation Challenges and Issues for Congress*. Washington, D.C.: Congressional Research Service, 2005,

32   "ODNI Fact Sheet: Forging an Intelligence Community that Delivers the most Insightful Intelligence Possible." Office of the Director of National Intelligence

interests."[33] According to former Director of National Intelligence Michael McConnell, "The director of National Intelligence probably would've been more appropriately named the coordinator of National Intelligence."[34]

To handle this challenging mission, the DNI manages the integration of the nation's intelligence collection through seven core organizations: Integration Management Council (IMC), National Intelligence Managers (NIMs), National Intelligence Council (NIC), Mission Integration Division (MID), National Counterterrorism Center (NCTC), National Counterproliferation Center (NCPC), and the National Counterintelligence Executive (NCIX).[35] The DNI's stated goal is to effectively integrate foreign, military and domestic intelligence in defense of the homeland and of United States interests abroad. In order to accomplish this overarching goal, the ODNI has several mission responsibilities, including technology development, training and financial management for the IC, an others. But, perhaps the most relevant of the DNI's responsibilities to the domestic counterterrorism effort is to "establish objectives and priorities for collection, analysis, production, and dissemination of national intelligence."[36]

The DNI is staffed largely by permanent employees of other IC agencies. For instance, senior officials are selected by the CIA to represent the ODNI overseas, and senior FBI field personnel represent the DNI in domestic environments outside of Washington, DC.[37] For domestic counterterrorists, the NCTC provides authoritative analysis at a strategic level and produces the majority of strategic-level analysis products, including National Intelligence Estimates.[38] Because of its prominence for local-level counterterrorists, NCTC will be explored more fully below.

---

33   "CIA Wins Turf Battle Over DNI: But is it Over?" Federal News Radio

34   Matthew Harwood. "CIA Defies its Boss and Wins Turf War." *ASIS International*, accessed November 17, 2012

35   "Office of the Director of National Intelligence::Organizational Chart." Office of the Director of National Intelligence

36   "Office of the Director of National Intelligence: About the ODNI." Office of the Director of National Intelligence

37   Mueller, 2011. Statement Before the House Permanent Select Committee on Intelligence

38   "Office of the Director of National Intelligence::Organizational Chart." Office of the Director of National Intelligence

Like the DNI, the National Counterterrorism Center (NCTC) was established in the IRTPA.[39] NCTC was conceived and intended to address a key finding of the 9/11 Commission: "Breaking the older mold of national government organizations, this NCTC should be a center for joint operational planning and joint intelligence, staffed by personnel from the various agencies."[40] Reporting to both the president and the Director of National Intelligence (DNI), the NCTC is charged with a mission to "lead our nation's effort to combat terrorism at home and abroad by analyzing the threat, sharing that information with our partners, and integrating all instruments of national power to ensure unity of effort."[41]

Unfortunately, as a practical matter, NCTC is relegated to "suggesting" rather than "leading" the counterterrorism effort because "neither the NCTC director nor the assistant to the president for homeland security and counterterrorism can direct departments and agencies, even on matters of CT programs and resources."[42] Nine years after 9/11, the need to consider both domestic radicalization and unity of effort raised the concern of national leaders including chairman of the Homeland Security Committee and its ranking member Senator Susan Collins. Collins "expressed concern that no single U.S. agency is in charge of identifying and stopping the recruitment of U.S. citizens to carry out terrorist attacks."[43] "[W]e have a lot of good people, a lot of good agencies [and] a lot of activity, she argued but there still doesn't seem to be an overall strategy nor accountability built in, nor a means of assessing the success."[44]

The FBI is the lead federal agency for counterterrorism investigations. The FBI, in contrast to DHS, is highly centralized. The FBI's Counterterrorism Division (CTD) closely guides counterterrorism investigations from across the country. Director Robert Mueller instituted this centralization in the immediate aftermath of September 11 due to the widely-held finding that FBI analytic and information-sharing failures contributed directly to the success

---

39   Masse, Todd M. *The National Counterterrorism Center: Implementation Challenges and Issues for Congress.* Washington, D.C.: Congressional Research Service, 2005

40   National Commission on Terrorist Attacks upon the United States, 403 .

41   US National Counterterrorism Center. "About the National Counterterrorism Center."

42   James R. Locher, III. *Toward Integrating Complex National Missions: Lessons from the National Counterterrorism Center's Directorate of Strategic Operational Planning.* Washington, D.C.: Project on National Security Reform, 2010

43   Chris Strohm. "Officials Warn of More Terrorist Threats within U.S." *National Journal Group, Congress Daily,*2010

44   Joedy Yager. *Washington Struggling to Rein in Increasing Homegrown Terrorism,* 2010

of the Al Qaeda attacks.[45] CTD is now singularly responsible for all FBI counterterrorism operations nationwide; it fulfills this responsibility through Joint Terrorism Task Forces (JTTF). An immediate reaction to September 11, centralization was instituted to ensure control of operations and to increase information flow in an organization that had previously operated largely as 56 independent investigative agencies with limited information from other offices. To further enhance information-sharing with the intelligence community, the CTD was physically co-located with the NCTC.

Expansion of the number of the FBI's joint terrorism task forces is, perhaps, the single most important accomplishment toward collaboration at federal and local levels since 9/11. This expansion also provides a tangible measure of increased communication: the number of JTTFs has grown from 33 in 2001 to more than 100 today.[46] JTTFs serve as the recognized and designated environment in which "federal to local operational partnerships" take place to detect, investigate, and disrupt terrorist threats or pursue perpetrators.[47] In the past, these task forces were guided by a national strategy that served as a "high level road map" encompassing the CTD's mandate to "protect the United States from terrorist attack."[48] The FBI published a national strategy in 2004, however, that strategy administratively expired in 2009. Since that time and due to an increased number of threat-driven scenarios, the FBI's counterterrorism mission has become almost entirely reactive. The CTD and the FBI's JTTFs are forced to respond quickly to a variety of eminent threats outside the construct of a long-range plan or strategic vision.

JTTFs do not have authority or a formal mechanism to disseminate information beyond participants in the task force. In the event of an overseas terrorist attack, or international event—for instance a coup d'état—state and local partner agencies might seek information regarding ongoing developments or "spot reporting" that is perceived to be available to JTTFs. Often such information is not available, and in other cases the information

---

45   National Commission on Terrorist Attacks upon the United States, 352.

46   Senate Judiciary Committee. *Nine Years After 9/11: Confronting the Terrorist Threat to the U.S: Statement of Robert S. Mueller III.* September 22, 2010, 2010

47   House Homeland Security Committee. *The Way Forward with Fusion Centers: Challenges and Strategies for Change 27 September 2007. Statement of Michael C. Mines Deputy Assistant DirectorDirectorate of Intelligence Federal Bureau of Investigation.* 2007

48   *FBI Strategic Plan 2004-2009.* Washington, DC: United States. Federal Bureau of Investigation, 2010

may be in a classified format that requires limited distribution. We have not yet become a true homeland security community. This has been the basis of comments from the International Association of Chiefs of Police:

> [T]he full benefits of intelligence sharing have not yet been realized because the process itself remains a mystery to many police officers, and some law enforcement executives consider their agencies too small or too remote to participate in criminal intelligence sharing. These obstacles to full participation could result in alarming gaps in the intelligence that guides our homeland security and crime fighting efforts.[49]

JTTFs collect information through a variety of means, including technical and human intelligence sources. But JTTFs enjoy only limited analytical capability for counterterrorism matters in support of local and regional issues or threats because intelligence collection priorities are generally related to foreign-focused national intelligence requirements, not societal factors that influence domestic radicalization.

Local officials sometimes benefit from JTTF intelligence, but they rarely receive products that contribute to local policy decisions. This may be part of the reason that some state and local organizations do not readily appreciate the value of JTTF participation. A 2008 survey of the International Chiefs of Police reinforces this point: its members concluded that the national counterterrorism strategy was developed "without sufficiently seeking or incorporating the advice, expertise or consent of public safety officials" at the state, local, and tribal level.[50]

The FBI also established field intelligence groups (FIGs), consisting of FBI agents, linguists, surveillance specialists, and analysts at every field division.[51] FIGs focus on cross-programmatic and all-source intelligence production and dissemination. According to FBI Director Mueller, FIGs have come to regularly share this intelligence with FBI partners in more than 18,000 law enforcement agencies around the country; additionally, they also collaborate closely with international counterparts, recognizing the imperative to be able to develop and disseminate information that will assist

---

49　International Association of Chiefs of Police." IACP Releases National Summit on Intelligence Report."

50　Ron Leavell. "The Evolution of Regional Counterterrorism Centers within a National Counterterrorism Network: Is it Time to Fuse More than Information?" M.A., Naval Postgraduate School, Center for Homeland Defense and Security, 2007

51　*National Strategy for Information Sharing: Successes and Challenges in Improving Terrorism-Related Information Sharing.* Washington, D.C.: United States. White House Office, 2007, 8

our partners.[52] Despite these accomplishments, it is not entirely clear that the FBI's homeland partners feel that they receive sufficient intelligence and analysis to enable effective homeland security operations.[53]

For this reason, many state and some local agencies have created and come to rely on their own intelligence centers that are not fully integrated with the national counterterrorism mission. Uncoordinated intelligence activities sometimes result in operational compromise and limit potential intelligence collection and, ultimately, the prevention of future attacks.[54] Since 2002, the Department of Homeland Security has provided homeland security grant funding to be used for preventive measures, including the establishment of intelligence fusion centers.[55] Fusion centers are state-administered joint intelligence hubs where state, local, and federal agents work in close proximity to receive, integrate, and analyze information into a system that can benefit homeland security and counterterrorism programs at all levels. Federal agencies play a supporting rather than a lead role.

Fusion centers are not standardized and have produced varying results. According to a report by the Congressional Research Service (CRS), many of the centers identify "prevention of attacks" as a high priority, but little "true fusion" or analysis of disparate data sources, identification of intelligence gaps, or proactive collection of intelligence against those gaps, which could contribute to prevention, actually takes place.[56]

The "FBI's role in and support of individual fusion centers varies depending on the level of functionality of the fusion center and the interaction between the particular center and the local FBI field office."[57] Many Fusion centers are not part of an integrated national or regional network at all, and some do not even have FBI representatives assigned. These conditions frustrate the flow

52   Senate Judiciary Committee. *Preparing for the Challenges of the Future: Statement of Robert S. Mueller, III.* 2008

53   Paul West and Julie Bykowicz. "Information-Sharing Still a Roadblock: Security Chiefs Tell O'Malley, Other Governors 'Paradigm Shift' among Agencies Needs to be done." *Baltimore Sun,* February 22, 2010

54   Jim Dwyer. "In Praise of Help that Hurts." *New York Times,* October 20, 2009

55   Department of Homeland Security. *One Team, One Mission, Securing our Homeland U.S. Department of Homeland Security Strategic Plan Fiscal Years 2008.* Washington, D.C.: Department of Homeland Security, 2008

56   John Rollins. *Fusion Centers: Issues and Options for Congress [Updated January 18, 2008].* Washington, DC: Library of Congress. Congressional Research Service, 2008

57   General Accountability Office. *Information Sharing: Federal Agencies are Sharing Border and Terrorism Information with Local and Tribal Law Enforcement Agencies, but Additional Efforts are Needed, Report to the Chairman, Committee on Homeland Security, House of Representatives .* Washington, D.C.: United States. General Accountability Office, 2009

of information to both the national level and state and local policymakers—those who deal with the public as part of their daily responsibilities and who are thus well positioned to spot and address circumstances that foment radicalization. DHS components participate at minimal levels in fusion centers, and this involvement is sometimes of limited value, due to the lack of secure compartmented intelligence facility space and accreditation that would allow them to process classified information. Until fusion centers and their personnel have access to classified information, their practical effectiveness in the counterterrorism mission is likewise limited. This may be a contributing reason for an additional finding by the Congressional Research Service (CRS) that many of the centers initially had purely counterterrorism goals but have increasingly gravitated toward an all-crime and even broader all-hazards approach.[58]

CHALLENGES PRESENTED BY THE CURRENT STRUCTURE

The current structure of the nation's counterterrorism effort confounds even the most dedicated efforts at a "whole government approach." This is not because of an unwillingness to cooperate or due to technical challenges that complicate sharing information, but because there is no unity of command for the counterterrorism mission. Consideration of whole-government strategies reveals inherent challenges for the United States' national security structure, and particularly the domestic counterterrorism effort: the Department of Homeland Security, National Counterterrorism Center, and the FBI all have legitimate and overlapping claims to primacy in "protecting the United States from terrorism" based on their charters and mission statements. Notably, while state and local governments participate in task forces administered by these agencies, they are not compelled to conduct counterterrorism operations within a national framework, as national strategies drafted by federal agencies do not necessarily incorporate state and local agencies into their planning processes.

The U.K. and the Netherlands, on the other hand, depend on thorough integration of similar authorities in the counterterrorism mission and consider a national effort crucial to preventing the development of terrorist groups. This is particularly evident when it comes to counterradicalization

---

58   Rollins. *Fusion Centers: Issues and Options for Congress* [Updated January 18, 2008], summary.

efforts. True collaboration and prevention of terrorism may be out of reach without a unified command and a holistic strategy that coordinates federal, state and local efforts.

Encouragingly, in 2010, a strategic review revealed that the United States faced systemic challenges because the "national security system is organized along functional lines (diplomatic, military, intelligence, law enforcement, etc.) with weak and cumbersome integrating mechanisms across these functions."[59] Until August 2011, there was no federal strategy that articulated a strategic aim to counter radicalization, and neither the Bush nor the Obama administration succeeded in coordinating efforts to counter radicalization across organizational boundaries.

The NCTC is responsible for "monitoring and assessing overall National Implementation Plan for the War on Terror (NIP) implementation as well as the impact of subordinate CT plans and guidance,"[60] but subordinate counterterrorism strategies, where they exist, do not matriculate from the NIP, and NCTC is not currently positioned to enforce its monitoring role.

Outside of DC, the United States has two basic structures though which the counterterrorism mission is addressed, with DHS and the FBI functioning at both ends of the organizational spectrum. DHS lacks both interconnectivity with its fusion centers and direct authority over resources that are "owned" by state and local agencies. The Department is instead charged with

> ...assisting state, local and private sector entities in disrupting potential terrorist activity and denying terrorists access to the United States at our land, air and sea ports of entry, as well as travel networks into and within the country... [However, despite DHS's role as] one of the Federal government's key counterterrorism agencies, beyond the Secretary and Deputy Secretary, DHS did not have a single coordinating entity for counterterrorism activities.[61]

This may seem a confusing alignment of resources to mission—in fact, overlapping DHS and FBI responsibilities and missions result in a fundamental challenge to effective and efficient prosecution of the homeland security mission. Instead of an integrated structure, the homeland security community

---

59   Locher, *Toward Integrating Complex National Missions: Lessons from the National Counterterrorism Center's Directorate of Strategic Operational Planning.*

60   *Eight Years After 9/11: Confronting the Terrorist Threat to the Homeland.* Hearing September 30, 2009

61   Department of Homeland Security (Bottom-Up). *Bottom Up Review Report: July 2010.* Washington, D.C.: Department of Homeland Security, 2010

has several separate structures that are not interlinked, a reflection of the amorphous nature of the current homeland security environment.[62] Further complicating the homeland security challenge, until the publication of NSS 2010 in April 2010, the counterterrorism community faced the dynamic nature and complexity of terrorism threats with no overarching strategy, multiple definitions of the homeland security mission, and overlapping jurisdictions that cause internecine rivalries, impede information sharing, and reduce efficiency. Both inside and outside of Washington, DC, the lack of clearly defined roles and missions creates confusion, provides no mechanism for resolution, and can result in missed opportunities to collect intelligence, explore alternative solutions to judicial intervention or exploit operational opportunities.

IMPLICATIONS OF THE STRUCTURE

While it is true that the formal, organized threat from bin Laden and core al Qaeda has been severely diminished by military force abroad and through law enforcement in the homeland,[63] the Salafi-jihadi narrative remains intact. Radicalization and polarization in the homeland are evidenced by the increasing numbers of individuals leaving the United States to join and fight in Islamist causes abroad and the relative increase in homegrown terrorist plots.

As previously stated, NSS 2010 was the first national strategy to acknowledge the growing threat of "homegrown" terrorism,[64] and the first strategy to include homeland security as part of a broader national security effort.[65] Logically flowing from the Bush Strategy and into the NSCT 2011, the strategy's evolution marks progress toward addressing guidance from the 9/11 Commission report: "our strategy must match our means to two ends: dismantling the al Qaeda network and prevailing in the longer term over ideology that gives rise to Islamist terrorism."[66] How NSCT 2011 will be implemented, however, remains to be seen.

---

62   Bellavita, Christopher. "Changing Homeland Security: What is Homeland." *Homeland Security Affairs Journal* 4, no. 2 (June, 2008)

63   Leiter. "The Aspen Institute: The Terror Threat Picture and Counterterrorism Strategy.".

64   Obama Administration. *National Security Strategy 2010*. Washington, Dc: Whitehouse.gov, 2010

65   Jake Tapper. "Brennan: President Obama's National Security Strategy Recognizes Threat of Homegrown Terrorists." *ABC News*, May 26, 2010, 2010

66   National Commission on Terrorist Attacks upon the United States, Thomas H. Kean, and Lee Hamilton. *The 911 Commission Report*, 363.

In August, 2009, John Brennan, the assistant to the president for homeland security and counterterrorism under President Barack Obama, assessed the homeland security atmosphere, saying:

> In the years since [the terrorist attacks of September 11], I have seen the significant progress made in safeguarding the American people—unprecedented coordination and information sharing between federal agencies and with state and local governments; improved security at our borders and ports of entry; disruption of terrorist recruitment and financing; and a degradation of al Qaeda's ability to plan and execute attacks.[67]

This commentary by a senior representative of a presidential administration (that, like most administrations, might be disinclined to compliment the accomplishments of its predecessor) speaks highly of the progress made by the homeland security community. It is widely accepted that the nation's security posture is improved relative to the status of homeland security prior to September 11, 2001, but why?

The sense that the homeland security community is moving in the correct direction is largely determined by evaluating critical mission areas. The Department of Homeland Security defines its strategic objectives:

- Prevent terrorist attacks within the United States;

- Reduce America's vulnerability to terrorism; and

- Minimize the damage and recover from attacks that do occur.[68]

The FBI in turn defines its strategic objectives for the counterterrorism mission:

- Prevent terrorist attacks against the United States and its interests;

- Deny terrorists and their supporters the capacity to plan, organize, and carry out logistical, operational, and support activities;

- Pursue appropriate sanctions against terrorists and their supporters;

- Provide incident response and investigative capability [investigation and intelligence]; and

---

67 Brennan, John O. and Stephen Flanagan. "Remarks by John O. Brennan, Assistant to the President for Homeland Security and Counterterrorism – as Prepared for Delivery "A New Approach to Safeguarding Americans " Washington, DC, August 6, 2009

68 *National Strategy for Homeland Security: Executive Summary.* Washington, D.C.: United States. Office of Homeland Security, 2002

- Identify and respond to weapons of mass destruction (WMD) threats and fully coordinate the investigative response of the U.S. government to a WMD threat or attack.[69]

Employing the above criteria, the fact that no major terrorism acts have occurred in the United States since 2001 and that several terrorist groups have been disrupted during the same period may indicate that the homeland security community has satisfactorily addressed the mission. The increased number of terrorist attempts toward the end of the decade, however, suggests that the correlation between resources applied to defend the nation, technological advances, increased information sharing and the absence of successful attacks is not a causal one.

Instead, the lack of successful attacks may indicate that no sophisticated attacks have been attempted, or that al Qaeda's strategy has changed to capitalize on American recruits with little training or experience. Such a strategy is less expensive in terms of time, resources, and risk than pre-September 11 al Qaeda operations, which took years to plan, employed highly trained explosives experts, were relatively expensive and subjected the terrorist operator and the operation to a high risk of compromise. Spreading Salafi-jihadi ideology and encouraging individual terrorist actions in support of a violent extremist agenda is one way al Qaeda can prosecute its "global jihad" with relatively little risk to the core al Qaeda organization.

Accepting that the threat has evolved is only part of the challenge. Devising and implementing a holistic counter-narrative to Islamist ideologies will necessarily include more than just law enforcement and intelligence agencies: community leaders, corporate partners, and nongovernment agencies must be integrated into such strategies. The U.S. government has not broached this challenge in a serious way; however, NSS 2010 could mark a significant shift in domestic policy. Certainly the roles and activities of counterterrorism agencies may change with a new counterradicalization mission that none has previously embraced.

The prominent roles of American "jihadists" like Adam Gadahn in Pakistan, Abu Mansour al-Amriki in Somalia, and Anwar Awlaki (now deceased) in Yemen may serve to attract other Americans who have lost confidence in the American system of government and reject western culture. Bruce Hoffman explained the impact of Salafi-jihadi propaganda to the United States Congress on May 24, 2011:

---

69   Federal Bureau of Investigation. FBI Strategic Plan 2004-2009.

Major Nidal Hasan, the Fort Hood shooter Faisal Shahzad, for example, in terms of the Times Square bombing, Umar Farouk Abdulmutallab, the Christmas Day bomber, and the list goes on. This [Inspire magazine] is a very effective tool. It is a way to animate, to mobilize, and, ultimately, I think, to activate or, actually, to engage individuals, just as you described, in low-level violence, that I say reflects an al-Qaeda strategy that is designed to throw at us this multiplicity of low-level threats, in hopes of creating so much noise, and so many distractions, that it is al-Qaeda's hope that bigger, more spectacular attacks or attempts will then prove more successful.[70]

Fellow counterterrorism expert Seth Jones concurred, "this struggle against al-Qaeda will continue, I think, to be a long one, partly because I think we are seeing a much more diffused organization across the globe."[71] If these experts are right, the appeal of Al Qaeda's ideology to citizens of the United States is indicative of a long-term threat to national security and a severe need for long-term strategies.

Political vitriol regarding the "Ground Zero Mosque" and the social divisions revealed through the proposed "Burn the Koran Day" in Gainesville, Florida in 2010, further indicate that the polarization of American society may be increasing. When the national media inflames such ingroup/outgroup conflict, American Muslims might logically wonder whether anti-Muslim bias is endemic to American society. So long as American Muslims believe that fellow Americans and the government's security apparatus are inherently biased against them, the battle of ideas promised by al Qaeda's doctrine will continue,[72] and Salafi-jihadi ideology will remain more resilient than its core leadership.

Today's strategic threat is bifurcated. The threat of Salafi-jihadi ideology includes not just the short-term physical assault on which the United States has focused since 9/11, but a tearing of the nation's social fabric by creating

---

70   *Future of Al-Qaeda: Hearing before the Subcommittee on Terrorism, Nonproliferation, and Trade of the Committee on Foreign Affairs, House of Representatives, One Hundred Twelfth Congress, First Session, may 24, 2011*. Washington, DC: United States. Government Printing Office, 2011

71   Ibid.

72   Lind, William S., Keith Nightengale, John F. Schmitt, Joseph W. Sutton, and Gary I. Wilson. "The Changing Face of War: Into the Fourth Generation." *Marine Corps Gazette* no. October (1989): 22-26. William Lind, the first to describe Fourth Generation Wars, articulated greatest concern for a form of warfare that combined terrorism, high technology, and the following additional elements: a nonnational or transnational base, such as an ideology or religion, a direct attack on the enemy's culture, and highly sophisticated psychological warfare, especially through manipulation of the media, particularly television news. These writers are probably the American military experts referred to by Abu Ubeid).

(or exacerbating) polarized identities. Polarized identities, in turn, result in the development, recruitment, and inspiration of new terrorists that might undermine the nation's way of life, its civil liberties and the way Americans live together.

Measuring domestic radicalization is, of course, a difficult challenge because the term "radical" implies deviation from a baseline and is a relative term, and voicing strong beliefs (with few exceptions) is a protected right afforded by the Constitution of the United States. "Violent extremists" and "terrorists" are likewise difficult to quantify in the U.S. population because such individuals logically seek to operate clandestinely. It can, however, be judged that "radicalization" and homegrown terrorists are on the rise in the United States through anecdotal evidence, as described below.

Number of Americans convicted or charged with "jihadi" related activity

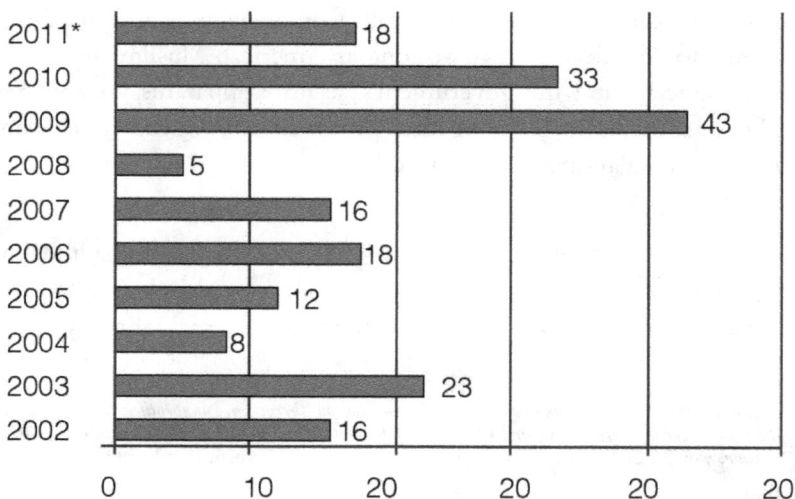

Year	Value
2011*	18
2010	33
2009	43
2008	5
2007	16
2006	18
2005	12
2004	8
2003	23
2002	16

The chart above reflects a count of "the 192 post-9/11 cases of Americans or U.S. residents convicted or charged with some form of jihadist terrorist activity directed against the United States, as well as the cases of those American citizens who have traveled overseas to join a jihadist terrorist group,"[73] * data collected through December 8, 2011. On December 21, 2011 Oytun Ayse Mihalik, of La Palma, California was charged with three counts of providing material support to terrorists. This subject was not included in the data assimilated by the New America Foundation at the time of writing.[74]

Some assess that domestic radicalization in the United States lags behind that observed in other Western nations. Even if this is true, 94 jihadist-inspired Americans were arrested or charged with terrorism between January 2009 and December 2011.[75] This figure alone, which represents almost half of 192 Americans arrested or charged for supporting Salafi-jihadi terrorism in the past decade, indicates that radicalization of Americans should be a major cause of concern.

The increasing number of U.S. citizens who are joining (or attempting to join) the Islamist camp may foreshadow increased violent extremism associated with this cause.[76] Examples of small group radicalization between 2009 and 2011 include (but are not limited to):

- American citizens departing the United States to fight with the al Qaeda-associated al Shabaab in Somalia;[77]

- Najibullah Zazi of Denver, Colorado, who led a plot to attack New York City's mass transit system;

- Colleen R. LaRose, a.k.a "Jihad Jane" and Jamie Paulin Ramirez of Philadelphia, Pennsylvania, and Denver, Colorado, respectively, who conspired to kill a Swedish artist for drawing a picture of the prophet Mohammed's head on the body of a dog;

- Waad Ramadan Alwan and Mohanad Shareef Hammadi, two Iraqi nationals who were afforded asylum in the United States and accused of trying to appropriate weapons for al Qaeda in Iraq.

---

73 Bergen, Peter, Andrew Lebovich, Matthew Reed, Laura Hohnsbeen, Nicole Salter, Sophie Schmidt, William Banks, et al. *Post-9/11 Jihadist Terrorism Cases Involving U.S. Citizens and Residents: An Overview*. Washington, DC: New America Foundation and Syracuse University's Maxwell School of Public Policy., 2011.

74 Associated Press. "California Woman Charged with Sending Money to Pakistan to Help Fund Attacks on US Military." *The Washington Post,* December 21, 2011, sec. National.

75 *Post-9/11 Jihadist Terrorism Cases Involving U.S. Citizens and Residents: An Overview*. Washington, DC: New America Foundation and Syracuse University's Maxwell School of Public Policy., 2011.

76 Matthew Levitt and Michael Jacobson. "Continuity and Change: Reshaping the Fight Against Terrorism." *Washington Institute for Near East Policy* Policy Focus No. 103, no. April 2010 (2010): May 10, 2010.

77 Patrisk Condon and Amy Forliti. "Missing Minnesota Somalis: Aspiring Fighters Or Dupes?" ABCNews.Com, July 7, 2009.

Americans should take little comfort in the fact that self-directed terrorists have not successfully conducted sophisticated attacks in the homeland to this point. The threat posed by homegrown terrorists is rapidly evolving with "characteristics that are constantly changing due to external experiences and motivational factors."[78] It is crucial that the United States consider strategies and structures that can align and re-align to address emerging threats.

During the last two decades, acts of domestic terrorism and spree killing in the United States vividly demonstrated that small, self-radicalized groups, even individuals, have the capacity to conduct attacks with devastating physical, social, and economic impact.[79] Complicating the challenge, self-radicalized terrorists may not be closely linked with foreign threat streams or directed by foreign terrorist organizations. Those types of nefarious associations make sophisticated collection techniques more readily available. For these reasons, and others, the identification of the self-radicalized terrorist is a daunting task for domestic intelligence services.

The extent of damage that can be inflicted by self-radicalized individuals is evidenced by the violent attack at Fort Hood, Texas, on November 5, 2009, where Army Major Nidal Hasan is alleged to have gone on a shooting spree, killing 13 people and wounded 30 others on Army base. A second example is the case of Faisal Shahzad of Bridgeport, Connecticut, who attempted to explode a car bomb in New York City on May 1, 2010. And, a third example, Carlos Bledsoe, was convicted of killing one soldier and wounding another in Little Rock, Arkansas on June 6, 2009. Bledsoe later wrote a letter to the judge who tried his case, one which clearly captures his full embrace of the Salafi-jihadi narrative:

> My lawyer has no defense... I wasn't insane or post traumatic nor was I forced to do this act. Which I believe and it is justified according to Islamic laws and the Islamic religion jihad -- to fight those who wage war on Islam and Muslims.[80]

---

78 Mark F. Guiliano. "Speech at the Washington Institute for Near East Policy." Washington, DC, 2011.

79 For instance, highly publicized violent attacks like the Oklahoma City bombing (1995), the Washington, D.C. sniper attacks (2002), and the Columbine school murders (1999) demonstrate the potential impact of "wannabe" and self-directed terrorists. It is likely that such acts, if conducted in a polarized social context by those subscribing to Islamist ideologies, might have an even more profound effect on society than previously experienced.

80 "Arkansas Recruiting Center Killing Suspect: 'this was a Jihadi Attack'." CNN.Com, 01/22/2010, 2010.

Due to the nature of the radicalization process, individuals may progress quickly from constitutionally protected activities to violent action, and they may vacillate between willingness and unwillingness to commit violence. Public source coverage of the alleged terrorists identified above reveals the motivation and corrupted religious justification for these acts, as their inspiration came from a fellow American citizen, Anwar Awlaqi.

Thus, the immunity or resilience to violent Islamist ideology has been demonstrably compromised in some segments of the American Muslim population. A 2010 summation of the terrorism threat goes directly at a concern for the homegrown threat:

> Al-Qaeda and its Pakistani, Somali, and Yemeni allies arguably have been able to accomplish the unthinkable—establishing at least an embryonic terrorist recruitment, radicalization, and operational infrastructure in the United States with effects both at home and abroad. And, by working through its local allies, the group has now allowed them to co-opt American citizens in the broader global al-Qaeda battlefield.[81]

The evidence provided above is anecdotal, but it supports the proposition by Jonathan Paris that the three most significant concerns to U.S. authorities should be:

1. Converts to Islam who become extremist;

2. Young American Muslims who travel abroad and meet AQ members or other extremists in Pakistan or the Middle East; and

3. Radicalized Muslims who have been alienated by U.S. foreign policy.[82]

Why are these concerns "most significant"? Because they indicate that the violent Islamists have successfully influenced some American citizens to join the "global jihad," despite diminishing support for al Qaeda around the globe.[83] How did this come about?

Adherents to Social Identity Theory might argue the increased level of radicalization is the result of a one dimensional counterterrorism strategy, because the United States' aggressive counterterrorism posture (unintentionally) created an overarching atmosphere of mistrust of the government by American Muslims. As the lessons of the United Kingdom

81 Bergen, Peter and Bruce Hoffman. *Assessing the Terrorist Threat: A Report of the Bipartisan Policy Center's National Security Preparedness Group.* Washington, DC: Bipartisan Policy Center, 2010.

82 Paris, Jonathan. "Discussion Paper on Approaches to Anti-Radicalization and Community Policing in the Transatlantic Space." Washington, DC, June 27-28, 2007, 2007.

83 Pew Global Attitudes Project. *Global Public Opinion in the Bush Years (2001-2008).*

and the Netherlands taught us, when Hard Power is employed too broadly in the domestic environment, it can result in alienation of the very constituency from which the government needs most support. This effect was evident in the early days of the Troubles in Northern Ireland and the early months of Dutch efforts to confront Moluccan terrorists as outlined in Chapters Three and Four. It may be that the responses to the 9/11 terrorist attacks by domestic law enforcement, the intelligence services and the general population were similarly perceived by much of the American Muslim population.

According to group dynamics theory, the American reaction to the September 11 attacks was predictable. Comprising approximately one percent of the American population, American Muslims had little contact with the general public, and the attackers had all been Arab Muslims. With relatively little intergroup exposure, Us/Them framing was bound to occur—a tactic bin Laden might well have counted on. The surprise attacks undermined feelings of security at both an individual and national level and resulted in a high degree of uncertainty about the future. Where and when would the terrorists attack next? The attackers had moved freely amongst the general population, in some cases for years. Which among the current population might also be a terrorist?

After all, his lieutenant Ayman Zawahiri's strategic thinking was "heavily indebted to vanguardism, a Leninist theory of revolution which posits that a small, revolutionary elite uses violence to rouse the people to fight against the government."[84] Zawhahiri had repeatedly encouraged (and participated in) terrorism against the Egyptian government in order to bait the government to harshly repress Islamist activists which would (hypothetically), in turn, motivate activists to join in overthrowing the existing government.

As the United States government and the American public responded to the 2001 attacks, their relationships with American Muslims and Americans of Arab and Southwest Asian extraction were, indeed, adversely affected. These groups came to see themselves as victims of discrimination, alienation, and prejudice from their fellow Americans and at the hands of various government organizations. A grievance cycle had begun. In response to sometimes violent racism and prejudice, some Arab- and Muslim-Americans developed (or had reinforced) a social identity more closely affiliated with their religion or ethnicity than their nationality.

---

84   International Research Center. . *Zawahiri Tries to Clear Name, Explain Strategy*. Washington, DC: Federation of American Scientists, 2008.

This type of social categorization is formed by contrast with other categories.[85] Approximately 65% of American Muslims were born outside the United States and more than 39% of this group immigrated to the United States in the last 20 years.[86] It is likely that many individuals within this population identify with the populations in regions where the United States is engaged in military conflict because they share common religious and cultural backgrounds. After all, in many cases, family and extended family, tribal or clan affiliations, ethnic similarities, and language provide a basis to identify with others from those regions. This may be particularly true if American Muslims feel alienated from the general public and disadvantaged. Therefore, it is likely that a more pronounced identification with "Muslim-ness" than "American-ness" is found in immigrant communities that are insular.

Immigrants lacking strong English language skills or those who veer from American mainstream culture are most vulnerable to the cultivation of ingroup/outgroup narratives and are more likely to accept stereotyping of the outgroup (the larger outgroup of relatively secularized, non-Muslim population, and particularly the police and federal agencies) because people engage in what they perceive as "strategically self-enhancing or self-protective identification."[87] The negative experiences that many American Muslims have endured in the wake of September 11 (mutually limited positive interaction between Muslims and the non-Arab, non-Muslim population, may tend to reinforce ingroup/outgroup polarization.)

Individual ingroup/outgroup categorization increased in the United States and throughout the Western world after the attacks on New York and Washington. Military strikes and law enforcement action impacted core al Qaeda dramatically, and al Qaeda morphed accordingly. Al Qaeda is no longer an externally based "jihadi organization with a chain of command to a jihadi movement—[it has become]…an ideology motivating dispersed groups internationally."[88] Increasing social polarization and the threat to social order was fueled by expanding violence from both "global jihadists" and Western

85   Michael A. Hogg "Social Categorization, Depersonalization and Group Behavior." In *Self and Social Identity*, edited by Marilynn B. Brewer and Miles Hewstone. 2nd ed., 203. Malden, MA: Blackwell Publishing, 2005, 203-206.

86   Pew Research Center. *Muslims in America: Mostly Middle Class and Mainstream.* Pew Research Center, 2007.

87   Dominic Abrams and Michael A. Hogg. "Collective Identity: Group Membership and Self-Conception." In *Self and Social Identity*, edited by Marilynn B. Brewer and Miles Hewstone. 2nd ed., 147. Malden, MA: Blackwell Publishing, 2005, 160.

88   Paris, Jonathan. "Discussion Paper on Approaches to Anti-Radicalization and Community Policing in the Transatlantic Space." Washington, DC, June 27-28, 2007, 2007.

military action. In answer to the British MI6 query in the immediate aftermath of 9/11, when the "mercury was struck" and the Salafi-jihadi call extended well beyond Afghanistan to the United States and other Western nations, it appears that for the next decade most of the domestic counterterrorism effort was unprepared to truly *prevent* terrorism. Here in the United States, the Salafi-jihadi call threatens homeland security and social order through the potential progression of continuing ethnic and religious conflict. We are engaged in a war of ideas, but the nation has not yet implemented or embraced a strategy, structure or effective means to combat violent extremist ideology.

RECENT CHANGES TO COUNTERTERRORISM STRATEGY

Subsequent strategies by the Obama Administration, issued in June and August of 2011 and a strategic implementation plan likewise failed to take on the daunting political task of establishing coordinating authorities for the counterterrorism and counterradicalization missions.[89] At the time of writing, counterterrorism efforts at the federal state, regional and local levels are coordinated on only a tactical, case-by-case basis.

The ideas behind the 2011 National Strategy for Counterterrorism are sound because they reflect an SIT-based approach. Not unexpectedly, the strategy entitled *"Empowering Local Partners to Prevent Violent Extremism in the United States* (ELP)." received a mixed response. The National Strategy for Counterterrorism was issued in June 2011 with al Qaeda and Salafi-jihadists squarely in its sights. This posture drew broad but qualified approval of the administration's counterterrorism policies, indicating that some maintain a preference for a one-dimensional, Hard Power, strategy and are suspicious of engagement with the "Muslim other":

> [W]hile I certainly support community involvement and initiatives, we must ensure that these do not become politically correct feel-good encounters which ignore the threats posed by dangerous individuals in the community. While we must assure the Muslim-American community that we will address real grievances, we

---

89   Homeland Security Advisory Council, Spring 2010. The establishment of a coordinating authority to manage the relationship between government and the local Muslim community is a consistent "smart practice" identified in this study, and included in recommendations by DHS's Homeland Security Countering Violent Extremism Working group.

must also remind its leaders that they must demonstrate leadership and cooperation. We should also encourage moderate Muslim-American leaders to step forward and assert themselves.[90]

The strategy may have received this caveated approval from U.S. Rep. Peter T. King, Chairman of the House Committee on Homeland Security, because in addition to Hard-Power tactics aimed mostly abroad, the strategy also alluded to a course meant to undermine the legitimacy of the Salafi-jihadi narrative and to attract potential recruits away from the al Qaeda's Salafi-jihadi ideology:

> [A]l-Qaʻida preys on local grievances and propagates a self-serving historical and political account. It draws on a distorted interpretation of Islam to justify the murder of Muslim and non-Muslim innocents. Countering this ideology—which has been rejected repeatedly and unequivocally by people of all faiths around the world—is an essential element of our strategy.[91]

Integrating the missions of federal, state and local agencies to counter terrorism, much less to counter radicalization, is an extremely complex challenge because most federal departments incorporate counterterrorism as only a part of their strategic plans. While national strategies set frameworks and communicate leadership visions, federal agencies, state and local governments do not collaboratively develop counterterrorism strategies. No agency coordinates whole government strategies at the local level. NSS 2011 acknowledges that "integrating and harmonizing the efforts of Federal, state, local and tribal entities remains a challenge,"[92] but offers only that the homeland security apparatus continues efforts to improve, and the homeland security apparatus is itself undefined.

Integration is even more of a challenge at the local level. Local governments and law enforcement organizations often cooperate with or participate in Joint Terrorism Task Forces and Fusion Centers, but in many cases—aside from JTTF and Fusion Center participation—local and state efforts to diminish the threat of terrorism are aimed at public safety, not national security concerns. In practice, a large segment of the homeland

---

90   King Statement on Obama Administration Violent Extremism Strategy. United States, Lanham: Federal Information & News Dispatch, Inc, 2011.

91   Obama Administration. "National Strategy for Counterterrorism (2011)." whitehouse. gov.

92   Ibid.

security community appears to have considered the "battle of ideas" as an external conflict based principally on foreign-policy issues or as a federal responsibility, at least until the spring of 2011.

NSS 2011 also emphasized a values-based approach to countering radicalization and hinted at how government might work with non-traditional and local partners to counter radicalization:

> Just as the terrorist threat we face in the United States is multifaceted and cannot be boiled down to a single group or community, so must our efforts to counter it not be reduced to a one-size-fits-all approach. Supporting community leaders and influential local stakeholders as they develop solutions tailored to their own particular circumstances is a critical part of our whole-of-government approach that contributes to our counterterrorism goals.[93]

On August 3, 2011, almost a decade after the al Qaeda attacks in New York and Washington, the administration published a much-anticipated domestic counterradicalization strategy entitled *"Empowering Local Partners to Prevent Violent Extremism in the United States* (ELP)." This strategy aligns directly with an SIT approach to preventing terrorism, as it articulates a vision of collaborative government, private and public entities working together at a local level. This new component of counterterrorism strategy was an encouraging move toward an SIT approach to counterterrorism in that it indicated a shift toward a balanced-strategy approach —one of the "smart practices" observed previously in our review the U.K. and the Netherlands. Ascertaining how the national strategy can be implemented from Washington, DC is, however, a challenge.

The administration's plan to empower local partners to prevent violent extremism in the United States sets forth these principles:

- We must continually enhance our understanding of the threat posed by violent extremism and the ways in which individuals or groups seek to radicalize Americans, adapting our approach as needed.

- We must do everything in our power to protect the American people from violent extremism while protecting the civil rights and civil liberties of every American.

- We must build partnerships and provide support to communities based on mutual trust, respect, and understanding.

- We must have honest dialogue between communities and government that is transparent and promotes community-based problem solving.

---

93   Ibid., 11.

- We must use a wide range of good governance programs—including those that promote immigrant integration and civic engagement, protect civil rights, and provide social services—that may help prevent radicalization that leads to violence.

- We must support local capabilities and programs to address problems of national concern.

- Government officials and the American public should not stigmatize or blame communities because of the actions of a handful of individuals.

- Strong religious beliefs should never be confused with violent extremism.[94]

Five months later, in December 2011, the *Strategic Implementation Plan for Empowering Local Partners to Prevent Violent Extremism* in the United States attempted to answer questions such as these. Unfortunately, the implementation plan, like the preceding documents, offers 1) no strong coordinating authority at either national or local levels, 2) no funding stream or requirement for any organization to dedicate funds to the project or 3) no common doctrine to ensure unity of effort, 4) no timelines or objectives to which a coordinating authority (if one existed) might hold participants accountable. These omissions reflect not so much a failure of ideas, but the political challenges that lay ahead for a top-down approach.

The media, too, has expressed skepticism of counterradicalization efforts, and the proposition of a new counterradicalization effort has been regarded with scrutiny. For example, writing for *The Nation*, Arun Kudnani, suggested:

> The lesson from European countries that have experimented with counter-radicalization policies is that unless intelligence-gathering and community engagement are clearly separated, community partners can end up being no more than government proxies, discouraging legitimate dissent on issues such as Western foreign policy and driving radical views dangerously underground. [95]

Such arguments against a policy to counter radicalization are flawed on several counts.

First, results in the Netherlands directly contradict such assertions. The threat of Salafi-jihadi terrorism is distinctly lower than before the Dutch counter- and deradicalization programs were implemented. Therefore, the correlation drawn by the author demonstrates a relationship between

---

94   Obama Administration (2011). *Empowering Local Partners to Prevent Violent Extremism in the United States*, 2-8.

95   Arun Kundnani. The FBI's 'Good' Muslims. *The Nation*, September 1, 2011, 2011.

government-community engagement and a decrease in violent rhetoric, but not a causal relationship between government-community engagement and diminished free speech or dissent.

Second, the United Kingdom acknowledged mistakes made by supporting not only moderate voices, but by also supporting (and funding) organizations with values contrary to those espoused by the government. The U.K. has since redoubled its efforts, with a more clear purpose. Prevent 2.0 aims to move the national effort closer to communities in a way that results in more effective government and more refined, local solutions to radicalization. The development of Prevent 2.0, implicitly acknowledges dissent from the population and acts to remedy legitimate community grievances, an outcome that is exactly the opposite of Kudnani's conclusion.

And finally, the suggestion that intelligence collection and community engagement should be separate argues *for* severe intrusion into the civil liberties of American citizens. Assuming government intelligence collectors cannot or should not develop a refined understanding of the context in which they work, the government would be forced to resort to a dramatic increase in electronic and physical surveillance, as the British were compelled to do in the early years of struggle against the PIRA.

Worse, isolating government agents from the American Muslim community might easily translate to the overuse of Hard Power, as illustrated in the Dutch cordon and search operations in Moluccan villages. Neither electronic nor physical surveillance provide sufficient insight to the full context that surrounds an individual or group's behavior (anyone who has ever had an e-mail message misinterpreted should be able to understand the value of context and interpersonal contact).

Only direct interaction with local communities affords the government a refined understanding of social context on which to base policy and operations, and only direct engagement by the community and those executing the counterterrorism mission affords the community the ability to voice dissent directly to government agents, rather than through third parties who might filter the community's concerns to serve their own political agendas.

The purpose of "intelligence" (whether obtained from overt dialogue, volunteers from the public, covert agents, electronic or physical surveillance) is to inform the decisions of policymakers. If intelligence collectors are isolated from the population most effected by government actions, then neither the public nor the government benefits.

It is disappointing that such critiques do not offer solutions, for if not the counterterrorists from government, civic organizations and the American Muslim community, who is to do the job of preventing terrorism? A collection of those who know both terrorists and the community have the capacity to develop solutions jointly if they can simultaneously maintain credibility with and the trust of those they serve. This is the only way counterradicalization can be effective.

Similarly, a Los Angeles Times editorial questioned the efficacy of a counterradicalization effort. The editorial suggested the case had not been made for "community outreach as an inoculation against extremism."[96] And yet, the whole point of an SIT approach is not to "inoculate against extremism," but to prevent extremists from turning to violence by partnering, as appropriate, with at-risk communities. Community outreach, strategic engagement nor Hard Power tactics alone can significantly change the threat posture in a liberal society. It is not the government's outreach that can prevent terrorism, rather it is positive change to the context in which potential terrorists live that can diminish the threat. Outreach is but one mechanism to generate positive contact and develop relationships between government officials and the communities they serve.

The evidence provided in U.K. and Dutch experiences addresses the concern that working with and through local communities might not be successful – both nations have achieved positive results – so there is reason to be optimistic about a Soft Power approach. But, the LA Times' assessment did make a valid point: "lone wolves" often "drop out" of or are rejected by their ingroups because the lone wolf considers the ingroup less extreme than necessary to attain its goals. While this observation contradicts the article's prior implication that counterradicalization programs have not proven their viability (lone-wolves drop out or are driven out of groups because they are more extreme than group will tolerate), the author is correct in stating that lone wolves will continue to emerge: they will develop and act across Islamist, right wing, left wing and single-issue terrorist groups (amongst others), as they always have.

It is clear that such individual actors pose a threat to public safety and their actions can be devastating to communities, but does the threat of a lone wolf terrorist constitute a serious threat to national security? Arguably,

---

96   "An Implausible Plan to Fight Terrorism through Community Outreach: A White House Paper Promoting Community Initiatives to Curb Radicalization is Commendable, but there is no Evidence to Suggest such Efforts Work " *Los Angeles Times,* 08/05/2011, 2011

individual actors do not present a threat to the nation's social fabric if lone wolves are seen for what they are—rejected by their ingroup. It is instead the isolation and polarization fueled by mistrust between groups and the violent feedback loop that could follow a lone wolf terrorist attack that represents a real existential threat to the nation. Community outreach and strategic engagement are necessary contributions to the nation's resilience to that type of threat.

Due to the potential harm that can be inflicted by even one terrorist, the lone wolf cannot be ignored. Lone wolves are difficult to spot precisely because they reject or are rejected by those in the mainstream, even by fringe "extremist" groups that are also non-violent. Their most extreme dialogue and actions cannot be observed by the mainstream because lone wolves normally withdrawal from the majority—they leave the mosque, the community center or school in which they no longer fit.

There are two principle ways for the practitioner to identify the lone wolf: the "inside-out" approach and the "outside-in" approach. An inside-out approach requires developing information about the subject from within the groups he or she is most closely associated with as he or she is developing a violent and extreme ideology. These social networks normally include friends, family, co-workers, fellow-congregants, etc. In order to garner information from these groups about the potential threat, the government must have or develop the trust of those in the network, or coerce individuals within this group to provide information. As demonstrated in the British and Dutch cases, security is enhanced when the community is not subject to broad application of coercive tactics. This means that Soft Power approaches are the preferred methods, especially in a domestic environment.

An outside-in approach calls for the intelligence community to identify suspicious behaviors through collection of information that is external to the subject's ingroup, but necessary for the terrorist to bring violent aspirations to fruition. For instance, terrorists' communications, financial transfers, information sharing platforms, purchase of bomb-making ingredients, and so forth, can help identify those who might have the intent to conduct an attack or materially support political violence. When suspicious activity is identified, government agents must still determine if the suspicious behavior is married with a violent ideology or criminal activity. In order to develop a fuller understanding of the subject's activities, government agents may be compelled to develop cooperation from those closely associated with the subject. Again, non-coercive tactics are preferable to achieve this end, for the same reasons articulated in the inside-out approach.

CVE should be *part* of a balanced and purposeful strategy that is both capable of disrupting terrorist activity and increasing resistance to violent ideologies, while extremism itself is not a concern. Practically speaking, "Strategic Engagement" allows counterterrorists from both the community and the government to communicate concerns to each other directly and to collaboratively develop strategies to influence the contexts that promote violent ideologies and protect civil liberties. With an effective strategic engagement effort, counterterrorists can work independently toward the same goals. Robert Lambert, a former leader within the U.K.'s Muslim Contact Unit (MCU),[97] described his unit's strategic engagement approach, noting that the approach resulted in the capacity and willingness of Muslim community groups to work:

> "...in a partnership devoid of coercion. This departure from coercive relationships [placed] the local London initiative at odds with conventional counterterrorism that relies instead on controlled relationships with paid informants."[98]

Might a similar approach alleviate some concerns of the Muslim community in the United States?

In at least some scenarios, non-coercive, collaborative relationships have been effective. From the author's experience working with Muslim communities to counter terrorism both domestically and internationally, the following points generally apply to successful strategic engagement:

1. Interpersonal engagement is most successful when it occurs between individuals perceived to have equal status community (authority, referent power, ability and willingness to mobilize others) within their own ingroups.

2. Continual interaction is very important. Government leaders must be willing to engage Muslim leaders at an interpersonal level. When mistakes are made, or offense is taken, it is important to acknowledge and correct wrongs, whether they are real or perceived.

---

97   The MCU was a specialized outreach component of the British Prevent program. Lambert makes a persuasive argument for engaging with the British Muslims who oppose terrorism, regardless of their opposition to British foreign policy.

98   Robert Lambert."Salafi and Islamist Londoners: Stigmatised Minority Faith Communities Countering Al-Qaida." Crime, *Law and Social Change* 50, no. 1-2 (Sep 2008, 2008): 73-89.

3. Informal settings are preferred. The author has both experienced and observed that messages are relayed more effectively in small groups where dialogue is possible. Public speeches and formal settings, on the other hand, offer a platform for venting, rarely produce tangible results and are prone to inflammatory media coverage.

4. It is important to differentiate between Community Relations (CR) and Strategic Engagement (SE), mutually supporting but separate functions. CR represents the most evident benefit to the community. SE helps identify the appropriate tools, tactics and strategies that are appropriate for local contexts. The need for the involvement of operational leaders is inherent in SE because only operational leaders have the legitimate authority to systemically impact the way counterterrorism operations are carried out.

The purpose of SE and CR outreach efforts should be to create the opportunity to develop positive contacts and deliver tangible benefits to communities. Strategic engagement should result in refined understanding and refined tactics that result in more efficient investigations and less unnecessary intrusion.

During the engagement process, it should be expected that counterterrorists will have divergent views on any number of topics, and that American Muslims might understand or even believe that some of the grievances espoused by terrorists are legitimate. In fact, in terms of SIT's cross-, de- and recategorization processes, extremists who reject violence are potentially the most viable partners for the counterterrorist precisely because they can speak with credibility to an audience of extremists. Where counterterrorists from government and the community find mutual benefit, opportunities for positive contact exist. Certainly this space includes the prevention of political violence, but it might also include matters of public safety, civil rights, education and cultural sensitivities. We can learn a lot from one another about how to be more effective, even if we do not always agree on every topic.

Model of CVE Roles

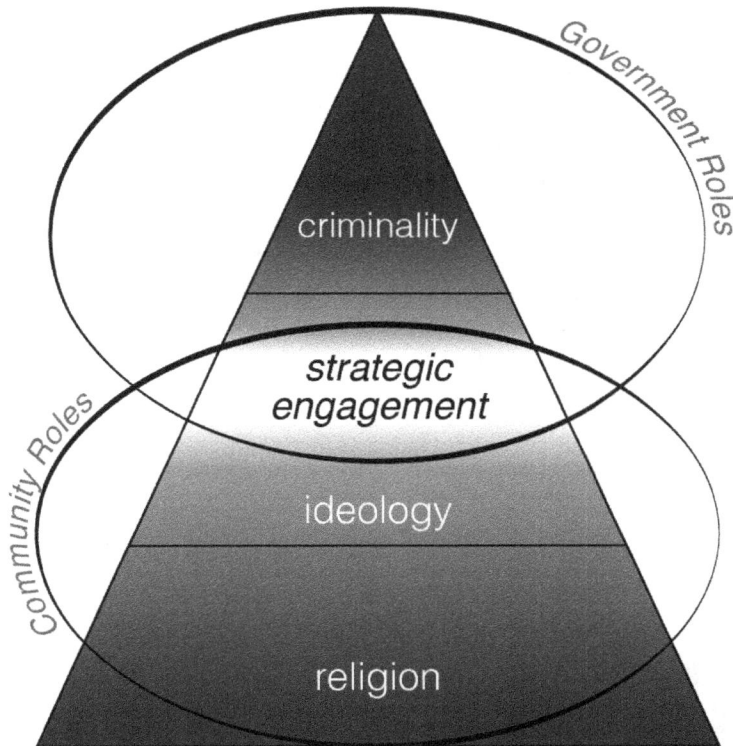

As depicted in the Model of CVE Roles above,[99] both the community and government have clearly defined roles for dealing with the terrorist threat. The government is legally responsible for enforcement of criminal laws and prohibited from policing religion, while counterterrorists from the American Muslim community feel morally compelled to protect their religion from Salafi-jihadi perversions that justify the killing of civilians and to protect their

---

99   This graphic representation of CVE Roles was developed at a joint presentation at the Naval Postgraduate School's Center for Homeland Defense and Security by Homeland Security Advisory Council member Mohamed Elibiary and the author on January 18, 2012. The model depicts a shared and practiced vision that proved successful in Southeastern Texas during the period of 2006-2012.

nation – and children – from violence. These roles of legitimate responsibility and natural concern overlap as the radicalizing subject or group progresses toward violent activity.

In all but a handful of instances, suspicious activity or indications of violent extremism do not result in violence or arrest. This may be because effective law enforcement served as a deterrent to terrorist activity. It could also be a result of incorrectly assessed "suspicious" behavior. A third possibility supported by SIT (without discounting the other two possibilities) is that the observed or reported suspicious behavior was the subject's response to certain contextual influences. With changing circumstances, subjects will seek ways to increase their own status, and that may mean shift in their approach to resolving internal conflicts; that is, the subject who demonstrates suspicious behavior may find solutions outside of the paradigm of violence or criminal activity. Perhaps his or her social identity altered from that of potential terrorist to something less dangerous. As such, for those interested in countering violent extremism and employing an SIT perspective, the key to diminishing violence is changing the context around an individual in a positive way—a way that makes non-violent solutions more attractive than violent action.

Counterterrorists must understand that the apparent goal of *Empowering Local Partners to Prevent Violent Extremism* in the United States is not to replace existing counterterrorism efforts, but to complement them. The introduction of Soft Power strategies is consistent with the evolution of Bush-era strategies (as described in the administration's updated strategy) and fully consistent with engaging in a battle of ideas (as recommended in *The 911 Commission Report*). By increasing the amount of positive contact with at-risk communities, government agents at the local, state and federal level might work together with community partners to change the context surrounding potential recruits to terrorism, thus reducing the number of new recruits and laying the groundwork for how the government and the American Muslim community will respond to one another in the wake of a successful attack.

Looking to the future, it is important to note that the 9/11 Commission Report took only the federal government under its lens. This was appropriate at the time, considering the federal government's responsibility to provide for the nation's common defense, because terrorist acts by foreign powers are fundamentally acts of war. It should also be noted that the structure necessary to execute a national strategy will necessarily include state and local authorities, nongovernment and community organizations. The evolution of the terrorist threat will likely result in fundamental changes to the way counterterrorism operations are defined and how the homeland security community fights terrorism.

It was important for the President and highest-level policymakers to consider a strategic question: does the United States face a greater threat from the few hundred al Qaeda members in the mountains of Pakistan and Afghanistan and their affiliates, or from the threat of social polarization and the violence at home, inspired by radical Islamist ideology? If, as NSS 2010 suggests, "[w]e are at war with a specific network, al-Qa'ida, and its terrorist affiliates who support efforts to attack the United States, our allies, and partners,"[100] then a sustained "hunt and kill or capture" policy may suffice. This statement, however, seems to conflict with current depictions of the present state of the terrorist threat, as provided by certain officials. The Director of the NCTC has stated, "[p]lots disrupted in [the domestic United States] during the past year were unrelated operationally, but are indicative of a collective subculture and a common cause that rallies independent extremists to want to attack the Homeland."[101] According to the Director of the FBI, "threats from homegrown violent extremists... who act without direction from a foreign terrorist organization—remain a concern,"[102] The secretary of DHS has stated, "It is clear that the threat of al Qaeda-style terrorism is not limited to the al-Qaeda core group, or organizations that have close operational links to al Qaeda."[103] After all, the formal, organized threat from bin Laden and core al Qaeda has been severely diminished by military force abroad and through law enforcement in the homeland.[104]

Despite progress against core al Qaeda and affiliated groups, the Salafi-jihadi narrative remained intact and has penetrated American society. "Last year [from September, 2009-September, 2010] was a watershed in terrorist attacks and plots in the United States, with a record total of 11 jihadist attacks, jihadist-inspired plots, or efforts by Americans to travel overseas to obtain terrorist training."[105]

100 Obama Administration. *National Security Strategy 2 010.* 20.

101 Senate Judiciary Committee. *Nine Years After 9/11: Confronting the Terrorist Threat to the Homeland: Michael Leiter Director of the National Counterterrorism Center*

102 Senate Judiciary Committee. *Nine Years After 9/11: Confronting the Terrorist Threat to the U.S: Statement of Robert S. Mueller III*

103 Senate Judiciary Committee. *Nine Years After 9/11: Confronting the Terrorist Threat to the Homeland: Statement of Secretary Janet Napolitano.*

104 Leiter, *The terror threat picture.*

105 Bergen and Hoffman. *Assessing the Terrorist Threat.*

Certainly the quantitative impact of American deaths caused by terrorism within the nation's borders during the last decade does not compare to 2001. On the other hand, the number of attacks and attempts has been multiplied tenfold, and with the technology available on-line, even unsophisticated terrorists have the capacity to conduct devastating attacks. Today's domestic threat from Salafi-jihadists is not the short-term impact of a dramatic physical assault, but the social and ideological impact of polarized identities. This polarization might divide the nation and directly affect our way of life if a cycle of religious and ethnic violence materializes. In addition to the prominence of Americans who have become leaders of al Qaeda and some of its affiliate organizations, al Qaeda engages in propaganda that undermines the status and credibility of the United States, and the impact is not limited by national boundaries – it is happening here in the United States.

American citizens with strong familial and ethnic ties in Pakistan, for instance, might be susceptible to Dr. Ayman al-Zawahiri's claims that America, via its influence with the government of Pakistan, actively prevented aid to flow to the victims of flooding in Pakistan.[106] Zawahiri's statement, of course, is true in the sense that al Qaeda members are actively targeted by United States and Pakistani government forces. Zawahiri's message, however, was not adequately countered, or better yet preempted, by broad messaging by the United States regarding efforts by the American military, Department of State, and nongovernment and charitable organizations that mobilized to deliver aid. This was an opportunity for the United States to engage in the war of ideas, a chance to inform those with family and friends still living (and suffering) in Pakistan that the United States and their fellow Americans were working to relieve suffering as well as to kill or capture murderous terrorists.

Unfortunately, the opportunity was lost. Instead of messages regarding efforts to deliver aid to Muslims abroad, the Muslim-American public was inundated by media coverage of the "Ground Zero Mosque" and "burn the Koran Day." On the horizon is the response to continuing Congressional hearings regarding the level of cooperation the United States government receives from the American-Muslim community,[107] recent revelations of an FBI analyst who allegedly "told his audience that the fight against al-Qaida is

---

106 al-Zawahiri, Ayman, Dr. *A Victorious Ummah, A Broken Crusade Nine Years After the Start of the Crusader Campaign.* Charleston, South Carolina: Nine Eleven Finding answers Foundation (NEFA), 2010.

107 Raymond Hernandez. "Muslim 'Radicalization' is Focus of Planned Inquiry." *New York Times,* 12/16/2011, 2010.

a 'waste,' compared to the threat presented by the ideology of Islam itself," [108] and the continuing threat of an al Qaeda attack. These incidents and the continuing threat accentuate the need to implement a Smart Power strategy.

108 Spencer Ackerman and Noah Shachtman. . *Video: FBI Trainer Says Forget 'Irrelevant' Al-Qaida, Target Islam.* Danger Room: What's Next in National Security: wired.com, 2011.

CHAPTER 6

BALANCING ACTS

WHAT CAN WE LEARN FROM OUR ALLIES AND SOCIAL IDENTITY THEORY?

"Perpetrators, collaborators, bystanders, victims: we can be clear about three of these categories. The bystander, however, is the fulcrum. If there are enough notable exceptions, then protest reaches a critical mass. We don't usually think of history as being shaped by silence, but, as English philosopher Edmund Burke said, 'The only thing necessary for the triumph [of evil] is for good men to do nothing.'"

–Martin Porter

In this study, we have explored how British and Dutch domestic counterterrorism strategies evolved across four parameters: their strategies, structure, the tools they employ and the impact of their strategies. We also reviewed how the United States homeland security community adapted the fight against terrorism and identified the nature of the continuing threats to domestic security. Before reviewing our findings, it is appropriate to acknowledge the study's weaknesses. First, this study included only two western nations. While the study's results were useful for identifying key considerations for counterterrorists, other scholars and practitioners are encouraged to test these findings. Because the entire argument for an approach to counterterrorism that is informed by Social Identity Theory is founded on the importance of context in local circumstances, real-world solutions must necessarily be tailored to local circumstances. Second, it is recognized that the legal and security structures of the United Kingdom and the Netherlands are fundamentally different than those of the United States. As discussed in the introduction, however, there are good methodological reasons for comparing these approaches, particularly considering this book's goal of identifying fundamental concepts and demonstrating their prima facie validity. Considering the immigration patterns of the United Kingdom and the Netherlands, where the preponderance of Muslim immigration preceded that of the United States, it may be that the lessons learned herein are more applicable to the next decade than the last. It may also be that our ability to successfully implement the suggestions below will dictate the nation's ability to truly prevent terrorism for coming generations.

LESSONS FROM OUR ALLIES

Since September 11, 2001, agencies conducting the counterterrorism mission in the United States have developed strategies independent of a national architecture and have favored enforcement action over Soft Power tactics.[1] Alternative strategies have been and are being applied by other Western governments with success. Chief among these nations are the United Kingdom—perhaps the country most experienced in combating insurgency and homegrown terrorism—and the Netherlands—one of the West's most liberal nations. The national security community should take the opportunity to learn from the mistakes of these nations as well as their successes. The "smart practices" common to the British and Dutch counterterrorism experience might serve as a road map to for the development of a national effort to mitigate the recruitment and radicalization of new terrorists. Counterterrorists in the United States should ask themselves how the smart practices identified in the pages of this book might be applied at the strategic, operational and local levels here in the homeland. The answers to these questions may define a strategy designed to impact not just the Salafi-jihadi threat but also to have a far-reaching impact when applied to other forms of terrorism.

As suggested by NSCT 2011 and Empowering Local Partners to Prevent Violent Extremism in the United States, a whole-government strategy might have profoundly positive implications for our national security, thereby and improving our way of life as citizens. Placed in an "eliminate-reduce-raise-create" grid,[2] the fundamental goals of a whole government counter-radicalization strategy are clearly defined in this way:

---

1   Joseph S. Nye. *Soft Power: The Means to Success in World Politics*. 1st ed. New York: Public Affairs, 2004, 14.

2   W. Chan Kim and Renée Mauborgne. *Blue Ocean Strategy: How to Create Uncontested Market Space and Make the Competition Irrelevant*. Boston, Mass.: Harvard Business School Press, 2005, 36.

Eliminate	**Raise**
• Cultural ignorance	• Community trust
• Religious justification of terrorism	• Quantity of information volunteered from at-risk communities
• The terrorists' ability to recruit increasing numbers of new terrorists	• Support for "mainstream" ideologies
	• Efficiency of counterterrorism effort by addressing the development of new threats
	• Number of non-violent alternative available to the disaffected
Reduce	**Create**
• Resonance of Islamist messaging	• Alignment with threat of homegrown terrorists
• The number of radicalizing influences	• Ability to identify and address grievances at state, local and federal levels
• Credibility of existing radicalizers	• Partnerships between government, NGO and at-risk communities
• Long term costs of deterrent force and technologies	• Multilevel problem-solving approaches

With the administration's strategy outlined in very broad terms, the homeland security community must determine how to implement counterterrorism and counterradicalization strategies. Why? The U.K.'s experience with PIRA indicates that ethno-nationalist organizations are long-lasting, but religiously-motivated terrorists tend to be even more resilient.[3] Al Qaeda's Salafi-jihadi ideology represents a hybrid of these motivations. As such, the narrative that inspires Salafi-jihadi violence is likely to be a multi-generational struggle—that is, unless positive steps are taken to counter violent extremism rather than simply continuing the pursuit of a one-track, Hard Power strategy.

Whether formally established or through a "coalition of the willing," counterterrorists from the government, NGOs and the American Muslim community must find ways to positively influence the local contexts that surround potential recruits to the Salafi-jihadi ideology. The lessons learned

---

3   Seth G. Jones and Martin C. Libicki, *How Terrorist Groups End: Lessons for Countering Al Qa'Ida.* Santa Monica, CA: Rand, 2008, 36-37 .

by the British and Dutch support adoption of strategies, structures and tactics that attract potential terrorists to a social identity that compares favorably to joining the global jihadists.

ORIENTATION TO THE WAR OF IDEAS

A precondition for success in the ideological confrontation being waged in the United States is an understanding of the American Muslim perspective, as it pertains to local and individual contexts. It may be true, especially in the United States that "anyone who wants to understand the roots of terrorism must come to grips with the simultaneous attraction and repulsion, love and hate that Islamic societies experience towards the United States."[4]

In many cases, hypocrisy in the foreign policy of the United States (real or perceived), paired with negative experiences with security services in their historical homelands and in the United States post-9/11, undermine American Muslims trust in the U.S. Government. This mistrust must be overcome in order to build partnerships to combat violent extremist ideologies.

Polarization between Muslims and non-Muslims complicates this challenge. Non-Muslim Americans are

> …galvanized by terrorist attacks and suicide bombings in Iraq, Israel, Palestine, Afghanistan, Pakistan and Indonesia … while the Muslim world is galvanized by the occupation of Iraq, abuses at Abu Ghraib and Guantanamo, and images of civilian deaths and destruction."[5]

As a result, many Muslim communities feel isolated, Muslim leaders may be suspicious of law enforcement, have concern regarding potential discrimination and misuse of information, and resent what they perceive as unfair treatment of Muslims in the United States.[6] Such concerns are exacerbated and/or exploited by some opportunistic advocacy groups and individuals who discourage Muslims from engaging independently with law enforcement.[7]

---

4   Fathali M. Moghaddam, *From the Terrorists' Point of View: What they Experience and Why they Come to Destroy.* Westport, Conn.: Praeger Security International, 2006, 15.

5   John L. Esposito and Dalia Mogahed, *Who Speaks for Islam? : What a Billion Muslims really Think,* (New York, NY: Gallup Press, 2007), 65.

6   This observation is consistent with the recent survey of Muslim attitudes in the Houston area.

7   CAIR. "American Muslim Civic Pocket Guide: Your Rights and Responsibilities as an American Muslim," .

According to the European Council's Counter-Terrorism Coordinator Gijs de Vries, those who would actively work to prevent terrorism must accept that "the key to tackling Islamist fundamentalism and terrorism from the Islamist community is in the hands of moderate Muslims."[8] While de Vries groups Islamist fundamentalism and terrorism together (contrary to the author's opinion) and doesn't define what a "moderate" Muslim is, the point he makes is important. Government agencies must win the support of fence sitters in the Muslim community. So, for government agents in the United States, the perceptions of the American Muslim community, in some ways, are the only really meaningful metric. If the Salafi-jihadi message appeals to disaffected American Muslims, then the threat of homegrown Salafi-jihadi terrorism will continue to grow. If American Muslims actively counter Salafi-jihadi messages, those vulnerable to recruitment will be more resilient and the threat of terrorist activity will decrease.

For this reason, the government—at all levels—must develop trusting alliances with Muslim leaders without compromising their credibility. But before setting out to build liaison, decision-makers should consider why the Islamist narrative resonates in America and in the contextual perspective of potential recruits. An understanding of the psychological and cultural influences that underpin radicalization should inform counter-radicalization strategies and may assist in anticipating the challenges and opportunities that lie ahead. Ultimately, the goal of engagement is to attract (or keep) the mass population's loyalty and to diminish the development or recruitment of more terrorists. Muslims who have assimilated into "mainstream society" might be able to provide great insight into the conservative and ultraconservative fringes of Islam, but may not lend expertise to the question "Why do people become terrorists?" Or "What is the best way to interrupt radicalization toward violence?" To prevent terrorism, the government must move beyond easy and amiable conversations to understand radicalism and the grievances from which it generates. It is crucial for the government to create safe platforms where frank conversations can be had between parties who are willing to accept criticism and resolve potential conflicts while simultaneously defending actions or acknowledging mistakes as necessary.

---

8   EurActiv Network, "Gijs De Vries on Terrorism, Islam and Democracy,".

ENGAGING IN THE DOMESTIC WAR OF IDEAS AND HOW THE U.S. SHOULD ADJUST

We are all subject to "radicalization" in some form. The global Salafi-jihadi movement poses a significant challenge to counterterrorists precisely because the radicalization phenomenon is indiscriminate and its indicators are subtle.[9] Whether an individual is being radicalized toward violence is hard to detect, especially in the process's early stages, unless those close to the radicalizing person understand which severe changes in behavior could signal danger. Too often, these behavioral cues, which may be overlooked as natural responses to Axis IV stressors, are recognized by those closest to the terrorist only in retrospect.

A growing amount of research explores the radicalization process, but so far no litmus test has emerged. Even the study of Americans who have been charged with or arrested for terrorism provides little help in developing a terrorist profile:

> Their average age is thirty. Of the cases for which ethnicity could be determined, only a quarter are of Arab descent, while 9% are African-American, 12% are Caucasian, 18% are South Asian, 18% are of Somali descent, and the rest are either mixed race or of other ethnicities. About half the cases involved a U.S-born American citizen, while another third were naturalized citizens. And of the 94 cases where education could be ascertained, two thirds pursued at least some college courses, and one in ten had completed a Masters, Ph.D., or another Doctoral equivalent.[10]

Truly, "they" are "us."

The most promising commonality of Western "jihadists," however, is that the terrorists encountered a "spiritual sanctioner" or "charismatic leader" who assisted their progression by bridging the self-identification and

---

9   Mitchell D. Silber and Arvin Bhatt, *Radicalization in the West: The Homegrown Threat.* New York: New York (City) Police Department, 2007. Silber and Bhatt describe this ideology as "the acceptance of a religious-political worldview that justifies, legitimizes, encourages, or supports violence against anything kufr, or un-Islamic, including the West, its citizens, its allies, or other Muslims whose opinions are contrary to the extremist agenda.... [R]ather than seeking and striving for the more mainstream goals of getting a good job, earning money, and raising a family, the indoctrinated radical's goals are non-personal and focused on achieving 'the greater good.' The individual's sole objective centers around the Salafi aim of creating a pure fundamentalist Muslim community worldwide" (21–22).

10   Bergen, et al., *Post-9/11 Jihadist Terrorism Cases Involving U.S. Citizens and Residents: An Overview,* 1.

indoctrination phases of radicalization.[11] The "charismatic leader" might be a personal contact, or, in previously mentioned cases, the charismatic leader could be a virtual personality who never has direct contact with the recruit.

Interaction with charismatic leaders known to be associated with terrorists is a likely point to identify those vulnerable to recruitment to violent extremism. This behooves the counterterrorist to develop allies in the ranks of those who have contact with individuals seeking spiritual guidance. In a Hard Power–only paradigm, these relationships are unlikely to form. This should be troubling for counterterrorists because it may also be the first and last opportunity for the law enforcement community to identify and intervene in the radicalization process before the recruit becomes a lost cause.

Despite identification of behavioral commonalities that might signal diversion from political dissent to violent activism, no single behavior (short of an overt act of terrorism) can positively identify the future terrorist. Further, any checklist developed will most likely include individuals who never actually engage in terrorism. Many of the behaviors that could indicate radicalization are constitutionally protected. Without an appreciation of baseline behaviors, it is difficult for the government official to identify aberrant behavior. This is why understanding individual and group behaviors within their social contexts is of utmost concern to the astute counterterrorist mind.

Fathali Moghaddam, Director of the Conflict Resolution Program at Georgetown University, suggests that rather than a "conveyer belt" process where individuals progress steadily from conservative religious beliefs to violent extremism, a person might vacillate between supporting and rejecting violence as a means to address grievances during the radicalization process.[12] According to Moghaddam, whether or not an individual becomes a terrorist depends on societal conditions that influence how a person perceives his or her personal and collective identities. Only by understanding behavioral changes *in context* can we hope to spot and intervene in the development of new terrorists and safeguard civil liberties. Societal conditions that affect American Muslims range widely from region to region and city to city within the United States; as such, each area faces different challenges, and will require different solutions.

---

11   Ibid. 1.

12   Fathali M. Moghaddam, *From the Terrorists' Point of View: What they Experience and Why They Come to Destroy*, (Westport, Conn.: Praeger Security International, 2006), 45-46.

In the United States, the Muslim population is understandably affected by cultural and emotional residue from their or their families' traditional homelands, which range broadly from Europe to Indonesia. In many Muslim-majority countries, corrupt and dictatorial governments generate a severe mistrust of government in general and law enforcement and intelligence agencies specifically. Government agents in the United States, in addition to generally being non-Muslims (and thus outgroup members), are typically regarded as a threat both to the individual and the ingroup. This is why persistent, purposeful engagement with centers of influence within the Muslim community is a critical step in the war of ideas. Overcoming resultant intergroup stereotypes should be a goal of every interaction with the Muslim community.

Converts to Islam present a particularly worrisome concern for counterterrorists. As in the cases of John Walker Lindh, Jose Padilla, Daniel Boyd, and others, these neophytes in Islam have an inherently limited knowledge of the religion and a limited understanding of nuanced theological arguments that underpin al Qaeda's religious justification for terrorism. Because converts are unable to critically evaluate the guidance provided by the "religious authorities" to which they subscribe, new converts to Islam may have a or feel a need to prove their orthodoxy; given that they are newcomers to the religion, language and culture they are particularly susceptible to the influence of charismatic leaders. Those who are prepared to act on the religious jurisprudence espoused by illegitimate "religious authorities" are most likely to be attracted away from terrorism by community members whom they view as credible. Clearly, religious jurisprudence is outside the scope of government's responsibility in the United States. This is the fundamental reason the government must develop partners in the Muslim community to confront terrorist ideologies.

THE RESONATING ISLAMIST-JIHADI NARRATIVE

The decision to engage in terrorism is a personal one, made within an individualized context: it is difficult and maybe impossible to predict who is or may become susceptible to the call of violent extremism. The messages that are common to statements published by al Qaeda and self-identified or convicted violent extremists, however, reveal basic ideas that are used to recruit some Muslims to violence.[13] For instance, soon after the failed attempt of the Christmas Day bomber, Umar Farouk Abdulmutallab, his self-proclaimed inspirational leader, Anwar Awlaki, published the second edition of *Inspire* magazine, an English-language Internet publication. In this magazine, Awlaki posited that the West is completely incompatible with the Muslim world, and sought to recruit individuals living in the West to "jihad" in order to fulfill what he interpreted to be a religious duty—killing those who did not follow his concept of true Islam.[14] Awlaki further encouraged others to kill by using a "pickup truck 'as a mowing machine, not to mow grass, but mow down the enemies of God.'"[15] Before Awlaki and his co-editor Samir Khan were killed by an airstrike on September 30, 2011, they had just published the seventh "Commemorative Edition" of the virtual magazine. Significantly, Awlaki and Khan were both American citizens.

Another example of the resonating Islamist narrative was presented by Faisal Shazad (who pleaded guilty to attempting to explode a vehicle bomb in New York's Times Square on May 1, 2010) at his sentencing appearance on October 3, 2010. Shazad advised the presiding judge and the American public:

> We are only Muslims trying to defend our religion, people, homes and land, but if you call us terrorists, then we are proud terrorists and we will keep on terrorizing you until you leave our lands and people at peace.[16]

In this instance and others like it, the fundamental theme that motivates Muslims to violent extremism is that Islam and Muslims are under attack by the West (and in particular, the United States)—a classic ingroup/outgroup framing that might easily appeal to a population isolated (or one that chooses to isolate itself) from the general public because of religious and, in many cases, ethnic differences. When an individual adopts this worldview, which

---

13   For a more detailed review of al Qaeda statements, video, and other al Qaeda propaganda, see the Nine Eleven Finding Answers Foundation (NEFA Foundation) website at http://www.nefafoundation.org, which provides an extensive list of al Qaeda propaganda.

14   Thomas Joscelyn, "Analysis: Anwar Awlaki's Message to Inspire Readers," *The Long War Journal* (2010)

15   Aljazeera, "Chilling Tips in Al-Qaeda Magazine: Yemen Offshoot Launches Second Edition of English Publication with Articles by Wanted US Cleric Anwar Al-Awlaki," Aljazeera.Net, October, 12, 2010.

16   Tom Hays and Larry Neumeister, "Times Sq. Bomber Sentenced, Warns of More Attacks," *Associated Press,* October 6, 2010.

might be reinforced by real or imagined experiences of persecution or victimization of self or the group to which he or she belongs, the individual is susceptible to a call to violent protest or retribution for perceived injustice.

According to David Gompert, writing for the RAND Corporation, for those who complete the radicalization journey, the result is marked by

> ...an impassioned, personal call to duty in defense of an embattled Islamic community spread around the globe, held to be under attack by the United States and its infidel accomplices.... The aim is nothing less than global holy war, leading to a new order—powerful, puritanical, and unified—throughout the Muslim world.[17]

Those who adhere to such Salafi-jihadi narratives pose a potential threat to the United States. Examples of homegrown terrorism over the past two years vividly demonstrate that individuals and groups within the United States are susceptible to the influence of Islamist political philosophy that proposes violence to resolve political grievances and misrepresents Islam to justify those acts. It is therefore easy to understand the government's desire to interdict proponents of this philosophy even when, within certain limits,[18] their freedom of speech is protected by the First Amendment to the Constitution of the United States.

CHALLENGES TO OVERCOME

Considering that only 35% of American Muslims were born in the United States and that 56% are under the age of 40,[19] the Muslim population's cultural immersion in the United States and its opportunities to assimilate or fully integrate with the general public is relatively limited, when compared to the Muslim experience in Europe and to other waves of migration in the United States. The events of September 11 and reactions by both the government and the public in the ensuing years impacted the American Muslim experience and increased social isolation. At the individual level, American Muslims express suspicion of government agencies and perceive sanctioned and systematic bias due to increased security protocol. Community

---

17   David C. Gompert, *Heads We Win*, International Security and Defense Policy Center, National Defense Research Institute, and Rand Corporation. RAND Research Brief. Vol. 9244, 1. Santa Monica, CA: Rand, 2007.

18   For detailed exploration of First Amendment case law and prohibitions on free speech, see Legal Information Institute, Cornell Law School (particularly "Government Restraint of Content of Expression")

19   Pew Research Center, *Muslims in America: Mostly Middle Class and Mainstream.* Pew Research Center, 2007.

roundtable discussions by the FBI and DHS revealed "frustration with what they [American Muslims] considered to be government profiling or discrimination on the basis of ethnicity or religion."[20] To many Muslims,

> ...it is clear that measures adopted by the government have had a profound impact on Muslims living in the United States. These measures have already disrupted the lives of thousands and left them in the grip of constant apprehension; they also have impeded the entry and full participation of the American Muslim community in the public square.[21]

The continued perception of bias and discrimination so many years after September 11 is particularly disconcerting from a security standpoint. Because the American Muslim population is young, the United States stands to face increasing numbers of young Muslims who experience an identity crisis over the next decade. Based on patterns observed in Europe, and particularly in the U.K. and the Netherlands, it is logical to project similar security challenges in the United States from some second- and third-generation Muslims as they grow up in a polarized context. Therefore, the steps taken (or not taken) now will have a direct impact on the threat of terrorism over the next generation.

BALANCED POWER STRATEGIES

Applied to counterterrorism, the purpose of Hard Power is essentially to diminish the enemy's ability to conduct physical attacks. The purpose of Soft Power is to stop the flow of new terrorist recruits, and to prevent the desire or perceived need to act violently. Neither tactic alone is likely to mitigate conflict entirely, but when exercised together in what Nye called "Smart Power,"[22] the odds of diminishing the terrorist threat are increased. According to many terrorism experts, Hard Power policies are mostly doomed to fail at truly *preventing* terrorism because they "only target those individuals whose

---

20   Department of Homeland Security. Roundtable. "Roundtable on Security and Liberty: Perspectives of Young Leaders Post 9/11: Houston, Texas and Washington, D.C.: Report for Government Officials and Policy Makers."). The author was present at this and subsequent meetings over a four year period. This frustration has been repeatedly and consistently expressed in interviews and successive roundtables by DHS and the FBI in the Houston area. Concerns are often specifically associated with screening processes at airports and ports of entry.

21   Yvonne Yazbeck Haddad and Robert Stephen Ricks, "Claiming Space in America's Pluralism: Muslims Enter the Political Maelstrom." In *Muslims in Western Politics*, edited by Abdulkadr H. Sino, 13. Bloomington, Indiana: Indiana University press, 2009.

22   Joseph Nye, "The Problem: A Smarter Superpower," *Foreign Policy* no. 160 (2007): 46-46-4.

identities have already been transformed" into terrorists.[23] Instead, a strategic approach—one that addresses the conditions that result in social polarization and ingroup/outgroup violence—is required to win an asymmetrical conflict.

The increasing phenomenon of homegrown terrorist plots indicates that by default, the United States has made a decision to surrender the ideological battlefield. Refusal, or reluctance, to fully engage in the ideological conflict at home is a poor policy choice because "terrorism will continue to be a social problem, and civil society-level initiatives perhaps not previously considered in a serious way will ultimately warrant much greater consideration."[24]

A historical review of terrorist groups supports this theory: terrorist groups were more likely to attain their goals than be destroyed when only coercive tactics were employed by the government. When political, intelligence, and policing strategies—strategies that appeal to the population's sense of fairness, morality and justice—were employed, terrorist groups were much more likely to fail.[25] This suggests that stopping terrorist acts and diminishing the recruitment of new terrorists requires active engagement between the government and the American Muslim population. As noted by the 9/11 Commission, the United States should "engage in the struggle of ideas."[26]

Since 2001, the United States has not integrated Soft Power in its domestic counterterrorism strategy. Instead, the United States has, by default, employed a counterterrorism strategy that leans almost exclusively toward Hard Power. This is likely the result of the lack of an overarching counterterrorism strategy. National Security Strategy 2010 provided a catalyst to develop an overarching strategy, but to win the battle of ideas, implementation of a holistic strategy is critical.

IMPERATIVE FOR BALANCED POWER

The challenge for the counterterrorist then, is to disrupt the radicalization process, to find ways of interfering with this narrative, and to develop a process whereby those vulnerable to the appeal of violent extremism can be attracted away from their destructive course early in the process. To

---

23   Moghaddam, *From the Terrorists' Point of View*, 127.

24   Horgan."Disengaging from Terrorism," 1 .

25   Jones and Libicki. *How Terrorist Groups End*, 18-30 .

26   National Commission on Terrorist Attacks upon the United States, Thomas H. Kean, and Lee Hamilton. *The 911 Commission Report: Final Report of the National Commission on Terrorist Attacks upon the United States*, 375.

be effective in the battle of ideas, the national security apparatus needs a balanced counterterrorism strategy—one that employs both Hard and Soft Power. Supporting this approach, Oliver Roy suggests[27]:

> The most effective way to combat terrorism is a combination of two levels: one level employs traditional intelligence and legal techniques to trace and neutralise cells and networks... The second level would hence be to destroy AQ's narrative, that is, to de-legitimise it.

Lessons learned in the U.K. and the Netherlands, as well as in asymmetrical conflicts overseas, demonstrate the complexity of the government's dilemma in confronting radicalization and the necessity of a balanced strategy:

> If they crack down too hard, they risk alienating the population and creating support for organizations where none previously existed. Failure to crack down, however, can decrease confidence in the state and make it easier for proto-insurgent [or terrorist] groups to mobilize would-be followers, since they need not fear that they will be arrested. In addition, a weak crackdown may lead rival communities to act on their own. If a group is singled out for repression because of its ethnicity, religion, or other features, the salience of that identity increases.[28]

In a liberal democracy, a repressive "crack down" is neither advisable nor desirable, as it runs counter to constitutional ideals. It is important for the government to distinguish between activities that pose a physical threat to lives or national security and activity that might encourage radicalization, or progression toward terrorist activity. It is incumbent on the government to interdict terrorist activity with Hard Power whenever a threat to public safety or national security is imminent, but even in these cases, Soft Power can be applied to influence community response by sharing factual information about the arrest.

Law enforcement provides an avenue to disrupt speech that promotes violence or supports the terrorist narrative, but Hard Power is rarely the only option for addressing such a threat; in fact, it may be the least preferred method of dealing with a radicalizer in most instances. As mentioned above, intelligence collection around those identified as radical and charismatic influencers can provide an opportunity to identify those who pose the threat of physical attacks. Unless exercised in an effort to disrupt an imminent

---

27   Olivier Roy, "Al Qaeda in the West as a Youth Movement: The Power of a Narrative," 21.

28   Daniel Byman, *Understanding Proto-Insurgencies: RAND Counterinsurgency Study--Paper 3*, Santa Monica: RAND Corporation, 2007.

attack, the application of Hard Power should be carefully considered in terms of balancing the extent of the disruption against the ability to collect intelligence. Law enforcement action that might be characterized as petty or harassing may temporarily disrupt the influencer's activity but could also increase the influencer's status: it may allow him to be portrayed as a martyr, increase his ability to raise funds, and draw sympathy from those with whom the West-versus-Islam narrative resonates. Hard Power should instead be applied in cases where strategic interests can be met and the radicalizer can be permanently disrupted or deported.

A nuanced understanding of how to shape the social context of the ideological conflict is therefore a necessary precondition to a counterradicalization strategy. For this reason, a successful national security strategy for counterradicalization must place heavy emphasis on the judgment of regional and local authorities—and these authorities must be responsible for developing relationships that can influence ideological environment. Regional and local authorities should commensurately be supported with training, and informed by a holistic "toolbox" of tactics based on the homeland security community's collective experience.

For example, such activity might be reasonably applied in the visa process in the United States. When foreign visitors promote or encourage violence against the United States or its allies as a legitimate method of political or religious expression, the "right" to visit might reasonably and immediately be terminated and the visitor deported without lengthy administrative process. Subsequent judicial consideration of asylum claims might be expedited to logical conclusion. By expediting these processes, the potential polarizing rhetoric of such a visitor (claims of prejudice and repression of Muslims by the government) could be limited, his credibility undermined, and the antagonistic visitor separated from the mass population. This action— revocation of the "right" to visit the United States—represents an aggressive Hard Power action that should only be taken after consideration of the subject's impact on the local Muslim population.

Alternatively, Soft Power tactics might accomplish the same goal by diminishing the status and credibility of the violent extremist messenger (and thus negatively impacting the visitor's influence and appeal to those vulnerable to recruitment), without generating increased hostility from the Muslim community toward the government. In this scenario, empowered leaders of the Muslim community might pressure peer groups through internal politics to counter the Islamist messenger publicly on both a social and theological level. Rejection of the messenger by his peer group might lead the individual to move away from the group in order to maintain the "integrity of his self-image,"[29] and it might diminish the radical's appeal to his followers by undermining his credibility and social status – any association with the alienated individual would logically lower the status of another within the group and thus such contact will likely be avoided.

It is likely that such rejection from the community would not be absolute, and while the radical messenger would have less appeal to a broad audience, he might still maintain influence in small social circles. This is an opportune time for the government to exercise Hard Power because the disruption of the radical's activity would be more palatable to the broad community.

FINDING NON-TRADITIONAL PARTNERS

Developing interpersonal relationships between government leaders and Muslim centers of influence is therefore a critical first step in building a network that can address ideological challenges. To diminish the appeal of terrorism, it is necessary to redefine the national effort to identify and fully engage with centers of influence of at-risk and immigrant Muslim populations. These referent leaders have more credibility with their ingroup than government agents and can therefore more effectively communicate the moral and theological foundations of an alternative ideology to Islamist extremists. With this influence, potential recruits might stall or reverse their progression toward terrorism and affiliation with terrorist ideologies in order to maintain positive self-esteem and acceptance by the normative ingroup.[30]

Further, organizational models suggest that some group leaders may be willing to adjust their personal goals to secure the loyalty of followers, recruit new members, or appeal to group members' needs. This provides opportunities for the engaged counterterrorist. If one takes a cognitive approach to building relationships with centers of influence and leverages the psychological need for positive self-esteem, it is possible to diminish the influence of radicalizing agents. In terms of asymmetrical conflict, this approach separates the ideological insurgent from the mass population.

---

29   Henri Tajfel, *Human Groups and Social Categories: Studies in Social Psychology*, New York: Cambridge University Press, 1981.

30   Kathleen A. Ethier and Kay Deaux, "Negotiating Social Identity when Contexts Change: Maintaining Identification and Responding to Threat," *Intergroup Relations: Essential Readings*, ed. Michael A. Hogg and Dominic Abrams (Philadelphia: Psychology Press, 2001), 254-266.

In some cases these centers of influence,[31] often imams (leaders within a mosque or influential nongovernment agencies or associations), express a personal desire and religious obligation to counsel individuals away from the path of violent extremism and toward a more mainstream interpretation of Islam.[32] Self-policing by the Muslim community is important and might be highly effective, although only self-reported and anecdotal information is available to support this claim. Nevertheless, according to the secretary of DHS, there are many cases where community leaders "helped disrupt plots and have spoken out against violent extremism. They play a central role in addressing this issue."[33] Muslim leaders must recognize that the risk of self-policing is literally a risk of life and death. Trusting relationships between the government and these centers of influence are likely to increase their willingness to bring radicalizing individuals, as well as individuals who "drop out" of the mainstream religious education, to the attention of law enforcement before the threat of violence becomes imminent.

Because the credibility of ingroup leaders is higher than government officials, within the ingroup, centers of influence can also be valuable partners in the wake of terrorist acts or government application of Hard Power (specifically, arrests). By communicating planned government actions to investigate a terrorist act, government agents might increase cooperation from the community by informing community leaders of the reason for the interviews and seeking the community leaders' input regarding any specific cultural sensitivity that might reduce cooperation. In the event of an arrest of a community member, communication with local leaders, distribution of leaflets regarding the arrest, and pre-planned media statements for federal, state and local officials immediately after the arrest would allow unclassified facts of a given case to be disseminated. Partnering with community leaders who have unparalleled credibility might communicate the facts of the case via an interpersonal network, mitigating the damage of messages from those who would intentionally sow discord and the Salafi-jihadi narrative.

---

31   Based on a survey of conservative Muslim leaders in the Houston area.

32   Committee on Homeland Security. *Working with Communities to Disrupt Terror Plots. Prepared Statement of Mohamed Elibiary*, Serial No. 111-58 Cong., 111th sess., March 17, 2010, 47-50.

33   Senate Judiciary Committee. *Nine Years After 9/11: Confronting the Terrorist Threat to the Homeland: Statement of Secretary Janet Napolitano.* September 22, 2010, 3.

BUILDING A NETWORK

In order to counter and confront Islamist ideology, it is important for the United States to look within its own borders, as well as externally, in order to identify radicalizing influences. "Intermediaries—charismatic individuals— often help persuade previously law-abiding citizens to radicalize or even become violent jihadists. Social networks, virtual or actual, support and reinforce the decisions individuals make as they embrace violent jihad as does perusal of online materials."[34] But perhaps more importantly at the regional and local levels, the security apparatus should assess and identify potential partners who have much higher influence with other Muslims than government agents. In turn, these alliances might be leveraged to have strategic impact.

Consistent with academic research, the U.K. and the Netherlands often initiate ingroup/outgroup contact privately between individual representatives of the government and the Muslim community, where intergroup influence is diminished and open dialogue can result in partnerships. Subsequent messaging to the Muslim ingroup by counterradicalization partners who lead ethnic or religious groups or subgroups might be more effective if conducted publically, because public ingroup messaging can assist in establishing group normative behavior.[35]

Data collected about Muslim attitudes at the international, national, and local levels indicate an imperative for the United States government to significantly increase direct interaction between government agents charged with enforcement responsibilities and the American Muslim population because face-to-face contact can be effective in improving intergroup relations if the contact occurs under cooperative conditions.[36]

Notably, Wilder's research also indicates that intergroup contact is more likely to change ingroup (Muslim) attitudes toward the outgroup (government) if the individual government agent is perceived as "typical" of the outgroup. This tends to contradict the notion that it is advantageous to create a workforce that "looks like" the vulnerable group. Individuals designated to represent the government in face-to-face, cooperative contacts need not look

---

34   Jerome P. Bjelopera and Mark A. Randol, *American Jihadist Terrorism: Combating a Complex Threat.* Washington, DC: Congressional Research Service, 2010.

35   Abrams, et al., "Knowing what to Think by Knowing Who You Are," 270.

36   Wilder, David A. "Intergroup Contact: The Typical Member and the Exception Rule," *Intergroup Relations*, edited by Michael A. Hogg and Dominic Abrams (Philadelphia: Psychology Press, 2001), 379.

or speak like the Muslim ingroup; in fact, in order to change Muslim attitudes about government agencies, the use of "atypical" representatives may have little effect, as the atypical representative will be viewed as an anomaly within the government agency and will thus be unable to shift opinions of the government because he or she varies from the stereotype.[37]

It is essential that face-to-face contact be initiated between leaders of the Muslim community and government agencies in order to establish credibility and commensurate status—a form of intergroup dialogue between individuals of similar perceived status.[38] Leader-to-leader contact, in effect, could create a new ingroup of counterradicalization partners who are perceived to have reciprocal influence. In a sense, such a group of leaders could function as its own tribal alliance. Membership in such a group, however, will include certain risks. Some of these group members will have seemingly conflicting goals—security and civil liberties, interpersonal alliances and political loyalties, for example. The ability to successfully form and maintain this kind of counterterrorism "tribe" necessarily requires a principled and nuanced approach.

TRUST

The fundamental requirement for a successful Soft Power strategy is trust, which should be developed through sustained, regular interaction. The larger the networks of trusting relationships, the more influence the network can have. If, for no other reason than this, government agents at all levels have a vested interest in and obligation to build trusting relationships with the Muslim community. Federal statutes address civil liberties, counterterrorism, Patriot Act authorities, immigration, and international travel—all issues at the forefront of concern for Muslim community leaders.[39] State and local officials like mayors, health and human service agencies, fire departments, public health, and emergency management officials also have a vested interest to succeed in building trust with the Muslim community because terrorism and radicalization can affect safety and quality of life in their states and communities. State and local officials are critical to the success of such efforts because of their regular interaction with the Muslim community.

---

37   Ibid., 379-380.

38   Amy S. Hubbard, "Cultural and Status Differences in Intergroup Conflict Resolution: A Longitudinal Study of a Middle East Dialogue Group in the United States," *Human Relations* 52, no. 3 (Mar. 1999).

39   Recent survey by the FBI of Muslim community leaders in the Houston area.

These government representatives must be willing to listen, seek to understand grievances, and constructively address those grievances where possible. Differences of opinion during engagement should be expected, and even encouraged, since rational discussion of terrorism can only assist the argument for nonviolent protest. Varying viewpoints will also likely derive from different ethnic groups and religious sects. In addressing Islamist group leadership or public forums, law enforcement officers should focus on each of the three levels identified in Social Identity Theory[40]:

> **Cognitive**: Those speaking to a group that has grievances should emphasize that the audience and the speaker respect the same "American" group goals (preventing political violence, diminishing radicalization, increasing tolerance in society).

> **Evaluative**: In discussing terrorism, concentrate on discussion of illegal or repugnant acts, i.e., targeting civilians with violence, matters that clearly conflict with "American" group goals.

> **Emotional**: Reinforce feelings of accomplishment by recounting the government-community joint efforts toward "American" goals (community assistance in disruption of terrorist activity, law enforcement investigation of civil rights complaints, social or interfaith projects).

Engagement with the Muslim community—even those who may harbor hostile or aggrieved feelings toward the government or law enforcement—should be a principal responsibility of government leaders responsible for counterterrorism missions. These counterterrorism officials should be positioned to have influence on local policies because their perspective would be informed by both formal intelligence products and knowledge of local dynamics. Likewise, the designated counterterrorism officials should be empowered to speak on behalf of participating agencies in a way that demonstrates their influence in local policies and the policies' consistency with national goals. The ideal target audience for this engagement consists of community members with similar influence and authority.

---

40   Brannan, Esler, & Strindberg, "Talking to 'Terrorists,'" 18.

Regular and sustained engagement of this type can result in the process of "recategorization (bringing members of two categories together under an inclusive, superordinate one), and decategorization (dissolving the problematic categories altogether, especially by facilitating contact between members of rival groups)."[41]

Recategorization can be affected through sustained intergroup contact between individuals from disparate ingroups who are committed to leading the effort to counter terrorism, particularly if these individuals are able to progress from formal meetings to more meaningful relationships within the group and between group members.

Decategorization, which is similarly dependent on intergroup contact, might be the result of collective efforts of the superordinate counterterrorist group that has recategorized. As centers of influence encourage and facilitate broader interaction, members of their associated sub-groups would be exposed to individuals from outgroups who act in contrast to accepted stereotypes, resulting in large-scale attitudinal changes.

Cross-categorization, the pluralist approach, presents opportunities for contact outside a security paradigm. For instance, when American Muslims and government agents meet where religious identities are less salient (in business settings, parent-teacher meetings, sporting events, etc.), intergroup contact provides the opportunity to learn about one another. Cross categorization has less direct applicability to government strategies than recategorization and decategorization, but an awareness of this model of conflict mitigation increases the likelihood of positive outcomes. Participation in crossed categorization experiences might also assist in identifying superordinate projects in which the American Muslim community and individuals from the general public or government can work together.

---

41   Ibid, 19.

Within these frameworks, the government should actively seek leaders who are credible sources of information and influence to the American Muslim community. In so doing, the government may gain the capacity to anticipate community concerns and the ability to address community grievances in their early stages, before they progress to more entrenched feelings of discord, greatly reducing the number of individuals with political grievances who might otherwise progress toward violent expression.

Muslim leaders who have been interviewed in the Houston, Texas-area almost unanimously identify the need to educate the Muslim American community about government agencies, and the need to educate government agents, especially law enforcement and security agencies, regarding Islam and cultural sensitivities. Encouragingly, these same conservative imams report that they are willing to cooperate with the government by hosting and providing training, and in some cases they have demonstrated willingness to report even members of their self-defined "group" that they believe to be "radicalized." This cooperation, however, is contingent on trusting relationships. Notably, not all those interviewed held positive views of the government, security, or law enforcement—but where positive assessments were reported, the most important factor defining the relationships was the amount of contact between government agents and the individual leader.[42]

In many instances, the immigrant population that arrives in the United States has migrated out of respect for the individual freedoms and opportunities provided by a free, capitalist society. However, they also sometimes carry with them an inherent distrust of intelligence and police officers, based on their experiences in their native countries where national authorities have great power and a different perspective on security. This apprehension must be overcome, as relationships with local leaders can dramatically assist the government. One misstep can set back these interpersonal relationships, which is why it is important for government contact to be consistent and sustained. The outreach effort is more than just "community policing." The suggested approach for the counterterrorist is at an operational, rather than tactical level. Efforts in this arena should be a major police effort that is coordinated with and supported by Joint Terrorism Task Force (JTTF) managers and intelligence analysts. Community leaders must be made aware of intra-government communication, which is to be expected if those interested in counterradicalization seek to affect positive change from both the community and the government.

---

42   Survey of self-described conservative imams in the Houston area.

Recurrent contact between groups is necessary for building trust and resilience; sitting around a table only to discuss grievances is not enough to counter terrorism. Engagement must be seen to produce tangible rewards. For instance, in the Houston area, informal conversations between FBI agents and strategic engagement partners from the Muslim community resulted in increased positive interaction and tangible benefit for the Muslim community. Working together, a counterterrorism supervisor and several agents met with centers of influence to identify projects that might provide educational opportunities for Muslim parents. Operational leaders facilitated the attendance of community outreach specialists who, in turn, arranged training for Muslim parents on how to protect children from Internet predators and classes to older adults about how to protect oneself from identity theft. By developing relationships outside the counterterrorism paradigm, both FBI agents and community members came to see one another in different contexts.

The benefits to working with non-traditional partners and the process of purposeful engagement should be expected to yield:

1. A better understanding of how communities might react to recent or expected developments—a pending arrest or proposed policy shift, for instance;

2. A sense of partnership in a common goal (preventing violence) and reassurance for community partners that the government aims to avoid unwarranted intrusions; and,

3. Confidence that the government is prepared to aggressively respond to threats to the community, an expectation every citizens should enjoy.

Beyond these benefits, and only when carefully considered, relationships built with community leaders can provide additional tools for counterradicalization efforts. For instance, parallel tracks of investigation and counterradicalization might be pursued collaboratively.

The objective of the counterterrorist is to exploit terrorists' weaknesses—their lack of resources—by depriving them of public support that would allow them to increase their resources.[43] Al Qaeda and other like-minded groups can be defeated, and violent extremism can be mitigated, but not through coercive power alone. Those charged with the counterterrorism mission should incorporate Soft Power tactics in national, regional, and local

---

43   David Tucker, "The Unconventional Threat to Homeland Security: An Overview," (unpublished). This reference was provided as a required reading at the Naval Postgraduates School's Center for Homeland Defense and Security in June 2008.

approaches to terrorism in order to attract partners from nongovernment and religious organizations who have high credibility for messaging and greater access to potential terrorists early in the radicalization process.

The benefit of dialogue and the exchange of ideas garnered through community outreach might be increased by involving Muslim leaders in the education of government officials who have regular contact with the community. Such involvement would demonstrate the government's willingness to consider community concerns, increase the status of those centers of influence that are willing to engage with the government within their own ingroup, increase job performance of government officials, and help refine contextual understanding of behaviors at the individual level.

By combining increased contact between the government and the Muslim community, fostering messages and actions that demonstrate a sincere intent to understand community issues, and demonstrating commitment to "serve and protect" both the Muslim community and the rest of the American public, counterterrorist agents can increase trust between groups whose relationship with each other might otherwise be incredibly fraught. The power of this shifting dynamic relies on its ability to deconstruct negative stereotypes.[44] The prospect of collaborative relationships between the government and the American Muslim community promises to undermine the resonance of the West-versus-Islam narrative, increase government understanding of radicalizing influences, and increase Muslim communities' confidence that the values of Islam and democratic society are ultimately compatible.

44   Marilynn B. Brewer and Samuel L. Gaertner, "Toward Reduction of Prejudice: Intergroup Contact and Social Categorization," *Self and Social Identity*, edited by Marilynn B. Brewer and Miles Hewstone. 2nd ed., (Malden, MA: Blackwell Publishing, 2005), 307-8.

CHAPTER 7

PRACTICAL APPLICATION

THE MARRIAGE OF LESSONS LEARNED AND SOCIAL IDENTITY THEORY

"In all fighting, the direct method may be used for joining battle, but indirect methods will be needed in order to secure victory. In battle, there are not more than two methods of attack—the direct and the indirect; yet these two in combination give rise to an endless series of maneuvers. The direct and the indirect lead on to each other in turn. It is like moving in a circle—you never come to an end. Who can exhaust the possibilities of their combination?"

-Sun Tzu

Through the lens of Social Identity Theory, the lessons of United Kingdom and the Netherlands teach that to prevent terrorism, we must change the context of those vulnerable to its appeal. It is not enough to kill, arrest, deport or otherwise deter the known terrorist—unless part of a balanced strategy, these tactics produce more threats than they eliminate. No single agency and no government can prevent terrorism unless the flow of new terrorists is cut off. A holistic and coordinated approach across federal agencies, between federal, state and local governments and in cooperation with trusted members of the Muslim community is necessary to realize true prevention. This is a tremendous challenge that cannot be implemented with the stroke of a pen in Washington.

A counterterrorist culture must be encouraged. Enforcement must become "intelligence minded," a condition that allows for aggressive response to imminent threats at one end of the force spectrum, and intervention by communities on the other. All the while, political and law enforcement leaders must take actions aimed at affecting the strategic threat—social polarization—and recognize that Hard Power has consequences that must also be addressed holistically. In many ways, prevention of terrorism can only be realized from the bottom up and through participatory government.

Over the past decade, the homeland security community has been, correctly, hell-bent on stopping the next terrorist attack by Salafi-jihadists. In many cases, integrated intelligence collection, analysis and aggressive operations prevented attacks in the homeland. At other times, plots have been incompletely disrupted because of failures in one or more of these counterterrorism components[1]. In some cases, like the attempted bombing of Northwest Airlines Flight 253 and the attempt to explode a vehicle bomb in Times Square,[2] the nation was lucky to avoid massive casualties. In 2009 at Fort Hood, Texas and at a military recruiting center in Little Rock, Arkansas, luck was not on our side. Both Nidal Hassan, the alleged spree-killer of American soldiers at Fort Hood, and Carlos Bledsoe, the convicted murderer of a soldier at a Little Rock, Arkansas recruiting center, are American citizens who are believed to have acted on Salafi-jihadi inspiration, not direction from external powers. These individuals who espoused Salafi-jihadi ideology were successful attacking in the American homeland. Where terrorist plots have been disrupted, the successes can be attributed in large part to the nation's focus on threats projected to the continental United States from abroad. For this reason, it causes concern that the terrorist threat to the domestic United States is increasingly by Americans, against Americans.

Because of the homeland security community's relative (though imperfect) success in thwarting terrorist plots from the external enemy, most agree that the nation is better prepared today to confront an imminent terrorist attack. Statistics seem to lend credibility to the argument that the homeland security community is more integrated today than ever. Before September 11, 2001, there were 35 joint terrorism task forces, today there are 104[3]; before 9/11 there were no fusion centers, now there are 73.[4] These joint environments increase the effectiveness of the community's efforts to secure to the homeland by increasing the exchange of information.

On the other hand, the progress made has not stopped the flow of new terrorists. Almost half (49%) of American citizens or residents charged or convicted for acts of "jihadi" terrorism since 9/11 were charged or arrested

---

1   Ben Conery and Valerie Richardson. "Blown Terrorist Case Led to Rushed Arrests" *Washington Times*, September 22, 2009, sec. National.

2   Al Baker and William K. Rashbaum. "Police Find Car Bomb in Times Square." *New York Times*, May 1, 2010, sec. NY/Region.

3   "Robert S. Mueller, III Director, Federal Bureau of InvestigationStatement before the Senate Committee on Homeland Security and Governmental AffairsWashington, D.C.September 13, 2011." Federal Bureau of Investigation.

4   "Fusion Center Locations and Contact Information." Department of Homeland Security.

between January 2009 and December 2011.[5] As we prepared for the threat from an external enemy (al Qaeda, the group), the threat morphed from that posed by a structured organization to a more ephemeral mix of networked and independent Salafi-jihadi movement.

This movement has attracted American citizens to its cause. For the most part, American Salafist-jihadists appear to have been drawn overseas, particularly to Pakistan, Yemen and Africa. What happens when they return home? And what of those living in the homeland who subscribe to terrorist ideology but have thus far been deterred from traveling abroad? What radicalizing factors might influence such these individuals to act violently here in the United States if they perceive violence as the only viable way to attain their goals or restore honor to their ingroup? These lone actors have been notoriously difficult to preempt, and small, self-radicalized groups present a similar challenge with an exponentially increased capacity for destruction.

The 9/11 Commission and the leadership of both the Bush and Obama Administrations recognized the potential for Salafi-jihadi ideology to attract recruits among American citizens. Both administrations also articulated their intent to increase engagement with the Muslim community in order to deprive terrorist organizations of new recruits. The Bush Administration's National Strategy for Combating Terrorism (NSCT 2006) framed the "Global War on Terror" as a "battle of ideas,"[6] proposing that al Qaeda-inspired terrorism emanated, not solely from opposition to American foreign policy, but also from "Political alienation…Grievances that can be blamed on others…Subcultures of conspiracy and misinformation…and an ideology that justifies murder."[7]

Similarly, the National Strategy for Counterterrorism (2011) posited, "to rally individuals and groups to its cause, al-Qa'ida preys on local grievances and propagates a self-serving historical and political account. It draws on a distorted interpretation of Islam to justify the murder of Muslim and non-Muslim innocents."[8] But while plots to attack Americans and American symbols can be confronted with military or law enforcement action, these attacks are only the most visible aspect of al Qaeda's strategy. Al Qaeda also

---

5   Bergen, et al. *Post-9/11 Jihadist Terrorism Cases Involving U.S. Citizens and Residents: An Overview.* Cases by Year. The report cited did not include the arrest of Oytun Ayse Mihalik, of La Palma, California on December 21, 2011.

6   *National Strategy for Combating Terrorism* [Updated 2006], 1.

7   Ibid., 19-20.

8   Obama Administration. "National Strategy for Counterterrorism (2011)," 3.

laid out a strategic vision to fight a fourth generation war—a war of ideas.[9] An important question for those in the homeland security community is, "Have we successfully confronted the ideological threat?" The statistics identified in Chapter 5 indicate that as a nation, we have thus far failed, or failed to seriously try.

Countering and Preventing Violent Extremism

If the Bush and Obama Administrations are correct in their consensus about the causes of Salafi-jihadi terrorism, and if homegrown terrorism is trending upward, then one might conclude that some segments of the American Muslim community perceive themselves politically alienated, unjustly treated, isolated from the general public such that misinformation thrives, and exposed to ideologies that justify murder. Such conditions, as noted by both administrations, call for engagement by the government with the American Muslim community to prevent terrorism.

This effort, termed "combating violent extremism" (CVE) or "preventing violent extremism" (PVE), should be understood as a method of confronting the ideological aspects of the Salafi-jihadist threat. According to the Salafi-jihadist framework, Islam and democracy are incompatible. This West-versus-Islam narrative underpins al Qaeda strategy and its appeal to American citizens who identify, at some level, with the sense of injustice (real or perceived) and the totalitarian ideology on which Salafi-jihadi ideology is based.

Why is a CVE strategy necessary? Because under conditions like those described above, 1) the government is at a true disadvantage in its efforts to stop terrorist attacks and, 2) the community and the public suffers when the government acts too aggressively or too passively to counter threats of terrorism. On one hand, counterterrorism actions that have too broad an impact undermine trust in government and play directly into the Salafi-jihadi narrative. On the other hand, a passive approach will undoubtedly result in terrorist attacks that can, in turn, be expected to exacerbate the conditions that foment terrorist ideologies. An inappropriate response can do more harm than good. Simply put, counterterrorists can do their job better if they have a better understanding of what and who constitute threats, and what and who are not. Further, CVE strategies offer more refined and subtle tools to challenge a narrative that contends that the West (and particularly the U.S. government) is hostile to those who practice Islam.

---

9   Lind, et al. "The Changing Face of War: Into the Fourth Generation," 22-26.

In August 2011, the Obama Administration published the "National Strategy for Empowering Local Partners to Prevent Violent Extremism in the United States" (ELP). That's not a particularly catchy title, but the document is important because it draws attention to a dramatic gap in the national counterterrorism effort. The ELP statement of intent posits that terrorism presents an existential threat to the social fabric of the United States, and it proposes a solution: "We surmount the many challenges that we face by remaining committed to the American ideals of freedom, equality, and democracy, which transcend differences of religion, ethnicity, and place of birth."[10] Excepting the domestic focus of the August document, the theme is not new; however, the promise of actually implementing the strategy is groundbreaking.

It is important at this juncture to note the specific language used in the strategy to counter radicalization to violence. Neither CVE nor PVE describe "radicalization" in and of itself as a targeted behavior or even a bad thing. Indeed, we are in many ways a nation of "radicals" – just look at some of the accusations from either party during our political campaigns. In fact, the ELP makes clear that "radicalization to violence" (violent extremism or terrorism) is the behavior that is considered unacceptable and should be targeted. This careful wording connotes both an effort to preempt violence and tacit acknowledgement that radicalization is acceptable unless it is paired with violence. The government must develop the capacity to positively influence those most susceptible to violent ideologies in a way that attracts those individuals away from violent acts.

It follows then, that preventing violent extremism (PVE), should be a national effort, across the whole of government, to 1) inhibit potential terrorists from forming or joining groups that justify or condone violence in the first place; 2) produce dissension in such groups as do exist; 3) facilitate exit from these groups; and 4) reduce support for groups that condone or support terrorism and delegitimize their leaders.[11]

These goals will no doubt raise concern with civil libertarian groups who argue that we need to create more refined enforcement policies to avoid repressing minorities. These same groups have historically represented the government's efforts to better understand American Muslims in a negative

---

10   Obama Administration. *Empowering Local Partners to Prevent Violent Extremism in the United States* (2011), 1.

11   Post, et al. "The Psychology of Suicide Terrorism." 17.

light, as veiled "intelligence-gathering."[12] Such arguments may seem a bit schizophrenic to the objectively informed reader, in that "the purpose of intelligence is to acquire information necessary to apply governmental power with greater precision."[13] CVE is not, in fact, broadly intrusive—it depends instead on overt and sometimes discreet relationships, straightforward, unvarnished discussion, and information-sharing among people with different perspectives but common goals. The purpose of CVE is to influence the contextual circumstances that contribute to violent extremism and restructure the way both "we" and "they" view one another.

It is nevertheless worthwhile to clearly differentiate between radicalization and violent extremism. Radicalization has several commonly understood meanings. For the purpose of this book, radicalization refers to a psychological process wherein one comes to favor or seeks to effect fundamental or revolutionary changes in current practices, conditions, or institutions through violence.

Due to the obvious risks inherent in the counterterrorism mission, CVE efforts must complement the exercise of Hard Power efforts like law enforcement and administrative actions that are traditionally used to disrupt terrorist activity. Ideally, only those who are engaged in or who conspire to engage in criminal activity should be exposed to Hard Power (arrest and prosecution in the United States, for instance), but until recently the homeland security community, as a whole, has not tried to implement Soft Power tools to confront the terrorist narrative. This effort is currently in its nascent stages.

Unlike on the fronts of the struggle against terrorism in countries like Pakistan, Afghanistan and Yemen, the U.S. government cannot use military strikes to address terrorist groups in the homeland. It is therefore critical that we come to understand this conflict in terms of an ideological competition. We remain in a battle for the hearts and minds of the rising generation of American Muslims, a generation that has grown up in the United States in the wake of 9/11, some of whom are affected by the "subcultures of conspiracy and misinformation" described in NSCT 2006.

---

12   Arun Kundnani, The FBI's 'Good' Muslims. *The Nation*, September 1, 2011.

13   Stephen Marrin. "Homeland Security Intelligence: Just the Beginning." *Journal of Homeland Security* (November, 2003).

CVE tools should therefore offer alternatives to developing threats, before potential terrorists come to morally justify political violence. A coordinated CVE strategy is required, and a mechanism to ensure collaboration is a necessity. To use Soft Power in accordance with existing laws, communities and/or non-governmental organizations, collaboration is requisite. The government has no legitimate role in policing individual religious beliefs or non-violent political expression. But in order to preempt violent action—to save lives—it is imperative that the government understands the nature of emerging threats. It is likewise critical for the government to understand and support those outside government who increase the community's resilience to violent ideologies. CVE practices thus compel the government and community to engage and communicate with one another.

At a strategic level, this means the government should publically state its values, transparently articulating what it considers and does not consider a threat. Next, government actions should be (and be perceived to be) consistent with these values. Where the government or its agents act in a controversial but lawful way, or develop disputed policies, the government should acknowledge criticism, accept responsibility for its actions and actively defend these actions via the same media that opposing narratives are voiced. This may mean verbal debate, through informal networks or via the Internet. It definitely indicates that government leaders should represent their agencies' policies and personally defend them or take definitive action to address legitimate concerns, the same way private companies might.

In order to speak credibly, government must increase its positive contact with the American Muslim community. Young students in public schools are often exposed to community outreach efforts. Career days, adopt-a-school programs and mentorship programs provide just a few examples where federal state and local agencies engage with the community. This is a community relations (CR) effort, and CR is a tool for counterterrorists. Too often though, this type of engagement defines the CVE effort, because CR carries little political risk and does not require a thorough understanding of either terrorist organizations or interpersonal contact with the "other." Thus, Community Relations (CR) can contribute to effective messaging, but it does not in itself constitute a CVE effort. CR, therefore, should be differentiated from CVE, as it is superficial. If CR is the only method of engagement, it will be unsuccessful because CR can be perceived as the government's disingenuous attempt to manipulate.

If the aim of a community outreach program is to counter violent extremism, then it should be purposeful and integrated in to a counterterrorism strategy; this might best be described as "Strategic Engagement." To combat violent extremism, counterterrorism messaging (via CR and Strategic Engagement) needs to reach well beyond the general Muslim population. Strategic Engagement should include centers of influence regardless of their support or opposition to government policies. This creates an environment where counterterrorists from government and the community can identify challenges, create solutions and check progress. While "moderate" Muslims may represent the majority of the population, the conservative and ultra-conservative subset of the American Muslim community is more likely to have access to those vulnerable to terrorist ideologies. They also are also most capable of shaping the context around the vulnerable. This is important, because influential members within the social network of those who are openly critical of government policies can speak more credibly to their audience when the time comes to intervene in the radicalization process.[14]

The principal requirement for CVE, then, is trust. Trust between the government and the American Muslim population is unlikely to develop where sustained, recurring and purposeful communications do not exist; this point is also true of collaboration between federal state and local government agencies. Perceived trustworthiness has been demonstrably tied to "the impression of shared goals,"[15] between high- and moderate-power actors.[16] This suggests it is important for government leaders to seek engagement with community leaders. When one demonstrates empathy—the ability to understand, if not sympathize, with another's condition—it affords the ability to speak frankly about local grievances within the American Muslim community and the security concerns of the government.

It is important that those charged with CVE missions demonstrate a sincere drive to work with the Muslim community and have the power to affect change. Counterterrorists from the government and the community must be committed to finding creative solutions for grievances where the concerns are valid and be prepared to explain to each other why the concerns will not be addressed. This again implies that those responsible for CVE

---

14   Abrams, et al. "Knowing what to Think by Knowing Who You are: Self-Categorization and the Nature of Norm Formation, Conformity and Group Polarization." 270-288.

15   Olekalns, Mara, Feyona Lau, and Philip L. Smith. "Resolving the Empty Core: Trust as a Determinant of Outcomes in Three-Party Negotiations." *Group Decision and Negotiation* 16, no. 6 (Nov, 2007; 2007): 527.

16   Ibid., 527.

must have the authority to effect change in their organization and in local policies. Federal agencies should play an important role in this process, based on the federal government's constitutionally-defined mandate to provide national defense.

But even the title of the ELP strategy identifies the necessity of a local approach. Local approaches to CVE are critical because the decision to engage in terrorism is ultimately one made by an individual or a group of individuals. What entities are better placed to alter the circumstances around those radicalizing to violence than local communities and local government?

In order to prevent or disrupt the development of new terrorists, those vulnerable to, or already in the throes of, radicalization to violence must be influenced at the individual or small group level. An overarching national strategy cannot provide precise solutions to individual circumstances precisely because local contexts and immediate social networks underpin social identities. Precise solutions to attract the vulnerable away from violent ideologies should be developed at the local level, where individual contexts can be affected through the use of a mix of federal and local tools: policies, influential social networks, credible ingroup members, family and friends. Of course, what a national strategy can do is provide the framework and tools to support local strategies. The 2011 ELP strategy provides such a framework.

The PVE framework is thus the logical evolution of a long-standing vision for the battle of ideas. It is consistent with the counterterrorism vision articulated by both the Bush and Obama Administrations, and thus should be viewed as a pragmatic, rather than political approach to stopping the flow of recruits to Salafi-jihadi terrorism.

Despite its laudable vision, however, the ELP does not provide a mechanism to coordinate either national or local efforts. The Strategic Implementation Plan for Empowering Local Partners to Prevent Violent Extremism in the United States (SIP), published in December 2011 answered this concern. While the SIP articulates an excellent vision for preventing violent extremism, and assigns lead and supporting roles to different agencies, it also exhibits significant flaws that are likely to undermine its goals. The implementation plan is not binding on any agency because there is not an associated funding stream and there is no way to ensure the strategy is coordinated at local levels. The strategy suggests United States Attorneys "have begun leading federal engagement efforts" within their jurisdictions.[17] While this understanding may be prevalent in Washington, it raises concerns regarding whether politically-appointed positions that are regularly vacant should lead an effort that requires sustained commitment. It also begs the question, do U.S. Attorneys lead this effort uniformly and based on doctrine, or are the efforts more haphazard and based on individual personalities or political leanings?

Until there are mechanisms in place to ensure integration across federal, state and local levels, and until funding from these entities is tied to CVE efforts, the ELP strategy and the SIP serve merely as suggestions. This has led and will continue lead to expensive duplication efforts by city, county and federal agencies and poor execution of a vision with much potential.

Uncoordinated collection and competition between agencies also complicate analysis, result in disparate threat assessments, and lead to inappropriate or uncoordinated actions to address those threats. Worse, uncoordinated messaging might diminish the credibility of those partnering with the American Muslim community.

How can a coordinated approach to countering violent extremism be ensured at the local level? A coordinating entity that brings together federal, state and local agencies, as well as non-governmental groups representing the local American Muslim community must be created. Those participating may be formally designated as leaders, or simply committed to countering violent ideologies. At the national level, the authors of the SIP did just this: they assembled a task force of representatives from the most obviously necessary departments and agencies to develop the SIP.[18] Should not the same approach be taken at the local area? A similar entity should exist to coordinate CVE efforts that combine CR and Strategic Engagement, provide support where needed and ensure alignment of strategic and tactical goals, ideals that the current structure of the United States' counterterrorism effort does not support.

---

17   Obama Administration. "Strategic Implementation Plan for Empowering Local Partners to Prevent Violent Extremism in the United States." 8.

18   Obama Administration. "Strategic Implementation Plan for Empowering Local Partners to Prevent Violent Extremism in the United States." 3. The following departments and agencies were involved in the deliberations and approval process: the Departments of State (State), the Treasury, Defense (DOD), Justice (DOJ), Commerce, Labor, Health and Human Services (HHS), Education (EDU), Veterans Affairs, and Homeland Security (DHS), as well as the Federal Bureau of Investigation (FBI) and the National Counterterrorism Center (NCTC).

In order to implement the ELP at both national and local levels, the following objectives should be considered.

STRATEGIC REALIGNMENT

The counterterrorism strategy of the United States is misaligned with the evolving threat from terrorism. After an extensive review of the circumstances surrounding the attacks of September 11, 2001, the first reflection by the 9/11 Commission was that "in the post-9/11 world, threats are defined more by fault lines within societies than by territorial boundaries between them."[19] This observation should serve as a foundation for developing a national strategy to address the root cause of homegrown terrorism: social polarization. The bipartisan commission issued its findings with multiple observations, opinions, and recommendations, summarized in a single sentence: "We believe the 9/11 attacks revealed four kinds of failures: in imagination, policy, capabilities, and management."[20]

The NCTC and DHS were created to enhance the nation's ability to synthesize, analyze, and coordinate operations, but the structure of these organizations does not facilitate coordination outside of Washington. Neither NCTC nor DHS has a strong and authoritative mechanism to coordinate activities at the operational level, where implementation occurs. Because they have little footprint outside of Washington, these entities can do little to ensure that strategic plans and policies are implemented throughout the country, particularly across federal and state jurisdictions. Neither NCTC nor DHS has an overarching counterterrorism strategy or coordination authority that reaches to the local level.

The FBI coordinates counterterrorism investigations via a network of JTTFs, but JTTF strategies have emphasized mitigation of existing threats, rather than examining the underlying social conditions, real or perceived, that result in an individual's radicalization. Furthermore, with 56 field offices and more than 100 JTTFs, the span of control for the FBI's Counterterrorism Division and its Directorate of Intelligence (which provides analysis and intelligence) is exceptionally broad. This condition can yield high degrees of uncertainty and argues for a diminished span of control at upper levels of management, as large spans of control tend to lead to poor communication,

---

19   National Commission on Terrorist Attacks upon the United States, Thomas H. Kean, and Lee Hamilton. The 911 Commission Report : *Final Report of the National Commission on Terrorist Attacks upon the United States*, 361.

20   Ibid. 339.

which can, in turn, lead to bad decisions.[21] Each field office bases its actions and resource allocation on national threat priorities identified by FBI headquarters, but does so absent an overarching vision that integrates FBI and other federal agency efforts to combat radicalization.

The same inherent lack of coordination is evident between the federal government and state and local agencies. The existing structure does not encourage or facilitate the coordination of strategies across agencies, departments, and jurisdictions in a way that is most effective—though in some instances, mass of force is achieved (for instance, when manpower is shifted to a border region).

As suggested by the 9/11 Report, the United States ought to "engage in the struggle of ideas." In keeping with the external focus that permeated the government response, the 9/11 Report recommended taking only external measures toward that end.[22] In the 10 years since al Qaeda's attacks on the homeland, the United States has not ventured into the ideological arena in any meaningful way. Between 2002 and 2008, 93 individuals were subject to terrorism-related charges, an average of about 14 individuals per year. But in the next three calendar years, 95 American citizens or residents, an average of more than 33 per year, were indicted for jihadist-related crimes—an average increase of more than 135% per year.[23] For many, this is evidence that while the United States faced outward and employed mostly a Hard Power response, violent ideologies have been allowed to foment at home.

During the same period, clusters—or groups or cells—of would-be terrorists in Houston, Texas; Raleigh, North Carolina; and Alexandria, Virginia, concocted plans to join violent extremists fighting the United States military overseas but were disrupted by arrests. Considering the easy access to weapons (and targets) in the United States, it seems unlikely that these "wannabe terrorists" believe they are more likely to conduct a successful terrorist attack abroad than domestically. These Americans may have chosen to join the fight abroad because overseas conflicts were more salient to the identity of those "wannabe terrorists" than the condition of Muslims in the

---

21 Michael Keren and David Levhari. "The Optimum Span of Control in a Pure Hierarchy." *Management Science* 25, no. 11 (Nov., 1979): pp. 1162-1172.

22 National Commission on Terrorist Attacks upon the United States, Thomas H. Kean, and Lee Hamilton. *The 911 Commission Report : Final Report of the National Commission on Terrorist Attacks upon the United States*, 375–79.

23 *Post-9/11 Jihadist Terrorism Cases Involving U.S. Citizens and Residents: An Overview.* Washington, DC: New America Foundation and Syracuse University's Maxwell School of Public Policy., 2011.

United States, or that fighting abroad was an answer to dissonance caused by competing Salafi-jihadi and American identities. For whatever reason, the place where these individuals sought to join in battle against the United States was more important to them than attacking Americans in the homeland. It is all too easy, however, to imagine such individuals and groups making the determination that they might be more valuable to their cause by attacking targets in the United States. The United States can be thankful for this subtlety, but it cannot depend on it.

RECOGNIZING THE DOMESTIC THREAT

In contrast to the approach taken by the United States, soon after domestic attacks by al Qaeda and its affiliates in the U.K. and the Netherlands, British and Dutch security services looked inward—not for the purpose of self-blame, but to consider the potential for extended social conflict within their own societies.

National security components of both nations studied their own populations, considered the approaches of other nations and developed holistic strategies to bring the full force of government to bear in an ideological struggle against violent Islamist ideologies. The British and the Dutch then devised or expanded networked structures to support the strategy and designated a central authority—ultimately one person—to be responsible for coordinating and supporting the counterterrorism effort. Their networked structures incorporated Hard and Soft Power strategies that included local authorities and community leaders, tailored government action to local contexts, and shared best practices.

These nations judged that whole-government, balanced strategies required a framework that supported actions to simultaneously eliminate threats, reduce the flow of new terrorists, increase trust in government, and create contexts that influence radicalization. A coordinated effort that broadly impacts society is absent from the United States' domestic counterterrorism effort. Actions along these axes might be realized through effective implementation of a holistic strategy in the homeland.

In the U.K. and the Netherlands, broad approaches to counterterrorism provide an attractive alternative to Hard Power-only strategies. Principal benefits of a balanced strategy include:

- Information about community reactions and perceptions identified emerging trends;

- Consultation and partnership between government and the Muslim community, provided the assurance that terrorist activity, not the Muslim community, is the target of investigation. Consultation and partnership also enlists the community's capacity to demonstrate civic responsibilities; and

- The assurance that the police will forcefully clamp down on any backlash from non-Muslims.[24]

DEVELOP A TRULY PREVENTIVE STRATEGY THAT COORDINATES STATE, LOCAL AND FEDERAL EFFORTS

The counterterrorism structure of the United States does not adequately support a preventive counterradicalization strategy because it provides neither assurance that an overarching strategy is implemented at the local level, nor a mechanism for collaboration among governments, the public, and religious organizations to address grievances of local and national concern.

Regional, networked structures facilitate the exercise of imagination in learning organizations because lessons from localized experiences can be shared broadly and adjusted or improved in other locales. When innovation and response to new contingencies are required, as in a CVE effort, decentralized structures are clearly superior to hierarchical structures. Regional structures present a promising alternative to a highly centralized structure because lessons from local experiences can inform national policy makers of emerging domestic threats. In turn, trends might be more easily recognized at the national level—allowing for projective analysis. Regional structure and process, particularly in an age of electronic communication, serve to enhance both regional capabilities and organizational adaptability without diminishing access to valuable information or compliance matters at the central coordination point, the chief benefits of a hierarchy.[25]

Without a strong, unified command, it is exceptionally challenging for individual departments and agencies to act together. The NCTC and a homeland security council might serve as logical apex for regional organizations. At the regional and local levels, a dedicated multi-agency staff might effectively coordinate cross-agency actions. Such a multi-agency staff could also provide strategic analysis and long-range planning for a

---

24   Paris. "Discussion Paper on Approaches to Anti-Radicalization and Community Policing in the Transatlantic Space," 14.

25   Aleksander P. J. Ellis, John R. Hollenbeck, Daniel R. Ilgen, and Stephen E. Humphrey. "Asymmetric Nature of Structural Changes in Command and Control Teams: The Impact of Centralizing and Decentralizing on Group Outcomes." Washington, DC, Command and Control Research Program (U.S.), June 17-19, 2003, 14.

counterterrorism mission that requires continuous attention, adaptation and focus on individuals and groups impacted by elements of many different agencies.

HOLISTIC COUNTERTERRORISM STRATEGIES

A holistic counterterrorism strategy that is coordinated and implemented at the local level might allow government and community leaders to tailor approaches to counter radicalization and diminish the appeal of terrorist ideologies. The U.K. and Netherlands models demonstrate that joint-agency coordination at regional and local levels can help ensure that national strategies are resourced and prioritized correctly and, in turn, ensure that the central government is informed regarding the intricacies of the region.

Regional coordination points for "whole government" activities have the capacity to provide "full-service" responses to communities. Integration of a federal counterterrorism presence in local government agencies tends to ensure a "national" effort permeates the security structure. A network of homeland security representatives that are responsible for facilitating a whole-government response might allow the national counterterrorism apparatus to improve its overall capacity to reduce radicalization and increase security. Regional coordination might provide the following benefits:[26]

- Foster partnerships of police and citizens to involve the whole community in strategies to promote greater public safety;

- Take a problem-solving approach to identify and effectively address the underlying conditions that give rise to crime and disorder;

- Transform the organization to respond to community needs more effectively;

- Enhance understanding of interdisciplinary capabilities.

In developing an outreach strategy, it is critical to understand the threat that radicalization poses in one's area of operations. "In other words, what is lacking in our understanding of ideology is an awareness of the local, cultural and communication contexts that allow for, even encourage, the viral spread of these ideas."[27]

---

26 Mathew C. Scheider, Robert F. Chapman, and Michael F. Seelman. *Connecting the Dots for a Proactive Approach. United States,* 2003. Washington, DC: Office of Justice Programs National Criminal Justice Reference Service, 2003.

27 Steven R Corman, Bud Goodall, and Angela Trethewey. *Out of their Head and into their Conversation: Countering Extremist Ideology.* Tempe, Arizona: Consortium for Strategic Communication Arizona State University, 2009, 3.

REGIONAL AND LOCAL OUTREACH EFFORTS

Outreach and counter-radicalization policies must be developed and implemented locally. "Looking in from the outside won't do. Abstract knowledge of the situation, even when detailed, does not capture the affective tone of the place, its nonverbal features, its emergent norms, or the ego involvement and arousal of being a participant."[28] Solutions can be supported from Washington, and headquarters agencies can provide tools to address radicalization, but interpersonal trust between local government officials and the Muslim community will ultimately have more influence on radicalization than political statements and government messaging because the interpersonal relationship has "practical credibility."

COGNITIVE APPROACHES TO COUNTER-RADICALIZATION

The United States would benefit from counterradicalization efforts that build affinity to "American-ness" while diminishing the "pervasive crisis of identity being experienced by Islamic communities."[29] The hard-power-only approach in the United States has "spawned unprecedented levels of distrust toward law enforcement within the Arab and Muslim communities in the United States."[30] The practical reality of fourth-generation wars is that individual experiences influence group opinion by reinforcing or conflicting with ingroup/outgroup perceptions. "While terrorism is ultimately a group activity,[31] such a group will always comprise individuals, each of whom has a role to play in the movement. Anti-terrorism programs tend not to focus on individuals, but it is through understanding individual radicalization and its associated social and psychological qualities that effective ways of promoting disengagement can be developed."[32] Ideologies are "shaped by historical and

---

28   Philip Zimbardo and John Boyd. *The Time Paradox: the New Psychology of Time that Will Change Your Life*. New York: Free Press, 2008 , 322.

29   Moghaddam, Fathali M. From the Terrorists' Point of View : What they Experience and Why they Come to Destroy. Westport, Conn.: Praeger Security International, 2006, 26.

30   David Cole. *"The Preventative Paradigm and the Rule of Law: How Not to Fight Terrorism."* In *Muslims in Western Politics*, edited by Abdulkadr H. Sinno, 264-277. Bloomington, Indiana: Indiana University Press, 2009, 276.

31   From a psychological perspective, terrorists may act to avenge a perceived wrong that is associated with Western governments' actions against a group with which the terrorist identifies.

32   Horgan, John. "Disengaging from Terrorism."

cultural narratives, present perceived political and religious circumstances, and economic, social and familial realities. [Ideological frames are] enabled by everyday exchanges and interpretations of opinions, rumors, and accounts.[33]

Therefore, an immediate goal of those who execute counter-radicalization strategies should be to consistently generate experiences that conflict with the terrorists' frame of U.S. versus Islam conflict. When contact between law enforcement and the Muslim community is mostly based on suspicion and the parties view one another as potential adversaries, communication is inhibited. Counterterrorism investigators need to increase positive contact with the community to better understand the context of an individual's behavior. This concept is easily extrapolated to groups—and reinforces the point that government leaders should be directly engaged with leaders of the Muslim community to interrupt the psychological process that leads to radicalization.

The most efficient way to counter the appeal of terrorism and diminish radicalization, then, is for federal, state, and local government leaders to identify and fully engage with centers of influence (referent leaders) of at-risk and immigrant Muslim populations. Leaders of the counterterrorism mission at local and regional levels must become directly engaged. These representatives must be prepared to listen, seek to understand grievances, and constructively address those grievances where possible. It is important that federal, state, and local activities be conducted in concert in order to avoid conflicting actions and ensure common messaging. This aspect of the counter-radicalization mission is critical because "many terrorists act in a pro-social manner, both believing themselves to be serving society and judged by their ingroup to be acting in its interest."[34] When governments provide a credible alternative to voice objection to existing policies and address community concerns, the argument for violent action is less compelling to the potential pool of extremists. The following model depicts a holistic approach to countering violent extremism:

---

33   Corman, Goodall, and Trethewey. *Out of their Head and into their Conversation: Countering Extremist Ideology*, 3.

34   Victoroff, Jeff. "The Mind of the Terrorist: A Review and Critique of Psychological Approaches," 1.

Approaches to Counterterrorism

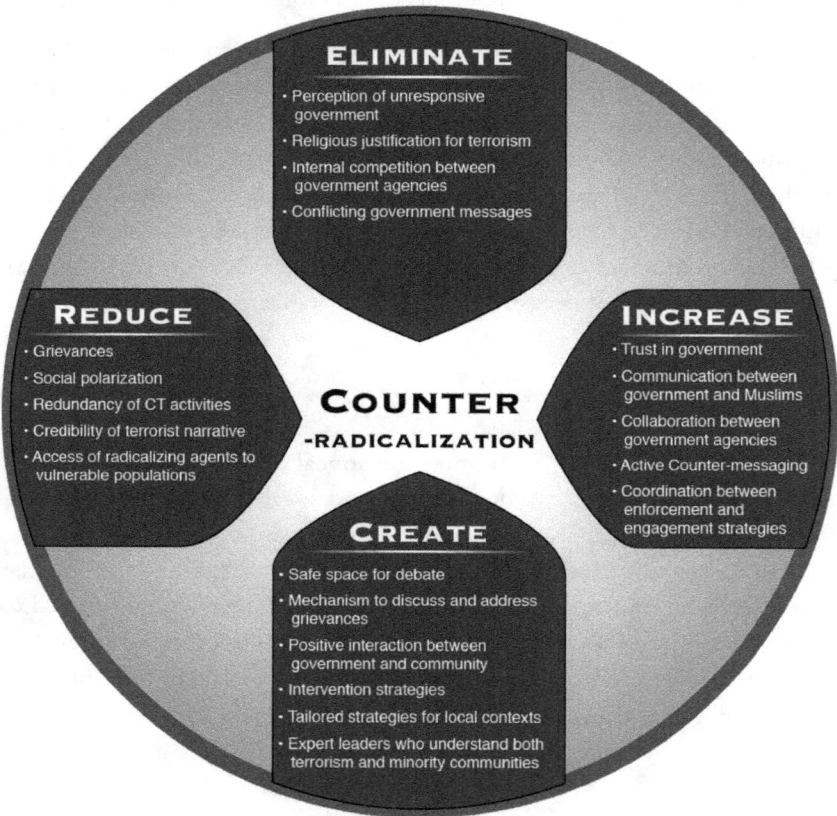

PARADIGM SHIFTS TO BE EMBRACED BY THE NEXT GENERATION OF COUNTERTERRORISTS

Decentralization and networks increase the likelihood of an organization's survival and success. On the other hand, a more decentralized and networked structure that enables contributing partners to capitalize on their individual strengths and apply them toward the group's superordinate goals is a necessity to counter violent extremism effectively. Each partner should be expected to leverage its individual network (ingroup) in a given region[35] in order to create a structure and functionality that can both quickly adjust to a fluid

---

35   Brafman and Beckstrom. *The Starfish and the Spider, 176*

environment and provide sufficient oversight to ensure that quality control is maintained. Well-developed networks are aware of local dynamics and can address emerging threats by bringing the right people, skills, and resources together at the right time and in the right place. Thus, a decentralized and networked structure provides qualitative value and innovation in a high-trust environment.[36]

Scientific studies and analysis might help overcome objections to a leader's sense of "giving up control" and encourage partnering with other organizations. It is well established that when compared to highly centralized organizational structures, networks are more adaptive and equally efficient. Networks are "superior in terms of learning new contingencies and developing innovative procedures."[37] Further, when multiple hierarchies are required to cooperate (for instance, within the current homeland security environment), "turf battles" and other forms of conflict tend to occur. This presents a challenge to the effective and efficient conduct of the counter-radicalization mission at the local level – where terrorists and solutions to terrorism are developed.

This means that formation of local and regional partnerships is in the interest of all parties because it positively impacts effectiveness and the bottom line, so long as accountability can be maintained. Therefore, it is important and in everyone's best interest to build and maintain trusting relationships that increase the speed of organizational actions. Such opportunities exist or can be realized where the interests of government, business and civil society overlap.[38]

"Interconnectedness" serves as a powerful tool for good or evil, dramatically lowers the cost of actions, and increases the potential for small numbers of people to have real impact on the masses. For these reasons, many organizations have a vested and tangible interest in contributing to

---

36   Stephen M. R. Covey and Rebecca R. Merrill. *The Speed of Trust: The One Thing that Changes Everything*. New York: Free Press, 2006, 13-29.

37   Ellis, Hollenbeck, Ilgen, and Humphrey. "Asymmetric Nature of Structural Changes in Command and Control Teams," 6.

38   Mark Gerenscer, Reginald van Lee, Fernando Napolitano, and Christopher Kelly. *Megacommunities: How Leaders of Government, Business and Non-Profits Can Tackle Today's Global Challenges Together*. New York: Palgrave MacMillan, 2008, 53.

joint projects: corporate consciousness is not wholly altruistic.[39] The value of the collective effort increases with each new member of a network, so there are important incentives for trusting and collaborating with others.

But, as noted by Tucker, "it does not take a network to fight a terrorist network,"[40] a wholesale reconstruction of the homeland security community is not required. While decision-making can be slow and hierarchical leaders may be isolated from changes in the environment, hierarchies also provide some advantages. For instance, the oversight necessary to ensure civil liberties are protected in a national security effort is best accomplished through a hierarchical organization because hierarchies provide accountability for each level of supervision. The same hierarchical structure that currently ensures compliance – a matter that is administrative and does not require knowledge of local contexts, might remain in place in a regional and networked structure. Centralized operations directed from remote headquarters with an expansive span of control, however, are likely to face severe challenges in combating violent extremism at a local level. The trick, it would seem is to find an organizational model that creates a hierarchy that is responsive to local and regional circumstances, attuned to local dynamics and able to work with local networks to accomplish strategic goals. Regional structures accomplish these goals –as evidenced in the U.S. military and fortune 500 companies.

HETERARCHIES AND NEW LEADERSHIP COMPETENCIES

Heterarchies may facilitate a solution to the challenges of overlapping interests, decentralized networks, and new leadership competencies. Those charged with the counter-radicalization mission, as opposed to the Hard Power aspects of counterterrorism, must recognize the impact of globalization across all economies and cultures. The counter-radicalization mission requires a greater understanding of factors that contribute to the radicalization process and the ability to influence those factors across a broad spectrum –federal, state and local policies may all require adjustment to change context for potential recruits to terrorism.

In some scenarios, federal law enforcement may not be the best choice to lead components of local counter-radicalization strategies. Some examples of areas where federal agencies are not best suited to lead counter-

---

39   Ori Brafman and Rod A. Beckstrom. *The Starfish and the Spider : The Unstoppable Power of Leaderless Organizations.* New York: Portfolio, 2006.

40   David Tucker. "Terrorism, Networks, and Strategy: Why the Conventional Wisdom is Wrong." *Homeland Security Affairs Journal* 4, no. 2 (June, 2008): 5.

radicalization efforts include local educational curricula, child welfare services and community policing initiatives. In other areas, like targeted outreach to vulnerable communities, threat and risk analysis, and assessment of volunteered threat information, the federal government should clearly play a more prominent role. The point here is that a coordinated enterprise allows for participants to share insight, best practices and resources to support the counter-radicalization effort.

These changes require a multi-faceted organization that can meet local challenges and address opportunities that might also have strategic impact. The current terrorist threat emerges from learning networks that present a difficult challenge for bureaucratic systems like the government hierarchies in the United States. When hierarchical systems are unlinked, they waste resources and "gaps" result. The threat posed by terrorists intensifies.

A heterarchical structure—somewhere between hierarchy and network—"provides horizontal links permitting different elements of an organization to cooperate, while they individually optimize success criteria."[41]

The combination of these themes—globalization, adaptability, and terrorism—is particularly relevant to today's counterterrorist because it emphasizes the potential impact of individuals on entire systems. The influence of these systems helps determine how individuals feel about their own security at personal and collective levels.

Implementing change in a way that plays to the strength of an interconnected world, across many disparate groups, can provide leverage in other situations. Collaboration among companies, nongovernment organizations, the government, and civil society provides the ingredients for a more resilient society where new trusting relationships are perpetually generated between people and groups. Through this interlinking a nation can become more cohesive, more efficient, and empowered to make positive change.

Once established, local engagement should inform regional assessments, which in turn might inform or refine national strategies. A unified joint coordination structure, one that coordinates Hard and Soft Power across multiple federal, state, and local agencies and interacts regularly with the Muslim community, would have the ability to identify grievances and assess threats and community reaction to the government's disruption tactics.

---

41   Karen Stephenson. Neither Hierarchy nor Network: An Argument for Heterarchy. *Entrenpreneur,* March 2009, 2009.

Unless the government engages with those directly impacted by radicalization, grievance mitigation and threat resolution is not possible. For some in the government, this will be a walk in the dark, fraught with discomfort and fear of change. Others have already begun the journey and deserve a coordinating mechanism to light the path ahead. The same is true of American Muslims. Our effort to address violent extremism will set a course for either the increased polarization of American society—which may lay only one successful terrorist attack ahead—or a future where interlinked and collaborating partners approach violent ideologies jointly.

NONTRADITIONAL LEADERSHIP

Leadership in the global environment requires investment in the community's success. The globalized environment demands a different kind of leader than found in traditional centralized hierarchies, where security and rule compliance are valued more than information and innovation. To function effectively in a decentralized and networked environment, organizational leaders must accept a collaborative posture: no single person can be in charge of every project; instead many people must play many roles.[42] Leaders of disparate organizations must be willing to take the risk of extending trust [43] and supporting change for others by releasing absolute control.[44]

The release of absolute control, however, does not equate to diminished responsibility for the leader. It is incumbent on leaders to exercise "smart trust," a decision-making process that combines a willingness to trust with an analytical assessment of just how much confidence one might have in a partner or partner organization. As people and organizations work together on superordinate goals, trust should increase, reputations will be built, and personal relationships that might be leveraged for different projects are formed. This interpersonal dimension is fundamental to success in the global environment due to the varying roles that leaders play.

Whether formally designated leader or serving in the capacity of informal influencers, the individuals who link collaborative entities are critical to successful ventures. A decentralized and networked organization is inherently a complex system, so those who serve as "catalysts" must be capable of

---

42   John M. Bryson. *Strategic Planning for Public and Nonprofit Organizations: A Guide to Strengthening and Sustaining Organizational Achievement* (Jossey Bass Public Administration Series). Revised ed. San Francisco, CA: John Wiley and Sons, Incorporated, 1995

43   Covey and Merrill. *The Speed of Trust.* 223.

44   Gerenscer, et al. *Megacommunities,* 200.

and intent upon understanding the perspectives of system partners[45] and affecting change. They serve as leaders and should be endowed by parent organizations with the authority to interact with the cross-interest group and to carry plans from the collective to the parent organization because their principal role is to inspire trust.[46] Here again, it is important for parent organization leaders to relinquish absolute control. Instead, the senior leader is responsible for creating an environment where work can be accomplished.

Effective communication within and among organizations can provide a thorough understanding of other component interests and their ability to affect outcomes. This is central to the network's ability to drive change. It is therefore important to win the trust and active participation of those leaders with high degrees of interest and power,[47] thereby validating a counterterrorist's focus on centers of influence when embarking on an effort to combat violent extremism.

The contributions of each member of "interest communities" bring additional insight and different resources that can be applied to local challenges. Incorporating different perspectives into such a process can unleash the project's potential,[48] and every effort should be made to incorporate divergent perspectives to better inform decisions. For this reason, continual expansion of the network might be an indicator of the effort's success.[49]

The importance of rejecting the notion of a "zero sum game" is critical to success in counterterrorism and particularly in counterradicalization efforts. This point cannot be overstated. As demonstrated by the British and Dutch counterterrorism efforts, the federal government, state and local governments, nongovernment agencies, and civil society in the United States can benefit when they work together to combat violent extremism, even though the full spectrum of benefits may not be readily apparent. Widely shared technology (like cell phones and the Internet) and nearly unfettered travel make for a high degree of awareness and contribution. These circumstances allow small inputs to have significant effects on a broad array of situations. Are we maximizing the talent and capabilities of our partners? The nation's security will be shaped by these small inputs, for better or worse.

---

45   Brafman and Beckstrom. *The Starfish and the Spider*, 125.

46   Covey and Merrill. *The Speed of Trust.*

47   Bryson. *Strategic Planning for Public and Nonprofit Organizations: 338.*

48   Brafman and Beckstrom. *The Starfish and the Spider*, 176.

49   Gerenscer, et al. *Megacommunities,*

CHAPTER 8

UNPLUGGING THE MACHINE

NECESSARY STEPS TO PREVENT VIOLENT EXTREMISM FOR THE NEXT GENERATION

"We believe the 9/11 attacks revealed four kinds of failures: in imagination, policy, capabilities and management."

-9/11 Commission

The addition of Soft Power tools to the existing Hard Power strategy provides real opportunities when engaging in the battle of ideas. Ideas cannot be arrested or targeted with bombs; ideologies, therefore, are best countered by creating experiences that conflict with preconceived stereotypes and the opponent's narrative. Polarization in some communities within the United States has already reached the precipice of violence. Attracting the confidence of the American Muslim population through a holistic, whole-government effort might provide the best avenue to mitigate long-term social divisions, violent extremism, and the retributive cycle that inevitably follows.

As demonstrated by experiences in the U.K. and the Netherlands, Soft Power enables society, and particularly vulnerable groups, to counter ideology at the base level (the "ground floor" of Moghaddam's "staircase to terrorism") because it changes the personal context of potential recruits to terrorism. A balanced-power approach also increases available options for dealing with threats and thus can be more effective than individual efforts.

STRATEGY: IMPLEMENT A BALANCED STRATEGY

- Soft Power tactics should be employed and coordinated between counterterrorism partners to counter the concept that Islam and democracy are incompatible. The government should support Muslim community leaders to achieve this goal.

- The president of the United States should establish a homeland security coordination group (HSCG) that reports to the NSC and functions similarly to the Joint Chiefs of Staff. The HSCG staff's principal responsibilities would be to create and update an overarching strategy and ensure that the strategy is sufficiently resourced (in terms of human capital) by agencies that participate in the HSCG's regional commands. The HSCG should likewise administer a dedicated funding stream for counter-radicalization activities and training.

- Homeland security agencies should work from an integrated and holistic strategy: Regional Outreach and Coordination Centers (ROC Centers) should be established to coordinate a "whole government" approach to counterterrorism and counterradicalization, tailoring actions to local contexts. The HSCG is the logical apex organization for this structure, although regional representatives from the ODNI might also fulfill this role, if the ODNI positions had similar authorities and resources.

- ROC Centers might replace some existing Fusion Centers and be blended in some cases with FBI Field Intelligence Groups, as a home for intelligence, operational response and policy makers to be housed under a single roof. It is logical that those who are compelled to deal with community fallout after major counterterrorist operations (state and local authorities) be able to plan for managing and setting the scene, media statements and community messaging associated with the enforcement action.

- ROC Center staffs should develop and coordinate two-pronged counterterrorism strategies that include both Hard Power and Soft Power tactics to address strategic goals. These strategies should identify priorities and actions across federal and local authorities within the region to mitigate terrorist activities.

- In order to implement these strategy changes, the National Security Council should create a working group composed of subject-matter experts with both academic and practical experience in counterterrorism, counterinsurgency policing, psychology and sociology.

- The NSC should implement a pilot program to test the strategy in an area (or areas) where both positive relationships and active engagement is ongoing, as well as in an area where government-community engagement has historically been challenging.

STRUCTURE: DEMAND "UNITY OF EFFORT" ACROSS GOVERNMENT AGENCIES

- The HSCG should initiate pilot ROC Centers to identify primary and secondary centers of influence and community grievances program at the regional level. The ROC Centers should initiate or expand relationships outside the government to create a diverse community of resources.

- The ROC Centers should work with key leaders to resolve legitimate grievances of the community and encourage projects affecting the centers of influence identified.

- Academic research regarding social dynamics should be conducted and published in unclassified form for public consumption. Partnering with local universities to conduct such research might lend credibility to this process because of the independent review processes.

TOOLS TO SHAPE THE IDEOLOGICAL BATTLEFIELD

- Key leaders of nongovernment organizations (NGO), religious groups, local policy makers, the private sector, the DHS, FBI, local law enforcement, and academia should jointly develop and support a curriculum to educate and inform the public regarding matters of community concern.

- Once ROC Center staffs are firmly established, the joint service entity should plan, coordinate, and oversee all aspects of the counterradicalization mission within their region. These staffs would implement their plans both as principals and through dedicated resources from participating agencies. Composition of these staffs would vary from region to region (determined by the overarching threat) but should include sufficiently senior officials from federal agencies, as well as state and local authorities, to coordinate and oversee activities of component agencies. Thus, the full array of tools available to the megacommunity could be applied to counter social polarization.

- The ROC Centers should generate or oversee production of locally relevant intelligence products that can serve to inform local strategists and local policymakers. Ideally, these bulletins would contain information that may be disseminated to the public. These products might improve communication with the Muslim community, increase awareness, and tend to deter terrorists who recognize that increased public awareness of threat means a more challenging operational environment for those with nefarious intent.

IMPACTING SOCIAL IDENTITY IN A POSITIVE WAY

- The DHS and FBI should coordinate more closely in efforts to bridge the gap between federal and state and local law enforcement, with an aim to develop domestic policing standards for the counterterrorism mission.

- Adoption or a return to community-policing models is an optimal condition that enhances intelligence collection and the public's trust of the government.

- New laws are needed to expedite the removal of noncitizens who are of concern to national security. Countering violent Islamist rhetoric in some instances is as easy as deporting noncitizens who promote violence. This is currently a multi-year process that allows an identified radicalizer to incite hatred and recruit terrorists, despite residing in the country illegally.

- Safe space for public debate of controversial issues should be created to allow grievances to be vented. Leaders of the ROC Centers and the HSCG should be prepared and empowered to address hard questions frankly and encourage critical debate from multiple perspectives.

CONCLUSION

"If you're a pragmatist, focused relentlessly on winning, you can't make policy or operational decisions at 30,000 feet. You have to come down, and get into the weeds, and understand the details of our counterterrorism tools at the operational level."[1]

—David Kris

The threat from homegrown Salafi-jihadi terrorists will not simply go away. Reminders of the continuing threat are abundant: an American citizen of Pakistani descent, Tarek Mehanna, was convicted on December 20, 2011 by a federal jury in Boston on four terrorism-related charges, including conspiracy to provide material support to terrorists, for allegedly traveling to Yemen in 2004 to receive terrorist training, as well as translating and disseminating jihadist propaganda online. Also on December 20, 2011, native-born Dylan "Mohammed" Boyd was sentenced to eight years and his brother Zakariya "Zak" Boyd, was sentenced to nine years in prison. Both pleaded guilty to a charge of conspiracy to provide material support to terrorists as part of a nine person terrorist cell in North Carolina. And, on December 21, 2011, Oytun Ayse Mihalik, a Turkish citizen legally residing in California, was charged with three counts of giving money to someone in Pakistan who knew the funds would be used to prepare and carry out attacks against American troops.[2] The individuals charged or convicted in these cases represent the complexity of the challenge facing the United States. These examples include males and a female; three were born in the United States. They are different ethnicities, resided in New England, the South and on the West Coast. The only commonalities among them appear to be adherence to a Salafi-jihadi ideology and their willingness to kill or materially support terrorism against the United States and its allies.

The deep resonance of the West versus Islam narrative promises that this threat will continue to grow, despite bin Laden's death, so long as the United States surrenders the ideological battlefield by pursuing only Hard Power solutions to terrorism. A one dimensional, Hard Power strategy fuels the Salafi-jihadi narrative that describes the West as an oppressive colonial force.

---

1   "Remarks as Prepared for Delivery by Assistant Attorney General David Kris at the Brookings Institution." *PRNewswire-USNewswire,* June 11, 2011.

2   Jennifer Rowland, "The LWOT: Tarek Mehanna Convicted On All Charges." *Foreign Policy* (January 3, 2012).

As al Qaeda has morphed from a group to a movement, so too must the nation's counterterrorism apparatus realign its approach to incorporate Soft Power to diminish the appeal of the violent Salafi-jihadi ideology.

NSS 2010 recognized the imperative to counter domestic radicalization and to empower communities to aid in the fight, but it does not delineate roles and missions. The same has been said of the National Strategy for Counterterrorism 2011 and *Empowering Local Partners to Prevent Violent Extremism in the United States*. Many agencies have, for years, been working with communities at risk; anti-gang task forces and "adopt a school" programs immediately spring to mind.

But counter-radicalization is an entirely new mission for domestic governance and counterterrorists. With limited resources and limited experience, the effort is at risk of being poorly implemented and poorly executed. And yet, to do nothing is not an option. Regional and local approaches are critical. Population density, the existence of ethnic enclaves, and socioeconomic standing of immigrant populations differ from place to place. Radicalization is evident in rural as well as metropolitan areas. Police forces, particularly in tough economic times, may be unable to support community policing models, and Muslim populations may relate in virtual rather than in geographic communities. As the experiences of the British and Dutch have demonstrated, to successfully win the battle of ideas, the United States needs tailored approaches that:

1. Align with domestic as well as external threats;

2. Ensure "unity of effort" across government agencies and include nongovernment and religious community leaders;

3. Provide tools to shape the ideological struggle; and

4. Aim to diminish ingroup/outgroup polarization by supporting social identities that are consistent with both Islam and national allegiance.

Regional Outreach Coordination Centers (ROC Centers) represent an opportunity to coordinate engagement activities and tailor local approaches across all levels of government, while simultaneously increasing cooperation between government agencies and creating a new space for government-community collaboration.

ROC Centers should be staffed by senior representatives of federal, state, and local organizations who are also recognized as subject matter experts in counterterrorism, policing, and sociology. Charged with principal responsibility for coordinating Hard and Soft Power strategies, the ROC

Centers should orchestrate community outreach and counterradicalization initiatives of participating agencies, serving as a nexus to nongovernment agencies and religious groups with an interest in counter- and deradicalization efforts. Members of these ROC Center teams would alternate taking lead roles, based on the nature of an individual program and individual specialties. They might also provide enhanced outreach (in more complex deradicalization efforts) and training to partner agencies at regional and local levels, and partner with academic institutions to study social influences that impact the region.

While it is unrealistic to expect ROC Centers to offer a panacea for the challenge of terrorism, such an organization would have the capacity to understand local contexts and develop sustained relationships more effectively than any existing structure. Therefore, ROC Centers offer an enhanced capacity to develop tailored strategies to mitigate the growth of violent extremism. Finally, such a group is well positioned to support counter- and deradicalization efforts by the Muslim community through trusting relationships because the ROC Centers would be both informed by and separate from those responsible for the application of Hard Power.

Each new terrorist threat brings with it the potential for media frenzy and bitter political posturing that could preclude the development of a truly preventive counterterrorism policy. This book recommends ROC Centers be considered in detail now, while the opportunity to realign and positively engage is viable.

INDEX

BIBLIOGRAPHY

18 USC CHAPTER 113B - TERRORISM, (2010): 18 USC 2331 - Terrorism.

Abrams, Dominic and Michael A. Hogg. "Collective Identity: Group Membership and Self-Conception." In *Self and Social Identity,* edited by Brewer, Marilynn B. and Miles Hewstone. 2nd ed., 147. Malden, MA: Blackwell Publishing, 2005.

Abrams, Dominic, Margaret Wetherell, Sandra Cochrane, Michael A. Hogg, and John C. Turner. "Knowing What to Think by Knowing Who You are: Self-Categorization and the Nature of Norm Formation, Conformity and Group Polarization." In *Intergroup Relations: Essential Readings,* edited by Hogg, Michael A. and Dominic Abrams, 270-288. Ann Arbor, Michigan: Edwards Brothers, 2001.

Abu 'Ubeid, Al-Qurashi. *Fourth Generations Wars.* Washington, DC: The Middle East Media Research Institute, 2002.

Ackerman, Spencer and Noah Shachtman. *Video: FBI Trainer Says Forget 'Irrelevant' Al-Qaida, Target Islam.* Danger Room: What's Next in National Security. wired.com, 2011.

Aho, James. "The Terrorist Identity: Explaining the Terrorist Threat." *Contemporary Sociology* 36, no. 4 (2007): 372-373.

Akerboom, E. S. M. "Counter-Terrorism in the Netherlands." *Tijdschrift Voor De Politie (Police Magazine)* no. June (2003).

Akerboom, Erik. *Countering Violent Extremist Narratives.* The Hague: Netherlands National Coordinator for Counterterrorism (NCTb), 2007.

al-Anani, Khalil. *Working Paper Number 4: The Myth of Excluding Moderate Islamists in the Arab World.* Washington, DC: The Sabhan Center at the Brookings Institution, 2010.

Alarabiya.net. "UK Police Probe Muslim Youth for Radical Views." Alarabiya. Net, March 29, 2009.

Aljazeera. "Chilling Tips in Al-Qaeda Magazine: Yemen Offshoot Launches Second Edition of English Publication with Articles by Wanted US Cleric Anwar Al-Awlaki." Aljazeera.Net, October, 12, 2010

Alonso, Rogelio. "The Modernization in Irish Republican Thinking Toward the Utility of Violence." *Studies in Conflict & Terrorism* 24, no. 2 (2001): 131.

al-Zawahiri, Ayman, Dr. *A Victorious Ummah, A Broken Crusade Nine Years After the Start of the Crusader Campaign.* Charleston, South Carolina: Nine Eleven Finding answers Foundation (NEFA), 2010.

Ana Belén Soage. "Hasan Al-Banna and Sayyid Qutb: Continuity Or Rupture?" *The Muslim World* 99, no. 2 (Apr 2009, 2009): 294-311.

"An Implausible Plan to Fight Terrorism through Community Outreach: A White House Paper Promoting Community Initiatives to Curb Radicalization is Commendable, but there is no Evidence to Suggest such Efforts Work " *Los Angeles Times,* 08/05/2011, 2011.

Arab News.com. "'Prevent' Strategy: The UK's "Prevent" Strategy to Target Young British Muslims Who might be Susceptible to Radicalization and Recruitment by Al-Qaeda is Fraught with Dangers." *Arab* News.Com.

"Arkansas Recruiting Center Killing Suspect: 'this was a Jihadi Attack'." CNN. Com, 01/22/2010, 2010.

Associated Press. "California Woman Charged with Sending Money to Pakistan to Help Fund Attacks on US Military." *The Washington Post,* December 21, 2011, sec. National.

Baker, Al and William K. Rashbaum. "Police Find Car Bomb in Times Square." *New York Times,* May 1, 2010, sec. NY/Region.

Baker, Peter, Helen Cooper, and Mark Mazzetti. " Bin Laden is Dead, Obama Says " *New York Times,* 05/01/2011, 2011.

Baldor, Lolita C. "US must Deal with Homegrown Terror Problem." *Associated Press,* September 10, 2010,

Bar-Tal, Daniel. "Sociopsychological Foundations of Intractable Conflicts." *The American Behavioral Scientist* 50, no. 11 (Jul 2007, 2007): 1430-1436, 1438-1453.

Bayat, Asef. "When Muslims and Modernity Meet." *Contemporary Sociology* 36, no. 6 (2007): 507-507-511.

Bellavita, Christopher. "Changing Homeland Security: What is Homeland." *Homeland Security Affairs Journal* 4, no. 2 (June, 2008).

Benford, Robert. "An Insider's Critique of Social Movement Framing Perspective." *Sociological Inquiry* 67, no. 4 (1997): 409-430-16.

Bergen, Peter. "Bergen: Time to Move on from War on Terror." CNN.

Bergen, Peter and Bruce Hoffman. *Assessing the Terrorist Threat: A Report of the Bipartisan Policy Center's National Security Preparedness Group.* Washington, DC: BIPARTISAN POLICY CENTER, 2010.

Bergen, Peter, Andrew Lebovich, Matthew Reed, Laura Hohnsbeen, Nicole Salter, Sophie Schmidt, William Banks, et al. *Post-9/11 Jihadist Terrorism Cases Involving U.S. Citizens and Residents: An Overview.* Washington, DC: New America Foundation and Syracuse University's Maxwell School of Public Policy., 2011.

bin Laden, Usama. "Usama Bin Laden: "Declaration of War Against the Americans Occupying the Land of the Two Holy Places" August 1996." Nine Eleven Finding Answers (NEzfA) Foundation.

bin Laden, Usamah, Ayman al-Zawahiri, Abu Y. Taha, Mir Hamza and Rahman Fazlul. "Bin Laden, Others Sign Fatwa to "Kill Americans Everywhere.""

Bjelopera, Jerome P. and Mark A. Randol. *American Jihadist Terrorism: Combating a Complex Threat.* Washington, DC: Congressional Research Service, 2010.

Brafman, Ori and Rod A. Beckstrom. *The Starfish and the Spider: The Unstoppable Power of Leaderless Organizations.* New York: Portfolio, 2006.

Brannan, David W., Philip F. Esler, and N. T. Anders Strindberg. "Talking to "Terrorists": Towards an Independent Analytical Framework for the Study of Violent Substate Activism." *Studies in Conflict & Terrorism* 24, no. 1 (2010): 3-24.

Brennan, John O. and Stephen Flanagan. "Remarks by John O. Brennan, Assistant to the President for Homeland Security and Counterterrorism – as Prepared for Delivery "A New Approach to Safeguarding Americans " Washington, DC, August 6, 2009.

Brewer, Marilynn B. "Reducing Prejudice through Cross-Categorization: Effects of Multiple Social Identities." In *Reducing Prejudice and Discrimination*, edited by Oskamp, Stuart, 165-183. Mahwah, NJ: Erlbaum, 2000.

Brewer, Marynn B. and Samuel L. Gaertner. "Toward Reduction of Prejudice: Intergroup Contact and Social Categorization." In *Self and Social Identity*, edited by Brewer, Marilynn B. and Miles Hewstone. 2nd ed., 298. Malden, MA: Blackwell Publishing, 2005.

Brewer, M. B. "When Contact is not enough: Social Identity and Intergroup Cooperation." *International Journal of Intercultural Relations* 20, no. 3/4 (Jul 1996, 1996): 291-303.

Brewer, Marilynn B. and Miles Hewstone. *Self and Social Identity*. Perspectives on Social Psychology. Malden, MA: Blackwell Pub., 2004.

British Security Minister Outlines Key Elements of New Prevent Agenda. International Centre for the Study of Radicalization, 2011.

Brouwer, Marina. "The Moluccan Dream – Still Alive at 60." Radio Netherlands Worldwide, April 26, 2010, 2010, on 10/10/2011." *Radio Netherlands Worldwide,* April 26, 2010.

———. "The Moluccan Dream – Still Alive at 60." *Radio Netherlands Worldwide,* April 26, 2010, 2010.

Brown, Amy Benson and Karen Poremski. *Roads to Reconciliation: Conflict and Dialogue in the Twenty-First Century*. Armonk, N.Y.: M.E. Sharpe, 2005.

Bryson, John M. *Strategic Planning for Public and Nonprofit Organizations: A Guide to Strengthening and Sustaining Organizational Achievement (Jossey-Bass Public Administration Series)*. Revised ed. San Francisco, CA: John Wiley and Sons, Incorporated, 1995.

Byman, Daniel. *Understanding Proto-Insurgencies: RAND Counterinsurgency Study--Paper 3*. Santa Monica: RAND Corporation, 2007.

Byng, M. "Complex Inequalities." *The American Behavioral Scientist* 51, no. 5 (Jan, 2008): 659.

CAIR. "American Muslim Civic POCKET GUIDE "Your Rights and Responsibilities as an American Muslim."

Cantle, Ted. *Community Cohesion: A Report of the Independent Review Team Chaired by Ted Cantle (Cantle Report)*. London: UK: Home Office, 2001.

Carlile, Alex. *Report to the Home Secretary of Independent Oversight of Prevent Review and Strategy (also Referred to as the Lord Carlile Report), as Provided in Prevent 2011.*: United Kingdom. The Stationery Office Limited on behalf of the Controller of Her Majesty's Stationery Office, 2011.

———. *Report to the Home Secretary of Independent Oversight Or Prevent Review and Strategy (also Referred to as the Lord Carlile Report.)*. London: United Kingdom. The National Archives, 2011.

Chen, Chao C., Xiao-Ping Chen, and James R. Meindl. "How can Cooperation be Fostered? The Cultural Effects of Individualism-Collectivism." *The Academy of Management Review* 23, no. 2 (1998): 285-285-304.

"CIA Wins Turf Battle Over DNI: But is it Over?" Federal News Radio.

Clapper, James R. "Unclassified Statement for the Record on the US Intelligence Community Worldwide Threat Assessment James R. Clapper, Director of National Intelligence." Office of the Director of National Intelligence,

Clark, John. "NORTHERN IRELAND: A Balanced Approach to Amnesty, Reconciliation, and Reintegration." *Military Review* 88, no. 1 (Jan/Feb, 2008; 2008): 37-37-49.

Clifford, Bob. "Kill a Leader, Murder a Movement? Leadership and Assassination in Social Movements." *The American Behavioral Scientist* 50, no. 10 (Jun, 2007; 2007): 1370-1370-1375,1377-1394.

Clutterbuck, Richard L. *The Long, Long War; Counterinsurgency in Malaya and Vietnam*. New York: Praeger, 1966.

Cole, David. "*The Preventative Paradigm and the Rule of Law: How Not to Fight Terrorism.*" In *Muslims in Western Politics*, edited by Sinno, Abdulkadr H., 264-277. Bloomington, Indiana: Indiana University Press, 2009.

" The Salafist Challenge: Coming Out of the Arab Woodwork." *The Economist* (04/30/2011, 2011): 49.

Committee on Homeland Security. *Working with Communities to Disrupt Terror Plots. Prepared Statement of Mohamed Elibiary.* Serial No. 111-58 Cong., 111th sess., March 17, 2010, 2010.

Condon, Patrick and Amy Forliti. "Missing Minnesota Somalis: Aspiring Fighters Or Dupes?" ABCNews.Com, July 7, 2009, 2009.

Conery, Ben and Valerie Richardson. "Blown Terrorist Case Led to Rushed arrests." *Washington Times,* September 22, 2009, sec. National.

Coolsaet, Rik. "EU Counterterrorism Strategy: Value Added Or Chimera?" *International Affairs* 86, no. 4 (2010): 857.

Corman, Steven R., Bud Goodall, and Angela Trethewey. *Out of their Head and into their Conversation: Countering Extremist Ideology*. Tempe, Arizona: Consortium for Strategic Communication Arizona State University, 2009.

Countering International Terrorism: The United Kingdom's Strategy July 2006. London: HM Government, 2006.

Covey, Stephen M. R. and Rebecca R. Merrill. *The Speed of Trust: The One Thing that Changes Everything*. New York: Free Press, 2006.

Cunningham, George. "Importance of Friendship Potential in Reducing the Negative Effects of Dissimilarity." *The Journal of Social Psychology* 148, no. 5 (2008): 595-595-608.

———. "The Influence of Group Diversity on Intergroup Bias Following Recategorization." *The Journal of Social Psychology* 146, no. 5 (2006): 533-533-47.

Curtis, E.,IV. "A History of Islam in America: From the New World to the New World Order." *The Journal of American History* 97, no. 3 (Dec, 2010): 775.

DARNTON, JOHN. "I.R.A. Said to be Close to Truce to End Violent Ulster Campaign." *New York Times,* 1994.

Davis, Paul K. and Michael J. Jenkins. *Deterrence and Influence in Counterterrorism: A Component in the War On al Qaeda.* Santa Monica, California: RAND, 2002.

Demant, Froukje and Beatrice De Graaf. "How to Counter Radical Narratives in the Case of Molaccan and Islamic Radicals." *Studies in Conflict and Terrorism* 33, (2010): 408.

Demant, Froukje, Marieke Slootman, Frank Buijs, and Jean Tillie. *Decline and Disengagement: An Analysis of Processes of Deradicalization.* Amsterdam, NL: Institute for Migration and Ethnic Studies (IMES), University of Amsterdam, 2008.

Department of Homeland Security. *One Team, One Mission, Securing our Homeland U.S. Department of Homeland Security Strategic Plan Fiscal Years 2008.* Washington, D.C.: Department of Homeland Security, 2008.

Department of Homeland Security (Bottom-Up). *Bottom Up Review Report: July 2010.* Washington, D.C.: Department of Homeland Security, 2010.

Department of Homeland Security (Grant Program). *Fiscal Year 2010 Homeland Security Grant Program Guidance and Application Kit.* Washington, D.C.: Department of Homeland Security, 2009

Department of Homeland Security. Roundtable. "Roundtable on Security and Liberty: Perspectives of Young Leaders Post 9/11: Houston, Texas and Washington, D.C.: Report for Government Officials and Policy Makers."

Department of State. "Patterns of Global Terrorism 1996." Department of State.

Diagnostic and Statistical Manual of Mental Disorders Third Edition, Revised (1989). Third Edition (Revised) ed. Washington, DC: American Psychiatric Association, 1989.

Diagnostic and Statistical Manual of Mental Disorders, Fourth Edition. IV ed. Washington, DC: American Psychiatric Association, 1994.

Dickson, Brice. "Counter-Insurgency and Human Rights in Northern Ireland." *Journal of Strategic Studies* 32, no. 3 (2009): 475

Dilanian, Ken. "U.S. Looks at Ways to Head Off Home-Grown Extremism." *Los Angeles Times,* May 26, 2010, 2010.

Director of National Intelligence. *Declassified Key Judgments of the National Intelligence Estimate: Trends in Global Terrorism: Implications for the United States.* Washington, DC: Director of National Intelligence, 2006.

Donner, J. P. H. and J. W. (Letter No 30) Remkes. *Counterterrorism: LETTER FROM THE MINISTER OF INTERNAL AFFAIRS &KINGDOM RELATIONS AND THE MINISTER OF JUSTICE.* The Hague: NCTb, 2004.

Donohoe, Laura K. "Britain's Counterterrorism Policy." In *How States Fight Terrorism: Policy Dynamics in the West*, edited by Zimmerman, Doron and Andreas Wenger, 17. Colorado: Lynne Reinner Publishers, Inc, 2007.

Dwyer, Jim. "In Praise of Help that Hurts." *New York Times,* October 20, 2009.

Eight Years After 9/11: Confronting the Terrorist Threat to the Homeland. Hearing September 30, 2009 sess., September 30, 2009.

Elliot, Andrea. "Why Yasir Qadhi Wants to Talk about Jihad." *New York Times,* March 17, 2011, sec. Magazine.

Ellis, Aleksander P. J., John R. Hollenbeck, Daniel R. Ilgen, and Stephen E. Humphrey. "Asymmetric Nature of Structural Changes in Command and Control Teams: The Impact of Centralizing and Decentralizing on Group Outcomes." Washington, DC, Command and Control Research Program (U.S.), June 17-19, 2003.

Emerson, Steven. *American Jihad: The Terrorists Living among Us.* 1 Free Press pbk ed. New York: Free Press, 2003.

Esposito, John L. and Dalia Mogahed. *Who Speaks for Islam?: What a Billion Muslims Really Think.* New York, NY: Gallup Press, 2007.

Ethier, Katleen A. and Kay Deaux. "Negotiating Social Identity when Contexts Change: Maintaining Identification and Responding to Threat." In *Intergroup Relations: Essential Readings*, edited by Hogg, Michael A. and Dominic Abrams, 254-266. Philadelphia: Psychology Press, 2001.

EurActiv Network. "Gijs De Vries on Terrorism, Islam and Democracy." EurActiv.Com, March 4, 2005, 2005.

European Union. *Council Framework Decision of 13 June 2002 on Combating Terrorism*. Luxembourg: Publications Office of the European Union, 2002.

European Union (Counterterrorism Strategy). *The European Union Counter-Terrorism Strategy*. Brussels: Council of the European Union, 2005.

European Union. Action Plan. *EU Plan of Action on Combating Terrorism*. Brussels: Council of the European Union, 2004.

European Union. Transnational Terrorism and the Rule of Law. *The EU Counterradicalization Strategy: Evaluating EU Policies Concerning Causes of Radicalization (EU Counter-Radicalization Strategy)*. Luxembourg: Publications Office of the European Union, 2008.

Fahim, Kareem, William K. Rashbaum, and Tim Stelloh contributed reporting. "Former City Resident is Accused of Trying to Join Terrorists." *The New York Times,* October 27, 2010, sec. A; Metropolitan Desk.

FBI Strategic Plan 2004-2009. Washington, DC: United States. Federal Bureau of Investigation, 2010.

Federal Bureau of Investigation (Quick Facts). "The Federal Bureau of Investigation: Quick Facts."

Feldman, Noah. "Why Shariah?" *New York Times,* March 16, 2008, 2008.

Fishman, Brian. "Al-Qaeda War Close to Over, Say US Experts.", *Sunday Nation,* December 9, 2011.

Frenkiel, Olenka. "Dutch Moluccans Appeal for Solidarity." *BBS News,* March 8, 2001.

Fusion Center Locations and Contact Information. Department of Homeland Security

Future of Al-Qaeda: Hearing before the Subcommittee on Terrorism, Nonproliferation, and Trade of the Committee on Foreign Affairs, House of Representatives, One Hundred Twelfth Congress, First Session, May 24, 2011. Washington, DC: United States. Government Printing Office, 2011.

Garamone, Jim. "Al Qaeda Leader's Letter Questions Zarqawi Tactics." *American Forces Press Service,* 10/17/2005, 2005.

Gardham, Duncan. "Terrorist Andrew Ibrahim was turned in by the Muslim Community." Telegraph.Co.Uk, July 18, 2009.

General Accountability Office. *Information Sharing: Federal Agencies are Sharing Border and Terrorism Information with Local and Tribal Law Enforcement Agencies, but Additional Efforts are Needed, Report to the Chairman, Committee on Homeland Security, House of Representatives.* Washington, D.C.: United States. General Accountability Office, 2009.

Geraghty, Tony. *The Irish War: The Hidden Conflict between the IRA and British Intelligence.* Johns Hopkins ed. Baltimore: Johns Hopkins University Press, 2000; 1998.

Gerenscer, Mark, Reginald van Lee, Fernando Napolitano, and Christopher Kelly. *Megacommunities: How Leaders of Government, Business and Non-Profits Can Tackle Today's Global Challenges Together.* New York: Palgrave MacMillan, 2008.

Gigerenzer, Thalia. "Muslim American Artists Strive to Bridge a Chasm." *New York Times,* Dec 17, 2010.

Gledhill, Ruth. "Muslim leaders 'failing to tackle extremists'." *Times Online,* March 30, 2010.

Global Terrorism Database, National Consortium for the Study of Terrorism and Responses to Terrorism (START). "Global Terrorism Database, National Consortium for the Study of Terrorism and Responses to Terrorism (START)."

Gompert, David C., International Security and Defense Policy Center, National Defense Research Institute, and RAND Corporation. *Heads We Win.* RAND Research Brief. Vol. 9244. Santa Monica, CA: Rand, 2007.

Goure, Daniel. "Homeland Security." In *Attacking Terrorism: Elements of a Grand Strategy,* edited by Cronin, Audrey Kurth and James M. Ludes, 261. Washington, D.C.: Georgetown University Press, 2004.

Gregory, Kathryn. *Provisional Irish Republican Army (IRA) (Aka, PIRA, "the Provos," Óglaigh Na hÉireann) (UK Separatists).* Washington, D.C.: Council on Foreign Relations, 2010.

Grossman, Cathy Lynn. "Number of U.S. Muslims to Double." *USA TODAY,* Jan 27, 2011.

———. "U.S. Muslims Try to Counter Negative Perceptions." *USA TODAY,* Jan 27, 2011.

Guiliano, Mark F. " Speech at the Washington Institute for Near East Policy." Washington, D.C., 2011.

Haddad, Yvonne Yazbeck and Robert Stephen Ricks. "Claiming Space in America's Pluralism: Muslims Enter the Political Maelstrom." In *Muslims in Western Politics*, edited by Sino, Abdulkadr H., 13-34. Bloomington, Indiana: Indiana University press, 2009.

Haslam, S. Alexander and John C. Turner. "Extremism and Deviance: Beyond Taxonomy and Bias." *Social Research* 65, no. 2 (1998): 435-435-448.

Hays, Tom and Larry Neumeister. "Times Sq. bomber sentenced, warns of more attacks." *Associated Press,* October 6, 2010.

Hernandez, Raymond. "Muslim 'Radicalization' Is Focus of Planned Inquiry." *New York Times,* December 16, 2011.

Hewstone, Miles, Mark Rubin, and Hazel Willis. "Intergroup Bias." *Annual Review of Psychology* 53, no. 00664308 (2002): 575-575-604.

Hoffman, Bruce. "Al-Qaeda has a new strategy. Obama needs one, too." *Washington Post,* January 10, 2010.

————. *Inside Terrorism*. Revised & enlarged edition. New York: Columbia University Press, 2006.

————. "The Myth of Grassroots Terrorism: Why Osama Bin Laden Still Matters." *Foreign Affairs* no. May/June (2008): 2.

————. "The Use of the Internet by Islamic Extremists." *RAND, Testimonies* CT-262-1, no. Congressional Testimonies (2006).

Hogg, Michael A. "Social Categorization, Depersonalization and Group Behavior." In *Self and Social Identity*, edited by Brewer, Marilynn B. and Miles Hewstone. 2nd ed., 203. Malden, MA: Blackwell Publishing, 2005.

Hogg, Michael A. and Dominic Abrams, eds. *Intergroup Relations: Essential Readings*. Philadelphia: Psychology Press, 2001.

Hogg, Michael and Deborah Terry. "Social Identity and Self-Categorization Processes in Organizational Contexts." *Academy of Management Review* 25, no. 1 (2000): 121-121-140.

Homeland Security Advisory Council. "Countering Violent Extremism (CVE) Working Group." Department of Homeland Security.

"Home Office Business Plan 2011-2015", Home Office.

Horgan, John. "Disengaging from Terrorism." *Jane's Intelligence Review* (2006).

Hornsey, Matthew and Michael Hogg. "The Effects of Status on Subgroup Relations." *The British Journal of Social Psychology* 41, no. 01446665 (2002): 203-203-18.

Hornsey, Matthew, Louise Majkut, Deborah Terry, and Blake McKimmie. "On being Loud and Proud: Non-Conformity and Counter-Conformity to Group Norms." *The British Journal of Social Psychology* 42, no. 01446665 (2003): 319-319-35.

House Homeland Security Committee. *The Way Forward with Fusion Centers: Challenges and Strategies for Change, 27 September 2007. Statement of Michael C. Mines Deputy Assistant Director, Directorate of Intelligence, Federal Bureau of Investigation.* 2007.

Hubbard, Amy S. "Cultural and Status Differences in Intergroup Conflict Resolution: A Longitudinal Study of a Middle East Dialogue Group in the United States." *Human Relations* 52, no. 3 (Mar, 1999; 1999): 303-303-325.

Huddy, Leonie. "From Social to Political Identity: A Critical Examination of Social Identity Theory." *Political Psychology* 22, no. 1 (March 2001): 127-156.

Hughes, Chris. "Iraq War 'Caused Terrorism in Uk'; Says Ex-Boss of MI5." *The Mirror,* July 21, 2010, sec. NEWS.

Hunger, J. David and Louis W. Stern. "An Assessment of the Functionality of the Superordinate Goal in Reducing Conflict." *Academy of Management Journal (Pre-1986)* 19, no. 000004 (Dec, 1976; 1976): 591-605.

Huntington, Samuel P. "The Clash of Civilizations." *Foreign Affairs* 72, no. 3 (1993): 48.

Innes, Martin. "Policing Uncertainty: Countering Terror through Community Intelligence and Democratic Policing." *Annals of the American Academy of Political and Social Science* 605, no. Democracy, Crime, and Justice (May, 2006): 222-241.

Institute for Migration and Ethnic Studies (IMES) Research: Strictly Orthodox Muslims Pose no Threat to Dutch Democracy. Amsterdam, Netherlands: University of Amsterdam, 2010.

"Intelligence Collection Disciplines (INTs)." Federal Bureau of Investigation.

"Intelligence Defined." Federal Bureau of Investigation.

International Association of Chiefs of Police. "IACP Releases National Summit on Intelligence Report."

International Research Center. *Zawahiri Tries to Clear Name, Explain Strategy*. Washington, DC: Federation of American Scientists, 2008.

Jane's Islamic Affairs Analyst. "Europe's Emerging Solutions to Radical Islam." IHS Jane's Defense & Security Intelligence & Analysis. (2009)..

Jane's Provisional IRA. "Groups - Europe - Dormant, United Kingdom: Provisional IRA (PIRA)." Jane's Terrorism and Insurgency Centre.

Janse, Ronald. "Fighting Terrorism in the Netherlands; a Historical Perspective." *Urecht Law Review* 1, no. 1 (2005).

Jenkins, Brian Michael. *Would-be Warriors: Incidents of Jihadist Terrorist Radicalization in the United States since September 11, 2001*. Occasional Paper. Vol. OP-292-RC. Santa Monica, CA: Rand, 2010.

Johnson, David and Roger Johnson. "New Developments in Social Interdependence Theory." *Genetic, Social, and General Psychology Monographs* 131, no. 4 (2005): 285-285-358.

Jones, Seth. "How Terrorist Groups End." Santa Monica, California: Rand Corporation, 2008.

Jones, Seth G. *In the Graveyard of Empires: America's War in Afghanistan*. New York: W.W. Norton & Company, 2009.

Seth G. Jones (2012). "Think Again: Al Qaeda: A year after Osama bin Laden's death, the obituaries for his terrorist group are still way too premature." *Foreign Policy*, 04/29/2012,

Jones, Seth G. and Martin C. Libicki. *How Terrorist Groups End: Lessons for Countering Al Qa'Ida*. Santa Monica, CA: Rand, 2008.

Joscelyn, Thomas. "Analysis: Anwar Awlaki's Message to Inspire Readers." *The Long War Journal* (2010).

Kapitan, Tomis. "Can Terrorism be Justified?". http://www.niu.edu/phil/~kapitan/pdf/CanTerrorismbeJustified.pdf

Keren, Michael and David Levhari. "The Optimum Span of Control in a Pure Hierarchy." *Management Science* 25, no. 11 (Nov., 1979): pp. 1162-1172.

Khatab, Sayed. "Arabism and Islamism in Sayyid Qutb's Thought on Nationalism." *The Muslim World* 94, no. 2 (2004): 217-217-244.

Kim, W. Chan and Renée Mauborgne. *Blue Ocean Strategy: How to Create Uncontested Market Space and make the Competition Irrelevant*. Boston, Mass.: Harvard Business School Press, 2005.

King Statement on Obama Administration Violent Extremism Strategy. Lanham: Federal Information & News Dispatch, Inc, 2011.

Knickmeyer, Ellen and Jonathan Finer. " Insurgent Leader Al-Zarqawi Killed in Iraq." *Washington Post,* 06/08/2006, 2006, sec. Council on Foreign Relations Reports.

Kohut, Andrew. *Anti-Americanism: Causes and Characteristics.* Washington, DC: Pew Research Center for People and the Press, 2003.

Kramer, Roderick. "A FAILURE TO COMMUNICATE: 9/11 AND THE TRAGEDY OF THE INFORMATIONAL COMMONS." *International Public Management Journal* 8, no. 3 (2005): 397-397-416.

Kruglanski, Arie W. and Shira Fishman. "The Psychology of Terrorism: "Syndrome" Versus "Tool" Perspectives." *Terrorism and Political Violence* 18, (2006): 193-215.

Kundnani, Arun. "The FBI's 'Good' Muslims." *The Nation* (September 1, 2011, 2011).

———. "Spooked! How not to prevent violent extremism." *Institute of Race Relations* (October 17, 2009).

Kydd, Andrew H. and Barbara F. Walter. "The Strategies of Terrorism." *International Security* 31, no. 1 (Summer, 2006): 49-80.

Lambert, Robert. "Salafi and Islamist Londoners: Stigmatised Minority Faith Communities Countering Al-Qaida." *Crime, Law and Social Change* 50, no. 1-2 (Sep 2008, 2008): 73-89.

Leavell, Ron. "The Evolution of Regional Counterterrorism Centers within a National Counterterrorism Network: Is it Time to Fuse More than Information?" M.A., Naval Postgraduate School, Center for Homeland Defense and Security, 2007.

Leiter, Mike. "The Aspen Institute: The Terror Threat Picture and Counterterrorism Strategy." Aspen, Colorado, Federal News Service, 2010.

Levitt, Matthew and Michael Jacobson. "Continuity and Change: Reshaping the Fight Against Terrorism." *Washington Institute for Near East Policy* Policy Focus No. 103, no. April 2010 (2010): May 10, 2010.

Lewis, Bernard. "The Roots of Muslim Rage" *Atlantic Monthly* 266, no. 3 (1990): 60.

Lind, William S., Keith Nightengale, John F. Schmitt, Joseph W. Sutton, and Gary I. Wilson. "The Changing Face of War: Into the Fourth Generation." *Marine Corps Gazette* no. October (1989): 22-26.

Locher, James R., III. *Toward Integrating Complex National Missions: Lessons from the National Counterterrorism Center's Directorate of Strategic Operational Planning*. Washington, D.C.: Project on National Security Reform, 2010.

Lord, Carnes. " Reorganizing for Public Diplomacy." In *Information Strategy and Warfare: A Guide to Theory and Practice*, edited by Arquilla, John and Douglas A. Borer, 118. New York: Routeldge, 2007.

Lynch, Mark. "Rhetoric and Reality: Countering Terrorism in the Age of Obama, p.3." Center for a New American Security, Washington, DC.

Maher, Shiraz and Martyn Frampton. *Choosing our Friends Wisely: Criteria for Engagement with Muslim Groups*. London: Policy Exchange, 2009.

Marrin, Stephen. "Homeland Security Intelligence: Just the Beginning." *Journal of Homeland Security* (November, 2003).

Masse, Todd M. *The National Counterterrorism Center: Implementation Challenges and Issues for Congress*. Washington, D.C.: Congressional Research Service, 2005.

McCauley, Clark and Sophia Moskalenko. *Friction: How Radicalization Happens to Them and Us*. New York: Oxford University Press, 2011.

McKinley, James C., Jr. "U.S. Judge Blocks a Ban on Islamic Law." *New York Times,* Nov 30, 2010.

Mellis, Colin. *Amsterdam and Radicalization the Municipal Approach.* The Hague: National Coordinator for Counterterrorism, 2007.

Metz, Steven. *Rethinking Insurgency*. Carlisle, PA: Strategic Studies Institute, U.S. Army War College, 2007.

MI5. "Security Service MI5." https://www.mi5.gov.uk/output/uk-home-page.html

Migdal, Michael, Miles Hewstone, and Brian Mullen. "The Effects of Crossed Categorization on Intergroup Evaluations: A Meta-Analysis." *The British Journal of Social Psychology* 37, no. 01446665 (1998): 303-303.

Mogahed, Dalia. *Beyond Multiculturalism vs. Assimilation*. Princeton, New Jersey: The Gallup organization, 2007.

Moghaddam, Fathali M. *From the Terrorists' Point of View: What They Experience and Why They Come to Destroy.* Westport, Conn.: Praeger Security International, 2006.

————. *Multiculturalism and Intergroup Relations: Psychological Implications for Democracy in Global Context.* 1st ed. Washington, DC: American Psychological Association, 2008.

Moriarty, Gerry. "Statements of Regret Over Deaths do Not Signal IRA Desire to End Campaign for Every Person Killed by the IRA, Republicans Cite a Corresponding Atrocity by the "Other Side", Making an End to the Terrorist Campaign as Elusive as Ever." *The IrishTimes,* 03/25/1993, 1993.

Musaji, Sheila. *North American Muslims Determined to Counter Violence and Terrorism*: The American Muslim, 2010.

Muslim West Facts. *The Gallup Coexist Index 2009:A Global Study of Interfaith Relations With an in-Depth Analysis of Muslim Integration in France, Germany, and the United Kingdom.* London: Gallup Incorporated, 2009.

Naerssen, Ton Van. "Migration Associations and Multi-Local Politics: Rethinking the Case of Migrants from Indonesia in the Netherlands." The Hague, Netherlands, Institute of Social Studies The Netherlands, August 30-31, 2007.

National Commission on Terrorist Attacks upon the United States, Thomas H. Kean, and Lee Hamilton. *The 911 Commission Report : Final Report of the National Commission on Terrorist Attacks upon the United States.* Official government ed. Washington, DC: U.S. Government Printing Office, 2004.

National Commission on Terrorist Attacks Upon the United States. *Statement of Marc Sageman to the National Commission on Terrorist Attacks upon the United States July 9, 2003 the Global Salafi Jihad.* 2003.

National Strategy for Combating Terrorism [February 2003]. United States. White House.

National Strategy for Combating Terrorism [Updated 2006]. Washington, D.C.: United States Government, 2006.

National Strategy for Homeland Security: Executive Summary. Washington, D.C.: United States. Office of Homeland Security, 2002.

National Strategy for Information Sharing: Successes and Challenges in Improving Terrorism-Related Information Sharing. Washington, D.C.: United States. White House Office, 2007.

Senate Committee on Homeland Security and Government Affairs. *The Roots of Violent Islamist Extremism and Efforts to Counter it, before the U.S.: Testimony of Maajid Nawaz, Director of the Quilliam Foundation, London:* July, 10, 2008 sess., 2008.

Lower House of Parliament. *Anti-Terrorism Progress Report.* 29 754 no. 196. Cong., session year 2010-2011 sess., 2011.

———. *Fourteenth Progress Report on Counterterrorism.* The Hague: National Coordinator for Counterterrorism, 2011.

———. "Government Presents National Counterterrorism Strategy for 2011-2015." National Coordinator for Counterterrorism. 2011.

———. *Thirteenth Progress Report on Counterterrorism*: National Coordinator for Counterterrorism (2011), 2011.

Netherlands Ministry of Justice. *Broad Government Anti-Radicalism and Radicalisation Approach.* The Hague: Netherlands Ministry of Justice, 2005.

Netherlands. Algemen Inlichtingen-en Veilighdsdienst (AIVD). "The Mission of the AIVD." The Netherlands

Netherlands. Hague Centre for Strategic Studies. "Counterinsurgency and Counterterrorism." The Hague Centre for Strategic Studies

Netherlands. Ministers of Justice and Internal Affairs & Kingdom Relations (Letter No.1). *Counterterrorism Policy 10-09-2004.* The Hague: National Coordinator for Counterterrorism, 2004.

Netherlands. Ministry of Justice (Broad approach). *Broad Government Anti-Radicalism and Radicalisation Approach*: NL Ministry of Justice, 2005.

Netherlands. National anti-terrorism coordinator. *Second Anti-Terrorism Progress Report.* The Hague: National anti-terrorism coordinator, 2005.

Netherlands. National Coordinator for Security and Counterterrorism. *Aliens Act, Published 01/05/2007.* .

———. . *11th Progress Report.* The Hague: National Coordinator for Counterterrorism, 2009.

———. *From Dawa to Jihad: The various Threats from Radical Islam to the Democratic Legal Order*: Netherlands Ministry of the Interior and Kingdom Relations, 2004.

———. "Mission of the NCTb." NCTb.

————. "NCTb: Themes; what is Terrorism?." NCTb.

Netherlands. Research and Documentation Centre (WODC). *Investigation: No Sharia Courts in the Netherlands*. The Hague: NL Ministry of Justice, 2010.

Niens, Ulrike and Ed Cairns. "Identity Management Strategies in Northern Ireland." *The Journal of Social Psychology* 142, no. 3 (2002): 371-371-80.

"Note Pinned to Body Threatened Dutch MP." *The Globe and Mail (Canada)*, November 5, 2004, sec. INTERNATIONAL NEWS; World in Brief.

Norton-Taylor, Richard. "The calamity of disregard: It is now chillingly clear: MI6's pre-Iraq warnings were swept aside by an obsessed White House." *The Guardian*, 08/04/2007, 2007.

Nye Jr., Joseph S. "Think Again: Soft Power." *Foreign Policy* (February 23, 2006).

Nye, Joseph S. *Soft Power: The Means to Success in World Politics*. 1st ed. New York: Public Affairs, 2004.

Nye, Joseph. "The Problem: A Smarter Superpower." *Foreign Policy* no. 160 (2007): 46-46-47.

Nye, Joseph S., Jr. "The Velvet Hegemon." *Foreign Policy* no. 136 (May/Jun 2003, 2003): 74-75.

Obama Administration. *Empowering Local Partners to Prevent Violent Extremism in the United States* 2011.

————. *"National Security Strategy"* (2010). whitehouse.gov.

————. "National Strategy for Counterterrorism" (2011). whitehouse.gov.

————. "National Strategy for Counterterrorism." United States.

————. "Strategic Implementation Plan for Empowering Local Partners to Prevent Violent Extremism in the United States."

O'Brien, Brenden. *The Long War: The IRA and Sinn Fein 1985 to Today*. Syracuse, NY: Syracuse University Press, 1999.

"ODNI Fact Sheet: Forging an Intelligence Community that Delivers the most Insightful Intelligence Possible." Office of the Director of National Intelligence.

"Office of the Director of National Intelligence: About the ODNI." Office of the Director of National Intelligence.

"Office of the Director of National Intelligence: Organizational Chart." Office of the Director of National Intelligence.

Olekalns, Mara, Feyona Lau, and Philip L. Smith. "Resolving the Empty Core: Trust as a Determinant of Outcomes in Three-Party Negotiations." *Group Decision and Negotiation* 16, no. 6 (Nov, 2007; 2007): 527-527.

O'Neill, Sean. "Special Branch Absorbed into Counter-Terror Unit." *The Times,* 2006.

"Panetta: US within Reach of Defeating Al-Qaida." *Associated Press,* 07/09/2011, 2011.

Paris, Jonathan. "Discussion Paper on Approaches to Anti-Radicalization and Community Policing in the Transatlantic Space." Washington, DC, June 27-28, 2007, 2007.

Pettigrew, Thomas. "Intergroup Contact Theory." *Annual Review of Psychology* 49, no. 00664308 (1998): 65-65-85.

Pew Global Attitudes Project. *Global Public Opinion in the Bush Years (2001-2008).* Washington, D.C.: Pew Research Center, 2008.

Pew Research Center. *Muslims in America: Mostly Middle Class and Mainstream*: Pew Research Center, 2007.

Poot, C. J., R. J. de Bokhorst, W. H. Smeenk, and R. F. Kouwenberg. *The Act on the Extension of the Scope for Investigation and Prosecution of Terrorist Crimes.* The Hague: WODC Wetenschappelijk Onderzoek- en Documentatiecentrum (translated Research and Documentation Centre), 2008.

Post, Jerrold M., Farhana Ali, Schuyler W. Henderson, Stephen Shanfield, Jeff Victoroff, and Stevan Weine. "The Psychology of Suicide Terrorism." *Psychiatry* 72, no. 1 (Spring, 2009; 2009): 13-13-31.

Preventing Violent Extremism: Next Steps for Communities. Rotherham, UK: Communities and Local Government Publications, 2008.

"Profile: Ayman Al-Zawahiri: Physician Considered to be the Brains Behind Al-Qaeda Began His Journey as a Dissident in Egypt." *Al Jazeera,* 06/16/2011, 2011.

Qutb, Sayyid. "Milestones, Chapter 5: LA ILAHA ILLA ALLAH-THE WAY OF LIFE OF ISLAM p.52, USA, Viewed), 2005." In *Milestones*, 52. Mississauga, Canada: Young Muslims, 2008.

Ramo, Joshua Cooper. *The Age of the Unthinkable*. pbk, 2010 ed. New York: Back Bay Books, 2009.

"RAND Database of Worldwide Terrorism Incidents." RAND.

Rassner, Martjin. "The Dutch Response to Moluccan Terrorism, 1970-1978." *Studies in Conflict and Terrorism* 28, no. 6 (2005): 481.

Ratcliffe, Jerry H. *Intelligence-Led Policing*. Canberra, Australia: Australian institute of Criminology, 2003.

Reicher, Stephen. "The Context of Social Identity: Domination, Resistance, and Change." *International Society of Political Psychology* 25, no. 6 (2004): 941-942.

———. "The Context of Social Identity: Domination, Resistance, and Change." *Political Psychology* 25, no. 6, Symposium: Social Dominance and Intergroup Relations (Dec., 2004): 921-945.

"Remarks as Prepared for Delivery by Assistant Attorney General David Kris at the Brookings Institution." *PRNewswire-USNewswire,* June 11, 2011.

Remkes, J. W. and J. P. H. Donner. *Addressing Radicalism and Radicalisation at Local and Judicial Levels*. The Hague: House of Representatives of the States General (Netherlands), 2005.

"Robert S. Mueller, III Director, Federal Bureau of Investigation Statement before the Senate Committee on Homeland Security and Governmental Affairs. Washington, D.C. September 13, 2011." Federal Bureau of Investigation.

Robison, Kristopher K., Edward M. Crenshaw, and J. Craig Jenkins. "Ideologies of Violence: The Social Origins of Islamist and Leftist Transnational Terrorism." *Social Forces* 84, no. 4 (Jun, 2006; 2006): 2009-2009-2026.

Rollins, John. *Fusion Centers: Issues and Options for Congress [Updated January 18, 2008]*. Washington, DC: Library of Congress. Congressional Research Service, 2008.

Rosenau, William, Bruce Hoffman, Andrew J. Curiel, and Doron Zimmerman. "Mike Whine, Community Security Trust Terrorism and Diasporas in the UK." RAND Corporation, 2007.

Rosenberg, Adam and Linda Trevino. "A Proposed Model of between-Group Helping: An Identity-Based Approach." *Journal of Managerial Issues* 15, no. 2 (2003): 154-154-174.

Ross, Lee. "The Intuitive Psychologist and His Shortcomings: Distortions in the Attribution Process." In *Advances in Experimental Social Psychology*, edited by Berkowitz, L. Vol. 10, 174-214. New York: Academic Press, 1977.

Rowland, Jennifer. "The LWOT: Tarek Mehanna Convicted on all Charges." *Foreign Policy* (January 3, 2012).

Roy, O. *Al Qaeda in the West as a Youth Movement: The Power of a Narrative*. Brighton: MICROCON, 2008.

Rubin, Mark and Miles Hewstone. "Social Identity, System Justification, and Social Dominance: Commentary on Reicher, Jost Et Al., and Sidanius Et Al." *Political Psychology* 25, no. 6, Symposium: Social Dominance and Intergroup Relations (Dec., 2004): 823-844.

Rule, Shelia. "Vught Journal; Remember the Moluccans? Is This a Last Stand?" *New York Times*, June 9, 1989, 1989.

Sageman, Marc. *Leaderless Jihad: Terror Networks in the Twenty-First Century*. Philadelphia: University of Pennsylvania Press, 2008.

———. *Understanding Terror Networks*. Philadelphia: University of Pennsylvania ress, 2004.

Senate Judiciary Committee. *Preparing for the Challenges of the Future: Statement of Robert S. Mueller, III:* 2008.

Scheider, Matthew C., Robert F. Chapman, and Michael F. Seelman. *Connecting the Dots for a Proactive Approach. United States., 2003*. Washington, D.C.: Office of Justice Programs National Criminal Justice Reference Service, 2003.

Scheuer, Michael. *Through our Enemies' Eyes: Osama Bin Laden, Radical Islam, and the Future of America*. Rev, 2 ed. Washington, D.C.: Potomac Books, Inc., 2006.

Scheuer, Michael. *Imperial Hubris: Why the West is Losing the War on Terror*. 1st ed. Washington, D.C.: Brassey's, 2004.

Schmidt, William E. "I.R.A. Declares Cease-Fire, Seeing 'New Opportunity' to Negotiate Irish Peace." *The New York Times*, September 1, 1994, 1994, sec. International.

Schwartz, Seth J., Curtis S. Dunkel, and Alan S. Waterman. "Terrorism: An Identity Theory Perspective." *Studies in Conflict & Terrorism* 32, no. 6 (Jun, 2009; 2009): 537-537-559.

Sciolino, Elaine and Schmitt, Eric. "A Not very Private Feud Over Terrorism." *The New York Times,* 06/08/2008, 2008, sec. The Nation.

Senate Judiciary Committee. *Nine Years After 9/11: Confronting the Terrorist Threat to the Homeland: Michael Leiter, Director of the National Counterterrorism Center.* Hearing September 22, 2010 sess., September 22, 2010, 2010.

Senate Judiciary Committee. *Nine Years After 9/11: Confronting the Terrorist Threat to the Homeland: Statement of Secretary Janet Napolitano.* September 22, 2010 sess., 2010.

Senate Judiciary Committee. *Nine Years After 9/11: Confronting the Terrorist Threat to the U.S: Statement of Robert S. Mueller III.* September 22, 2010, 2010.

Seta, Catherine, John Seta, and Jenifer Culver. "Recategorization as a Method for Promoting Intergroup Cooperation: Group Status Matters." *Social Cognition* 18, no. 4 (2000): 354-354-376.

Shepard, William. "Sayyid Qutb's Doctrine of Jahiliyya." *International Journal of Middle East Studies* 35, no. 4 (2003): 521-521-545.

Sherif, Muzafer. "Superordinate Goals in the Reduction of Intergroup Conflict." In *Intergroup Relations:Essential Readings*, edited by Hogg, Michael A. and Dominic Abrams, 64-288. Ann Arbor, Michigan: Edwards Brothers, 2001.

Silber, Mitchell D. and Arvin Bhatt. *Radicalization in the West: The Homegrown Threat.* New York: New York (City) Police Department, 2007.

Silke, Andrew. "Becoming a Terrorist." In *Terrorists, Victims and Society: Psychological Perspectives on Terrorism and its Consequences*, edited by Silke, Andrew, 30. West Sussex, England: Wiley & Sons, 2003.

Simons, Marlise. "Militants Recruiting Young Dutch Muslims for Foreign War." *New York Times,* May 31, 2002.

Simons, Marlise. "A Van Gogh Suspect is Linked to Islamists ; 8 More are Arrested by Dutch Police." *The International Herald Tribune,* November 4, 2004.

Smith, Paul. "A Critical Assessment of the US National Strategy for Counterterrorism: A Missed Opportunity? (ARI)." Real Instituto Elcano.

Soage, Ana Belén. "Hasan Al-Banna and Sayyid Qutb: Continuity Or Rupture?" *The Muslim World* 99, no. 2 (Apr 2009, 2009): 294-311.

Stephenson, Karen. "Neither Hierarchy nor Network: An Argument for Heterarchy." People and Strategy 32, no. 1 (March 2009, 2009)

Stevenson, Jonathan. "How Europe and America Defend Themselves." *Foreign Affairs* 82, no. 2 (Mar. - Apr., 2003): pp. 75-90.

Strindberg, Anders and Mats Warn. *Islamism*. United Kingdom: John Wiley and Sons Ltd, 2011.

Strindberg, Anders and Mats Wärn. "Realities of Resistance: Hizballah, the Palestinian Rejectionists, and Al-Qa'Ida Compared." *Journal of Palestine Studies* 34, no. 3 (2005): 23-23.

Strohm, Chris. "Officials Warn of More Terrorist Threats within U.S." *National Journal Group, Congress Daily,* 2010.

Sullivan, Eileen and Chris Hawley. "Angry Over Spying, Muslims Say: 'Don't Call NYPD'." *The Associated Press,* November 14, 2011, sec. Domestic news.

Syed, Anwar H. "Pakistan in 1997: Nawaz Sharif's Second Chance to Govern." *Asian Survey* 38, no. 2, A Survey of Asia in 1997: Part II (Feb., 1998): 116-125.

Taher, Abul. "Revealed: UK's First Official Sharia Courts." *The Sunday Times,* September 14, 2008, 2008.

Tajfel, H. and J. Turner. "An Integrative Theory of Intergroup Conflict. in (Eds.) (Pp. 94-109)." In *The Social Psychology of Intergroup Relations*, edited by Austin, W. G. and S. Worchel, 94-109. Monterey, CA: Brooks-Cole, 1979.

Tajfel, Henri. *Human Groups and Social Categories: Studies in Social Psychology*. Cambridge Cambridgeshire; New York: Cambridge University Press, 1981.

Tapper, Jake. "Brennan: President Obama's National Security Strategy Recognizes Threat of Homegrown Terrorists." *ABC News,* May 26, 2010.

Taspinar, Omer. *Europe's Muslim Street*. Washington, D.C.: Brookings Institute, 2003.

"The Burden of Victory: It's the Finest Moment of Obama's presidency—but it also raises uncomfortable moral questions." *Newsweek* (05/21/2011, 2011).

The Economist. "Special Report: The Enemy within - Muslim Extremism in Europe." *The Economist* 376, no. 8435 (Jul 16, 2005): 24.

The Future of the Global Muslim Population: Projections for 2010-2030. Washington, DC: Pew Research Center's Forum on Religion and Public Life, 2011.

"TERRORISM: Murder on the Milk Train." *Time Magazine* (December 15, 1075, 1975).

The Economist London. "Britain: Alone, Together." *The Economist. London* 360, no. 8230 (July, 14, 2001, 2001): 53.

The Organization for Security and Co-operation in Europe (OSCE). *POLIS - Policing OnLine Information System: Policing Profiles of Participating and Partner States-Netherlands*: The Organization for Security and Co-operation in Europe, 2009.

The Pew Forum on Religion and Public Life. *Little Support for Terrorism Among Muslim Americans*. Washington, DC: Pew Research Center, 2009.

Tobin, J. "The Mosque and the Mythical Backlash." *Commentary* 130, no. 3 (Oct, 2010): 24.

Tucker, David. "Terrorism, Networks, and Strategy: Why the Conventional Wisdom is Wrong." *Homeland Security Affairs Journal* 4, no. 2 (June, 2008): 5.

———. "The Unconventional Threat to Homeland Security: An Overview.".

United Kingdom. *Prevent Review: Summary of Responses to the Consultation*. London: National Archives, 2011.

———. "Annex A." In *Prevent (2011)*: The Stationery Office Limited on behalf of the Controller of Her Majesty's Stationery Office, 2011.

———. "Communities and Local Government." Home Office.

———. "Glossary." In *Prevent (2011)*: United Kingdom. The Stationery Office Limited on behalf of the Controller of Her Majesty's Stationery Office, 2011.

———. *Prevention of Terrorism Act 2005*, (2005):.

United Kingdom. Communities and Local Government Committee. *Preventing Violent Extremism: Sixth Report of Session 2009-10*. London: The Stationery Office, 2010.

United Kingdom. Creativity, Culture and Education. *Create/Participate*. London: Creativity, Culture and Education, January 1, 2010.

United Kingdom. HM Government. " PM's Speech at Munich Security Conference." HM Government.

United Kingdom. Home Office. "Home Office: Office for Security and Counter Terrorism." UK National Archives.

———. "Office for Security and Counter-Terrorism, about RICU." UK National Archives.

———. *Terrorism Act 2006*. London: UK Home Office, 2006.

United Kingdom. Home Office (Contest). "The UK Counter-Terrorism Strategy (CONTEST)."

United Kingdom. Home Office (Countering International Terrorism). *The United Kingdom's Strategy for Countering International Terrorism*. 2009 Crown ed. London: Prime Minister and the Secretary of State for the Home Department, 2009.

United Kingdom. Home Office (Counterterrorism). "Counter-Terrorism."

United Kingdom. Home Office (Current threat level). "Current Threat Level."

United Kingdom. Home Office (Prevent). "Prevent."

United Kingdom. Home Office: Office for Security and Counterterrorism (OSCT). *Channel: Supporting Individuals Vulnerable to Recruitment by Violent Extremists*: Home Office: Office for Security and Counterterrorism, 2010.

United Kingdom. Kent Constabulary. "Neighbourhood Policing: Visible, Accessible, Responsive."

United Kingdom. Metropolitan Police. "Metropolitan Police: Police Community Support Officers."

———. *Racial and Religious Hatred Act 2006,* (2006):.

United Kingdom. Security Service (Your Career). "Security Service MI5: Your Career."

United Kingdom:(Strategy for Countering International Terrorism). *Pursue Prevent Protect Prepare: The United Kingdom's Strategy for Countering International Terrorism*. London: United Kingdom, 2009.

United States Army. *FM 3-24.2: Tactics in Counterinsurgency*. Washington, DC: Department of the Army, 2009.

US National Counterterrorism Center. "About the National Counterterrorism Center."

U.S. Senate Homeland Security and Governmental Affairs Committee. *Homegrown Terrorism and Radicalization in the Netherlands: Experiences, Explanations and Approaches: Testimony by Lidewijde Ongering, Deputy National Coordinator for Counterterrorism*. Violent Islamist extremism: the European experience sess., June 27, 2007, 2007.

"Verbatim." *Time Magazine* (April 11, 2005, 2005).

Victoroff, Jeff. "The Mind of the Terrorist: A Review and Critique of Psychological Approaches." *The Journal of Conflict Resolution* 49, no. 1 (Feb 2005, 2005): 3-42.

Vindino, Lorenzo. "A Preliminary Assessment of Counter-Radicalization in the Netherlands." *CTC Sentinel* 1, no. 9 (2008): 12.

Wagner, Ulrich, Oliver Christ, Thomas F. Pettigrew, Jost Stellmacher, and Carina Wolf. "Prejudice and Minority Proportion: Contact Instead of Threat Effects." *Social Psychology Quarterly* 69, no. 4 (December, 2006): 380-390.

Walker, C. P. "The Jellicoe Report on the Prevention of Terrorism (Temporary Provisions) Act 1976." *The Modern Law Review* 46, no. 4 (Jul., 1983): 484-492.

Warner, Carolyn M. and Manfred W. Wenner. "Religion and the Political Organization of Muslims in Europe." *Perspectives on Politics* 4, no. 3 (Sep., 2006): 457-479.

West, Paul and Julie Bykowicz. "Information-Sharing Still a Roadblock: Security Chiefs Tell O'Malley, Other Governors 'Paradigm Shift' among Agencies Needs to be done." *Baltimore Sun,* February 22, 2010.

Wiktorowicz, Quintan. "A Genealogy of Radical Islam." *Studies in Conflict and Terrorism* 28, no. 2 (2005): 75-75-97.

Wilder, David A. "Intergroup Contact: The Typical Member and the Exception Rule." In *Intergroup Relations*, edited by Hogg, Michael A. and Dominic Abrams. Philadelphia: Psychology Press, 2001.

Yaeger, Carl H. "Menia Muria: The South Moluccans Fight in Holland." *Studies in Conflict & Terrorism,* 13, no. 3 (1990): 215.

Yager, Joedy. *Washington Struggling to Rein in Increasing Homegrown Terrorism* 2010.

Yilmaz, Hakan. "Islam, Sovereignty, and Democracy: A Turkish View." *The Middle East Journal* 61, no. 3 (2007): 477-477-493.

Zimbardo, Philip and John Boyd. *The Time Paradox: The New Psychology of Time that Will Change Your Life*. New York: Free Press, 2008.

Zimbardo, Philip G. *The Lucifer Effect: Understanding How Good People Turn Evil*. 2008 Random House trade pbk ed. New York: Random House Trade Paperbacks, 2008.

————. "A Situationist Perspective on the Psychology of Evil: Understanding How Good People Are Transformed into Perpetrators." In *The Social Psychology of Good and Evil*, edited by Miller, Arthur G., 21. New York: Guilford Press, 2004.

ABOUT THE AUTHOR

Brad Deardorff is a sixteen-year veteran of federal law enforcement and a graduate of the Naval Postgraduate School, where he earned a Master's of Arts degree in Security Studies from the Center for Homeland Defense and Security. Brad has been directly involved in counter-terrorist operations domestically and in more than twenty countries around the world.

www.ingramcontent.com/pod-product-compliance
Lightning Source LLC
Chambersburg PA
CBHW050342270326
41926CB00016B/3566